D0903365

Cisco Internet Architecture Essentials Self-Study Guide: Cisco Internet Solutions Specialist

Matt Recore

Jeremy Laurenson

Scott Herrmann

Cisco Press

Cisco Press
201 W 103rd Street
Indianapolis, IN 46290

Cisco Internet Architecture Essentials Self-Study Guide:
Cisco Internet Solutions Specialist

Matt Recore

Jeremy Laurenson

Scott Herrmann

Copyright© 2003 Cisco Systems, Inc.

Published by:
Cisco Press
201 West 103rd Street
Indianapolis, IN 46290 USA

Printed in the United States of America 1 2 3 4 5 6 7 8 9 0

First Printing September 2002

Library of Congress Cataloging-in-Publication Number: 2001090436

ISBN: 1-58705-044-7

Warning and Disclaimer

This book is designed to provide information about building a Cisco Internet infrastructure for e-business purposes. Every effort has been made to make this book as complete and as accurate as possible, but no warranty or fitness is implied.

The information is provided on an "as is" basis. The authors, Cisco Press, and Cisco Systems, Inc. shall have neither liability nor responsibility to any person or entity with respect to any loss or damages arising from the information contained in this book or from the use of the discs or programs that may accompany it.

The opinions expressed in this book belong to the author and are not necessarily those of Cisco Systems, Inc.

Feedback Information

At Cisco Press, our goal is to create in-depth technical books of the highest quality and value. Each book is crafted with care and precision, undergoing rigorous development that involves the unique expertise of members from the professional technical community.

Readers' feedback is a natural continuation of this process. If you have any comments regarding how we could improve the quality of this book, or otherwise alter it to better suit your needs, you can contact us through e-mail at feedback@ciscopress.com. Please make sure to include the book title and ISBN in your message.

Publisher	John Wait
Editor-In-Chief	John Kane
Cisco Systems Program Manager	Anthony Wolfenden
Acquisitions Editor	Brett Bartow
Managing Editor	Patrick Kanouse
Development Editor	Christopher Cleveland
Project Editor	Marc Fowler
Copy Editor	Marcia Ellett
Technical Editors	Bryce Lynn
	Bob Meindl
	Richard Ptak
	Peter Welcher
Team Coordinator	Tammi Ross
Book Designer	Gina Rexrode
Cover Designer	Louisa Klucznik
Compositor	Mark Shirar
Indexer	Tim Wright

CISCO SYSTEMS

Corporate Headquarters
Cisco Systems, Inc.
170 West Tasman Drive
San Jose, CA 95134-1706
USA
http://www.cisco.com
Tel: 408 526-4000
        800 553-NETS (6387)
Fax: 408 526 1100

European Headquarters
Cisco Systems Europe
11 Rue Camille Desmoulins
92782 Issy-les-Moulineaux
Cedex 9
France
http://www-europe.cisco.com
Tel: 33 1 58 04 60 00
Fax: 33 1 58 04 61 00

Americas Headquarters
Cisco Systems, Inc.
170 West Tasman Drive
San Jose, CA 95134-1706
USA
http://www.cisco.com
Tel: 408 526-7660
Fax: 408 527-0883

Asia Pacific Headquarters
Cisco Systems Australia,
Pty., Ltd
Level 17, 99 Walker Street
North Sydney
NSW 2059 Australia
http://www.cisco.com
Tel: +61 2 8448 7100
Fax: 161 2 9957 1350

Cisco Systems has more than 200 offices in the following countries. Addresses, phone numbers, and fax numbers are listed on the Cisco Web site at www.cisco.com/go/offices

Argentina • Australia • Austria • Belgium • Brazil • Bulgaria • Canada • Chile • China • Colombia • Costa Rica • Croatia • Czech Republic • Denmark • Dubai, UAE • Finland • France • Germany • Greece • Hong Kong • Hungary • India • Indonesia • Ireland Israel • Italy • Japan • Korea • Luxembourg • Malaysia • Mexico • The Netherlands • New Zealand • Norway • Peru • Philippines Poland • Portugal • Puerto Rico • Romania • Russia • Saudi Arabia • Scotland • Singapore • Slovakia • Slovenia • South Africa • Spain Sweden • Switzerland • Taiwan • Thailand • Turkey • Ukraine • United Kingdom • United States • Venezuela • Vietnam • Zimbabwe

Trademark Acknowledgments

All terms mentioned in this book that are known to be trademarks or service marks have been appropriately capitalized. Cisco Press or Cisco Systems, Inc. cannot attest to the accuracy of this information. Use of a term in this book should not be regarded as affecting the validity of any trademark or service mark.

About the Authors

Matthew Recore is a Senior Systems Engineer for Cisco, supporting the largest and most competitive accounts in the San Francisco region. He is Cisco's e-commerce specialist in Northern California. Matthew has taught several Quality of Service (QoS) boot camps for Cisco's largest IP Telephony customers, in addition to being a keynote speaker for Cisco at a recent networking event with Cisco's Ecosystem partners. He has also taught at University of California Davis and recently achieved the CCDP certification. Before joining Cisco, Matthew was a Senior Network Engineer for First Union, where he was responsible for core network and remote access network design and implementation. Matt Recore can be reached any time at matt@mattrecore.com.

Jeremy Laurenson, CCIE #8849, is a Consulting Systems Engineer and with Cisco Systems supporting Southern California with the Advanced Solutions Group. He is an IP Telephony Specialist working within some of the top accounts in California and he is a member of Cisco's internal convergence Technology Leadership Program.

Scott Herrmann is a Systems Engineer for Cisco Systems. His responsibilities include network design and support for Cisco customers, including LAN, WAN, IP Telephony, security, network management, wireless and CDN technologies, and the products that are related to these solutions. In addition to supporting customers, Scott educates other Cisco engineers in his assigned specialty of Network Management. Before joining Cisco, Scott was a Network Analyst and Network Engineer with Sutter Health, where he was responsible for network design, implementation, and troubleshooting.

About the Technical Reviewers

Bryce Lynn: After leaving the Computer Science Department at the University of California at Davis, Bryce spent several years learning the networking trade while working in network implementation and operations for Wells Fargo Bank. At the height of the dot-com boom, Bryce took a position as a Hosting Engineer for Organic, Inc., where he designed, implemented, and maintained server environments for large e-commerce web sites. Bryce is currently Lead Network Engineer for Organic's Corporate Information Services Department.

Bryce is also an avid softball player and will rarely turn down an offer to buy him a beer.

Robert J. Meindl is a Solutions Engineer with Cisco Systems reporting to the Vice President of U.S. Technical Operations. He creates and implements programs in support of the U.S. technical sales force. These include technical training and account support activities. Robert was previously a Systems Engineer for Cisco, providing pre- and post-sales technical support for Cisco's customer base, including several Fortune 500 financial corporations. He is knowledgeable in TCP/IP, OSPF, EIGRP, BGP4, Novell, DECnet, AppleTalk, DLSw, Bridging, Ethernet, FDDI, Token Ring, Frame Relay, Switched and Leased Lines, ATM, and Ethernet Switching. Robert specializes in large-scale network design, network security, and content networking. He has extensive project management, network design, support, and implementation experience. Robert holds a B.S. in Electrical Engineering from Layfayette College and an M.S. in Electrical Engineering from the University of Rhode Island.

Richard L. Ptak is President of Ptak & Associates, Inc., a leading industry analyst and consulting firm. Ptak & Associates works with clients in the infrastructure and business process management solution community to help them gain competitive advantage. Richard focuses on the component-based applications management market, management issues in Internet customer care, quality of service (QoS) management, network management, infrastructure management and integration. Richard has over 25 years of experience in the information technology industry. Prior to resuming his own consultancy, Richard was Senior Vice President at Hurwitz Group where he built a successful practice analyzing systems and applications and consulting. Prior to that, Richard was a Vice President at D.H. Brown Associates, where he was responsible for vision, strategy, production, and external communications for distributed systems and network management.

Richard frequently speaks at software industry conferences. His quotes have appeared in a variety of forums, including *Investor's Business Daily, Forbes, Wall Street Journal, San Jose Mercury News,* and the *Austin Statesman*. He contributes to such publications as *Business Communications Review, Journal of Information Systems Management, INTERNETWORK, InformationWeek,* and *NetworkWorld.* He is co-author of the recently published book, *Manager's Guide to Distributed Environments.* Richard holds a BS in Industrial Engineering from Kansas State University, an MS in Operations Research from Kansas State University, and an MBA in Finance and Marketing from the University of Chicago.

Dr. Peter Welcher, CCIE #1776, is an experienced senior instructor and consultant who has worked with a wide variety of products and technologies in complex environments, supporting many different industries. These projects include broad experience in network design, re-design, and implementation. Peter has also designed and helped implement network management architectures and Network Operations Centers for major corporations.

In addition to his CCIE credential, Peter is a Cisco Certified Instructor (CCSI #94014) who has authored several courses for Mentor Technologies and Cisco. He is currently in demand as a technical reviewer for books on topics relating to Cisco networking, design, and network management. His topic summaries (over 70 in number) in *CiscoWorld* magazine articles (see www.mentortech.com/learn/Welcher/papers/

index.htm) have been well received within the industry. The articles and Peter's excellent presentation skills have gained him quite a following in the industry.

Dedications

Matt Recore: I dedicate this book to my cabinet, composed of my incredible parents, Patty and Frank, my brother, Brian, my beautiful and loving girlfriend, Jennifer, and my close friends, Romacio and Hal.

Jeremy Laurenson: I dedicate my contributions in this book to Betsy, as well as the family and friends who have supported me despite the late nights and pages at 3:00 a.m.: Daniel, Robbi, Gloria, John, Jeff, Nina, and Dawn.

Scott Herrmann: To my father, Bruce, who has been a constant source of advice, encouragement, and inspiration.

Acknowledgments

Matt Recore: I thank Jeremy Laurenson, Scott Herrmann, Brett Bartow, Christopher Cleveland, Peter Welcher, Bob Meindl, and all those at Cisco Press for making this book happen. Your work has been outstanding. I thank Gary Christofferson, Steve Jacknow, and John Lampson for being very supportive managers during the year that we wrote this book.

Thank you Tony Robbins, Chris Manning, and James Serwanga for being such great coaches and setting an outstanding example.

Thank you to my special girlfriend, Jennifer. What a woman you are! How did I get so lucky to find you?

Thank you, Romacio and Hal, for being such great friends and for continually raising your standards.

Thank you, Mom and Dad, for instilling in me at an early age the belief that I can do anything, and for setting up a great home environment. I love you.

Thank you, God, for blessing and guiding me daily.

Jeremy Laurenson: I have to mention my team at Cisco—you are among the finest people I have had the privilege of working with, and you have made working for the finest company in the world both exciting and fun.

Scott Herrmann: Thank you, Matt Recore, for giving me the opportunity to contribute to this book. You are an excellent engineer and an outstanding person. Your work made this book what it is. I also thank everyone at Cisco Press for your guidance and patience while developing this book. It has been fun and very challenging. Finally, my gratitude goes to Brett Bartow, Executive Editor, for your assistance and dedication with all the authors as we pulled this book together.

Contents at a Glance

Introduction   xvii

Chapter 1   Internet System Architecture Overview   3

Chapter 2   Internet System Architecture Design Overview   25

Chapter 3   High Availability Overview   71

Chapter 4   Security Concepts and Design   95

Chapter 5   Content Delivery Networks   141

Chapter 6   Quality of Service   159

Chapter 7   Network Management   177

Chapter 8   Service Level Agreements   221

Appendix A   Answers to the Chapter Review Questions   239

Index   253

Table of Contents

Introduction   xviii

Chapter 1   Internet System Architecture Overview   3

Internet System Architecture Definition   5

Types of Internet Business Solutions   6
Customer Care Solution   7
e-commerce Solution   11
Supply Chain Management Solution and Architecture   14
e-learning Solution   15
Workforce Optimization Solution   19
e-publishing Solution   20

Summary   21

Review Questions   22

Chapter 2   Internet System Architecture Design Overview   25

Internet System Architecture Components   25

Cisco Internet System Reference Architecture Components   26
Perimeter Routers   26
Layer 3 Switches   28
Content Switches   34
Firewalls   41
CiscoSecure IDS Sensors and Directors   44
Content Engines   46
Content Routers   55
Server Placement for Web, Databases, and Application Servers   60

Benefits Realized After Implementing the Internet Systems Architecture   61
Capacity   62
Connectivity   62
Availability   63
Security   63
Quality of Service   63
Manageability—Network and System Management   64

Summary   65
Glossary of Key Terms in This Chapter   65

Review Questions   67

Chapter 3   High Availability Overview   71

    Benefits of Highly Available Systems   72

    Total Cost of Ownership Model   72

    Downtime and Availability   75

    Designing High Availability Architecture   76
        Defining Objectives   76
        Following a Top-Down Approach   77
        Developing an Availability Model   77
        Composing a Development Road Map   78
        Performing Design Verification   79

    The Two Design Approaches to Availability   79
        Networks and Systems Based on Fault Tolerant Devices   80
        Networks and Systems with Redundant Topologies   80

    E-Commerce Architecture   83
        Non-Redundant Design   83
        Redundant Design   83

    High Availability Design Enabling Technologies   84
        Load Balancers   84
        Ethernet Spanning Tree   85
        EtherChannel   86
        Hot Standby Routing Protocol (HSRP) and Virtual Router Redundancy Protocol (VRRP)   86
        Device-dependant Failover Mechanisms   87

    Non-network Considerations   88
        Operational Best Practices   88
        Server Fault Tolerance   89
        Power Considerations   89

    Failure Analysis and Recovery   89

    Summary   91

    Review Questions   91

Chapter 4   Security Concepts and Design   95

    How Important Is Security?   97

    What Is a Security Policy?   97
        The Need for a Security Policy   98
        Test and Implementation Considerations   100
        Monitor and Respond Considerations   100
        Manage and Improve Considerations   101

Types of Attacks   102
Packet Sniffers   102
IP Spoofing   103
Denial of Service   104
Password Attacks   106
Man-in-the-Middle Attacks   107
Application Layer Attacks   108
Network Reconnaissance   108
Trust Exploitation   109
Port Redirection   109
Unauthorized Access   110
Virus and Trojan Horse Applications   110

Conclusions About Attacks   111

Firewalls   111
Cisco PIX Firewalls   112

Virtual Private Networks   117
VPNs and Data Encryption   118
Cisco Devices that Support Encrypted VPN Access   122

Intrusion Detection   122
Cisco Intrusion Detection Solutions: Network-Based   125
Cisco Intrusion Detection Solutions: Host-Based   126

Access Control   127

Cisco SAFE Architecture   129
Cisco SAFE Architecture Main Module   130
Management Module   131
Server Module   133
Corporate Internet Module   134
Remote Access VPN Module   136
E-Commerce Module   137

Summary   139

Review Questions   139

Chapter 5   Content Delivery Networks   141

Traditional Web Growth   141

Anatomy of a Network   142
Bottleneck Points   143
Cisco Content Delivery Networks are the Solution   143

Cisco's Content Networking Architecture: Components   144
    Intelligent Network Services   145
    Content Switching   145
    Content Edge Delivery   150
    Content Routing or Global Server Load Balancing   151
    Content Distribution and Management   151

Applications of Content Delivery Networking   153
    Transparent Caching   153
    E-CDN   155

Content Filtering Solution   155

Summary   156

Review Questions   157

Chapter 6   Quality of Service   159

What is QoS?   159
    Network Demands Example   161

Planning for QoS   162
    Perform an Initial Policy Needs Assessment   163
    Perform a Network Characterization   163
    Perform an Application Characterization   164
    Define the Service Level   164
    Policy Testing and Validation   165

Implementing the Larger Scale Policy   166
    Deploying QoS   166
    QoS Device Manager   170
    QoS Application Points   170
    Cisco IOS QoS Tools/Categories   170

Summary   173

Review Questions   174

Chapter 7   Network Management   177

Network Management and the FCAPS Model   177
    Fault Management   178
    Configuration Management   178
    Accounting Management   182
    Performance Management   183
    Security Management   183

Fault Management   185
    Event Handling in a Fault Management System   186
    Key Functions in a Fault Management System   186
    Where to Implement a Fault Management System   188
    Reasons for Implementing a Fault Management System   188
    Troubleshooting in a Fault Management System   188

Performance Management   190

SNMP and RMON Overview   191
    Telnet   192
    SNMP   192
    RMON   201
    Syslog   202

Eight Guidelines for Managing a Network   203
    Starting with a Good Design and Secure Physical Location   203
    Identifying Critical Ports and Leaving the Rest Alone   204
    Setting Up Fault Monitoring   205
    Collecting Baseline Data   205
    Defining and Setting Thresholds   206
    Adjusting Thresholds   206
    Reducing Baseline Data Collection   206
    Revisiting and Gathering Baseline Data Regularly   207

Third-Party Network Management Tools   207
    Hewlett Packard's Openview   208
    IBM's Tivoli/Netview   208
    Computer Associate's Unicenter TNG   209

Cisco Network Management Solutions   209
    CiscoWorks 2000 Bundles   210
    QoS Policy Manager (QPM)   216
    Cisco Network Registrar (CNR)   216
    Access Control Server (ACS)   216

Summary   216

Review Questions   217

Chapter 8   Service Level Agreements   221

Service Level Management Chain   221

Business Synchronization   222
    Setting Expectations   223
    Measuring the User's View   224

What is a Service Level Definition?   224

Creating and Maintaining SLAs   225

Internal and External SLAs   226

Sample External Service Level Agreement   227

Common Core Requirements and Metrics of an SLA   228
Administrative Requirements   228
Technical Dependencies   228
Functional Dependencies   229
Network Availability Metrics   229
Network Performance Metrics   229
Operation Level Metrics   229
Cost   229

Design Integration   230
SLM Integration   230
Third-Party Integration Initiatives   230

Cisco Service Management Tools   230
Cisco Service Management Solution   231
Cisco Internetwork Performance Monitor   234
Cisco QoS Policy Manager Version 2.0   235

Summary   236

Review Questions   237

Chapter A   Answers to the Chapter Review Questions   239

Chapter 1 Review Questions   239

Chapter 2 Review Questions   240

Chapter 3 Review Questions   241

Chapter 4 Review Questions   242

Chapter 5 Review Questions   244

Chapter 6 Review Questions   245

Chapter 7 Review Questions   246

Chapter 8 Review Questions   250

Index   253

Introduction

Cisco Internet Architecture Essentials Self-Study Guide: Cisco Internet Solutions Specialist provides information necessary to complete the Cisco Internet Solutions Architecture fundamentals exam, as well as providing you with the knowledge you need when designing and building an Internet Solutions Architecture. It contains valuable tips and real-world advice from Cisco engineers who have been involved in building these solutions for years. It will help you understand all the components required to build a stable and reliable network infrastructure from power sources to service level agreements. You'll also learn about added services that can be built on top of the infrastructure to complement the infrastructure and add more overall value to the organization's network.

This book is most relevant to anyone interested in passing the Cisco Internet Solutions Specialist test, or anyone who wants to learn more about how real-world, Enterprise-class Internet Systems are architected and operated.

Organization/Chapter Organization

Figure I-1 shows a block diagram of a typical enterprise network. This book deals specifically with the portions of the network that are highlighted, however, the best practices and design guidelines in this book can be applied successfully to most parts of an enterprise network.

Figure I-1   *Typical Enterprise Network*

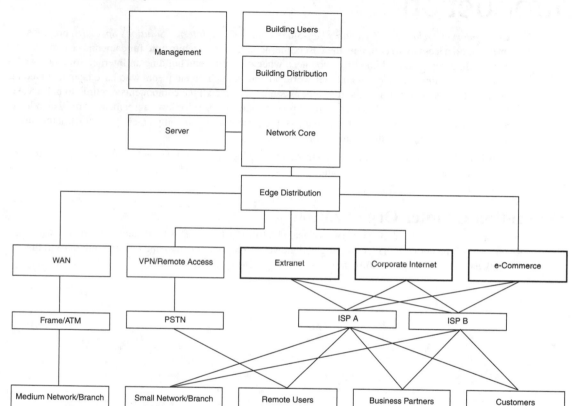

This book is divided into eight chapters dealing with different aspects relating to the overall Internet Solutions Architecture:

- **Chapter 1: Internet System Architecture Overview**—Provides an overview of what the Internet enables for businesses today, including business drivers and several common business solutions. The business solutions that are discussed are Customer Care, e-commerce, Supply Chain Management, e-learning, Workforce Optimization, and e-publishing.

- **Chapter 2: Internet System Architecture Design Overview**—Provides an overview of the components that make up the architecture, drilling down into each component to explain its significance and role in the architecture.

- **Chapter 3: High Availability Overview**—Discusses the needs for, and methods of, implementing highly available networks to support the Internet Business Solutions.

- **Chapter 4: Security Concepts and Design**—Discusses the security concerns, trends, and solutions relating to the Internet Business Solutions architecture. All of the recommendations coincide with the Cisco SAFE Architecture, which is a modular, end-to-end, continually evolving, security reference architecture.

- **Chapter 5: Content Delivery Networks**—Discusses Content Delivery Networks and how they allow an organization to better provide services to users, customers, and partners. This chapter breaks Content Delivery Networks into five components—Intelligent Network Services, Content Switching, Content Routing, Content Distribution and Management, and Content Edge Delivery. Some common architectures are discussed that utilize from some or all of the Content Delivery Networks components.

- **Chapter 6: Quality of Service**—Discusses the driving factors behind Quality of Service (QoS) and the different solutions to achieving end to end QoS throughout the Internet Business Solutions architecture.

- **Chapter 7: Network Management**—Discusses network management requirements and solutions—the ongoing maintenance of your Internet Business Solutions architecture.

- **Chapter 8: Service Level Agreements**—Discusses Service Level Agreements, including why they are necessary, how they are determined, and how you can support them in your Internet Business Solutions architecture.

As always, Cisco.com, Cisco's online presence, is available 24 hours a day at www.cisco.com/. This web site provides you with a wealth of additional information regarding solutions and architecture components. We highly recommend using Cisco.com when you are interested in finding out more.

In general, typing in www.cisco.com/go/<topic> will bring you to the latest information regarding the major topic you are interested in. The following list provides and describes some useful links we recommend you look at. The book's text provides more of these links.

www.cisco.com/go/ibsg
The Internet Business Solutions Group mission is to accelerate customer success in the Internet economy and develop long-term customer partnerships.

www.cisco.com/go/IQ
The Cisco IQ World Wide Web site demonstrates how Internet technology can solve critical business problems. It provides the guidance, insight, and knowledge you need to implement successful Internet business strategies for your organization.

www.cisco.com/go/avvid
Cisco Architecture for Voice, Video, and Integrated Data (AVVID) provides the framework for today's Internet business solutions. As the industry's only enterprise-wide, standards-based network architecture, Cisco AVVID provides the roadmap for combining your business and technology strategies into one cohesive model.

www.cisco.com/go/safe
The SAFE Blueprint is a flexible, dynamic blueprint for security and VPN networks, based on the Cisco AVVID, that enables businesses to securely and successfully take advantage of e-business economies and compete in the Internet economy.

www.cisco.com/go/qos
The Challenge—A communications network forms the backbone of any successful organization. These networks serve as a transport for a multitude of applications, including delay-sensitive voice and bandwidth-intensive video. These business applications stretch network capabilities and resources, but also complement and enhance every business process. Networks must provide secure,

predictable, measurable, and sometimes guaranteed services to these applications. Achieving the required QoS by managing the delay, delay variation (jitter), bandwidth, and packet loss parameters on a network, while maintaining simplicity, scalability, and manageability, is the secret to running an infrastructure that truly serves the business end-to-end.

Icons Used in This Book

Throughout this book, you will see the following icons used for common network devices

Router

Layer 3
Switch

Switch

PIX Firewall

Voice-Enabled
Router

Content
Switch

Route/Switch
Processor
(Layer 3 Switch)

Cisco 7500
Series Router

CSS11000
Content
Switch

Hub

Content
Engine

NetRanger
Intrusion Detection
System

Local Director

Access
Server

CiscoSecure
Scanner

IP/TV
Broadcast
Server

Cisco
CallManager

Cisco
Directory Server

PC

Laptop

CiscoWorks
Workstation

Web
Browser

Web
Server

Supercomputer

Relational
Database

Phone

IP Phone

Fax

File Server

Printer

Camera
PC/Video

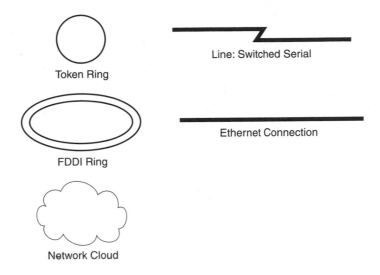

Token Ring

Line: Switched Serial

FDDI Ring

Ethernet Connection

Network Cloud

The conventions used to present command syntax in this book are the same conventions used in the *IOS Command Reference,* which describes these conventions as follows:

- Vertical bars (|) separate alternative, mutually exclusive elements.

- Square brackets [ ] indicate optional elements.

- Braces { } indicate a required choice.

- Braces within brackets [{ }] indicate a required choice within an optional element.

- **Boldface** indicates commands and keywords that are entered literally as shown. In actual configuration examples and output (not general command syntax), boldface indicates commands that are manually input by the user (such as a **show** command).

- *Italics* indicate arguments for which you supply actual values.

After reading this chapter, you will be able you to perform the following tasks:

- Define Internet system architecture.
- Explain the Cisco Customer Care Solution and its architecture.
- Explain the Cisco e-commerce Solution and its architecture.
- Explain the Cisco Supply Chain Management Solution and its architecture.
- Explain the Cisco e-learning Solution and its architecture.
- Explain the Workforce Optimization Solution.
- Explain the e-publishing Solution.

CHAPTER 1

Internet System Architecture Overview

The Internet began as the ARPANET during the cold war in 1969. It was developed by the U.S. Department of Defense (DOD) in conjunction with a number of military contractors and universities to explore the possibility of a communication network that could survive a nuclear attack. The ARPANET continued because the DOD, its contractors, and the universities found that it provided a very convenient way to communicate. Because of their efforts to continually search for a new and better way to communicate, you can communicate instantaneously with a person behind a computer on the other side of the planet. The Internet and its architecture have come a long way in a short amount of time. Figure 1-1 illustrates just how fast the Internet has grown compared to many other technological inventions such as the television, computer, and the radio.

Figure 1-1   *Internet Adoption Compared to Other Technologies*

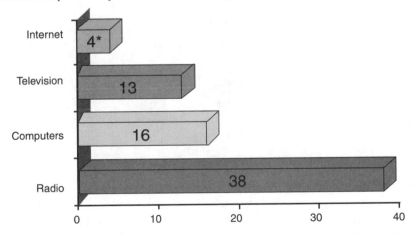

*Years to 50 Million Users

The many lessons learned have led the Internet to where it is today. This chapter walks you through where the technology was, where it is today, and where it is going in terms of the architectures and applications.

What is an Internet system architecture? To really understand what an Internet system architecture is you should know what an "Old World" architecture looks like. As Figure 1-2 illustrates, architectures of the past were splintered, static, proprietary, and riddled with legacy technologies that couldn't interoperate. Partner, supplier, customer, and employee systems existed like individual islands that weren't able to take advantage of each other. Machines were often located directly next to each other but couldn't communicate because of differing languages or protocols. The lack of integration led to many communication process inefficiencies.

Figure 1-2   *Old World Architecture*

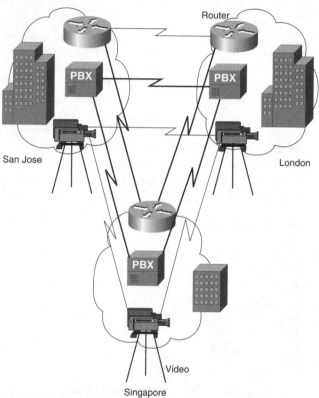

The old-world, splintered architecture is unacceptable today because it doesn't meet the needs of the business or any one interfacing with the business. Developers created the new Unified Internet system architecture and the "New World" applications that take advantage of this integrated architecture to correct the old architecture's lack of flexibility. Figure 1-2 showed some of the existing barriers of old-world architectures. The following chapters explore the characteristics of new-world architectures. This chapter focuses on what drives the "real" architecture applications that make companies money, reduce company costs, enhance productivity, improve employee effectiveness, improve customer satisfaction, and improve ecosystem relationships.

Internet System Architecture Definition

The Internet, Internet applications, and Internet architectures defined in this book enhance the quality of communication between people and organizations. When you think of an Internet system architecture from this point forward, envision a single, unified network infrastructure put in place to enhance the quality of communication. Unified in this context means mostly open standard-based technologies brought together to form an architecture to support open standard-based application communication. You can think of an Internet system architecture as a set of fundamental technologies that provide secure, manageable, reliable, ubiquitous access for all networked applications, enabling technologies and data. These technologies combine to create a single, connected network and system fabric platform to host distributed applications that cross traditional corporate boundaries and enable key constituents to work together.

Figure 1-3 illustrates an example Unified Internet System Architecture.

Figure 1-3 *Cisco's Architecture for Voice, Video, and Integrated Data*

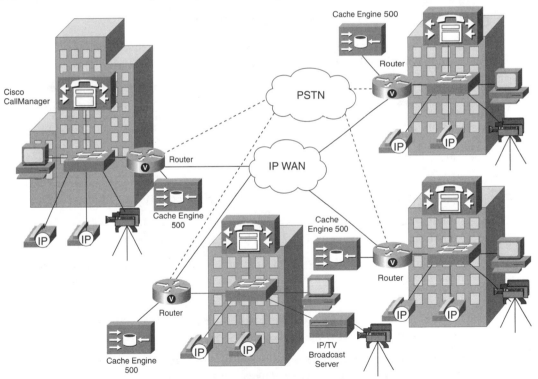

To be successful in today's hyper competitive, global marketplace, organizations need an edge. That edge is Internet-powered e-business practices. Organizations cannot afford to make major mistakes, nor can they sit idly by while their competitors establish market and mind share.

The network and system infrastructure of an organization involved in Internet business is key to ensuring its success. To deliver mission-critical applications such as Enterprise Resources

Planning (ERP) systems and new online applications such as integrated data, voice, and video, World Wide Web transaction processing, and videoconferencing, businesses need a highly available, scalable, secure, and application-aware network and system infrastructure—the Internet System architecture.

An Internet system architecture's primary goal is to support Internet-based solutions and applications. What drives a network architecture's requirements? The answer is always whatever the business is looking to accomplish and whatever applications are riding on the infrastructure. Those Internet-based solutions and applications include Customer Care, e-commerce, Supply Chain Management, e-learning, Workforce Optimization, and e-publishing. These Internet-based applications are changing people's standard of living, quality of life, and the way they live, learn, work, and play. Regardless of the economic time, CEOs and business managers around the world agree that the timely implementation of these Internet-based applications positively impact the future of their organization.

Types of Internet Business Solutions

Cisco has defined the following Internet business solutions to help customers reap the benefits of Internet-powered e-business applications:

- **Customer Care**—Customer service and customer relationship management tools and techniques and how they can be used to help acquire and retain customers

- **e-commerce**—Strategies and tactics for successfully conducting business online. This includes either business to business (B2B) or with customers in a World Wide Web-based manner (B2C)

- **Supply Chain Management**—Covers the entire procurement and order fulfillment process for customers, supplier partnerships, product life cycle, and product service

- **e-learning**—Defines Internet-powered learning solutions for organizations because one day training aspects for every job will be made available online

- **Workforce Optimization**—Everything from streamlining routine administrative tasks and managing complex business operations to improving communications and facilitating learning

- **e-publishing**—Cisco's e-publishing solution is a set of practices, partnerships, and tools to transform your e-business relationships by improving control over the way you create

Customers, employees, and partners are a company's greatest assets. The most successful companies recognize this and find innovative ways to accommodate the changing needs of their customers, employees, and partners. The companies profiled later in this chapter champion ways to continually improve their interactions with their customers, employees, and partners through Internet-based applications. Internet-based applications and Internet business solutions enhance a business's productivity by providing new ways to ensure customer loyalty, building and maintaining relationships with your suppliers and partners through real-time applications, and by improving employee efficiency through collaboration, distance learning, and centralized World Wide Web-based information. The rest of this chapter discusses the Internet business solutions that have been defined to increase a business's effectiveness.

Customer Care Solution

In the 20th century, Dr. Edwards Deming redefined the business world with his organizing principles on quality and cost. Companies have learned that quality and cost are key; however, a new revolution in business recognizes that the customer is key. Companies around the world are realizing that a solid customer care solution is not a should, but a must. Just a few years ago a 1-800 number and some call center agents were deemed sufficient to take care of a customer. Now because of the Internet, customers can contact an organization through several communication media. World Wide Web, e-mail, fax, telephone, and face-to-face are some of the major ways communication between a customer and an organization occurs. Without an integrated customer care solution, the customer sees a splintered, inconsistent view of the organization. For example, have you ever called a customer service number and been prompted for your account number only to find that when the agent takes the call, he or she asks for your account number again? Figure 1-4 illustrates how traditional customer care is often fragmented across multiple functional silos, customer contact points, and communications media. This fragmentation leads to inconsistent sales and customer service levels, fragmented customer messaging, missed sales opportunities, and inefficient business processes.

Figure 1-4   *A Typical Splintered Call Center*

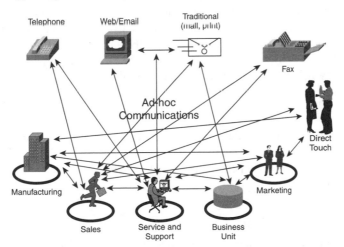

Customers choose organizations to do business with because of the feeling they get by working with that company. What's the difference between a satisfied customer and a customer who isn't satisfied? The answer is loyalty. A loyal customer becomes a "raving fan" customer and is the kind of customer all companies want. To create this type of customer, Internet-based companies meet current and future customer needs by seamlessly coordinating sales, customer service, marketing, support, and other customer-facing functions. These successful companies' customer care strategy integrates people, processes, and technology to create the best relationships with customers, distribution-channel partners, employees, and suppliers.

Some of the measurable business benefits of integrating customer interactions across marketing, sales, e-commerce, fulfillment, billing and provisioning, service, learning, and online communities include the following:

- Stronger relationships with customers and partners because of enhanced knowledge of the customer
- Improved customer satisfaction
- Increased brand awareness
- Reduced operating costs through increased employee productivity
- Efficiently scaled marketing, sales, and service functions
- Increased revenue, cross-selling, and up-selling
- Improved ability to retain existing customers and reach/acquire new customers
- Increased order accuracy and reduced cycle times

Case Study: Lands' End

With signature products like the men's button-down Oxford shirt, Lands' End has provided traditionally styled, classic casual wear to its mail-order customers since 1963. In 1995, the company became one of the first to embrace the Internet as a distribution channel. With fifteen mail orders on a "good day," according to founder Gary C. Comer, the company built its success around a guiding principle of excellence, and delightfully personalized one of the first catalogs to use the World Wide Web as a channel to customers. "The World Wide Web came along and we were intrigued by it," says Ann Vesperman, Vice President of Customer Services.

Challenge

Lands' End wanted to find a way to deliver "online service with a smile." Even though the company was a recognized leader in customer satisfaction, the goal was to ensure its World Wide Web site recreated the highly personalized, real-time interaction that built brand equity with customers over the phone.

Solution

Lands' End selected Cisco's Customer Interaction Suite (CIS) to integrate the company's Internet commerce, service, and telephone infrastructures to deliver voice/live agents on the World Wide Web. Now Lands' End successfully combines the personal value of human interaction with the information value of the World Wide Web. Customer service representatives can browse along with customers with Cisco's Follow-Me browsing technology. Customers can also browse with friends using Cisco's Shop With A Friend product.

Results

With the debut of the new service, Lands' End Live visitors could "Click to Talk" to a live agent directly from the World Wide Web or they could collaborate and shop with a friend via the World Wide Web. Sales for www.landsend.com more than doubled in one year from $61 million to $138 million with this new service in place. Over 38 million visitors have browsed the site during that time. Services are available 24 hours a day, 364 days a year. Specialty Shoppers are available 16 hours each day to help customers choose the right size, the right gift, or the right accessories to coordinate with their wardrobe.

In 2001, the Gartner Group named Lands' End the number one online retailer for World Wide Web-based customer care.

Figure 1-5 shows the end result of Lands' End's challenge to integrate quality customer care into its World Wide Web site.

Figure 1-5   *Lands' End World Wide Web-Based Customer Care*

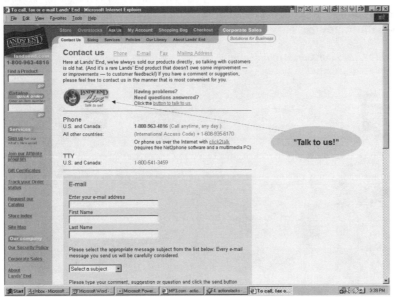

Cisco Customer Care Architecture

By combining Cisco IP telephony and contact center solutions, the Cisco IP Contact Center (IPCC) delivers an integrated suite of proven products that enables agents using Cisco IP phones to receive both time-division multiplexing (TDM) and Voice over IP (VoIP) calls. Because the IPCC was intended for integration with legacy call-center platforms and networks, it provides a migration path to IP-based customer contact while taking advantage of previous legacy PBX technology investments.

IPCC presents an operational view of customer data, internally and externally, regardless of contact method. An integral part of Cisco's Architecture for Voice, Video and Integrated Data (AVVID), the IPCC can be implemented in a single-site environment or integrated into a multi-site contact center enterprise. Specific capabilities include intelligent call routing, automatic call distribution (ACD) functionality, network-to-desktop computer telephony integration (CTI), interactive voice response (IVR) integration, call queuing, and consolidated reporting. The IPCC's open, standards-based architecture can also potentially support World Wide Web-based customer contact, including collaborative browsing, text chat, and e-mail response management. The IPCC utilizes a company's existing IP network, optimizing investments in a wide-area network (WAN) infrastructure and lowering administrative expenses. Geographic independence of both agent resources and IP-based application servers through the ubiquity of IP transport allows a business to easily extend the contact center enterprise boundaries to include branch offices, at-home agents, and knowledge workers.

Whether a company is expanding an existing operation or establishing its first site, the Cisco IPCC lowers total cost of ownership and capital-equipment investment, and allows for a single support staff, eliminating the overhead of multiple diverse data, voice, and video networks. Figure 1-6 illustrates the "New World" Customer Care architecture.

Figure 1-6   *"New World" Customer Care Architecture*

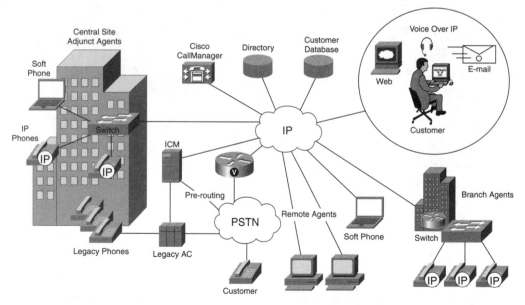

The Cisco Customer Care Solution's network and system architecture includes the following:

- Servers and interaction technologies, such as e-mail, co-browsing, and unified messaging

- Communications enablers, such as IP call switching, IP interactive voice response (IVR), intelligent contact management (ICM), and collaboration/click-to-talk

e-commerce Solution

Cisco's e-commerce Solution enables private enterprises and public institutions to conduct transactions online with suppliers, business partners, and customers through World Wide Web-based, interactive applications supported by a secure and robust systems and network infrastructure.

Cisco's e-commerce Solution provides a framework around strategies and tactics for successfully conducting business online. A complete e-commerce solution includes the Commerce Engine/Server (with the essential Before-You-Order, Order, and After-You-Order functions) and the associated Commerce Enabling Services (Service and Warranty, Financial Services, Logistics/Fulfillment) together with a secure and robust network foundation (Enabling Infrastructure and Foundation Infrastructure), as illustrated in Figure 1-7.

Figure 1-7   *Cisco's e-commerce Solution Framework*

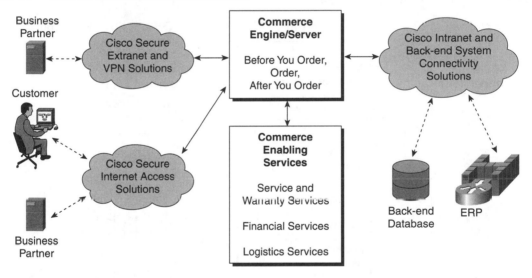

Cisco's full-service e-commerce solution model consists of six major components:

- **Pre-order/lead management/online marketing**—All of the pretransaction functions

- **Online ordering/customer service**—The order-related components of online transactions

- **Financial services functions**—The actual transaction-related functions

- **Service contract functions**—Provide customers with the ability to check on and order services

- **Logistics/fulfillment**—Fulfillment and distribution

- **Post-order management/non-technical customer support**—Order status, invoicing, returns, and parts replacement

Organizations can support their overall business objectives and profitability goals by viewing e-commerce as a strategic business tool. Some of the measurable benefits follow:

- Increased customer satisfaction resulting from improved order accuracy and customer service, and reduced cycle times

- Decreased operating costs

- Increased sales opportunities as a result of reaching existing and new markets more effectively

- Increased employee, customer, and channel partner productivity

The architecture outlined by Figure 1-8 shows the building blocks for a World Wide Web infrastructure business operation.

Figure 1-8   *e-commerce Business Architecture*

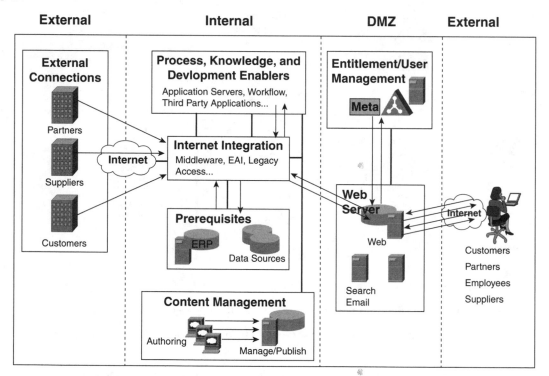

When you click on a World Wide Web site the following components are interacting behind the scenes to display the dynamic World Wide Web page unique to a your visit:

- **World Wide Web services**—This is considered the front-end or World Wide Web Layer of a World Wide Web site. World Wide Web servers (for example, Netscape, MS-IIS, and Apache), e-mail (such as SMTP, Notes, and Exchange), FTP (various), and search servers run as separate machines in this layer to spread the load. Server Load Balancers or Content Switches, covered in Chapter 5, "Content Delivery Networks," distribute requests across these servers.

- **User management/entitlement**—These are the centralized storage and management servers for user information. Usually stored in a Lightweight Directory Access Protocol (LDAP) capable server and integrated with back-end systems through a meta-directory system, these entitlement engines identify users and determine what resources they can use.

- **Application servers**—These servers typically perform the business logic. They can be general-purpose servers (Oracle App Server, Netscape App Server, BEA Weblogic, and so forth) or business application servers. Some overlap exists between these two categories, but they both have the same basic principles of load balancing, high-availability, database connectivity, state and session management, and content templating. The primary differentiator is if they come with a business application out-of-the-box.

- **Interaction enablers**—These applications provide the glue to connect the disparate services together in a guaranteed, scalable manner.

- **Prerequisite systems/information repositories**—These are the myriad of existing backend systems and databases that the company extends or leverages with the World Wide Web. Most data is stored in these. Typical system features include the capability to access, transform, and guarantee delivery in a publish/subscribe manner.

- **External connections**—Inter-enterprise process integration is handled through the interaction enablers over secure connections. This allows system-to-system/bi-directional person-to-system, guaranteed, and secure communication for streamlining business process integration.

Depending on the robustness of the implementation in each block, this architecture enables a customer to do everything from basic World Wide Web services, to complex, mission-critical applications.

As part of a complete Internet commerce solution, Cisco provides optimum network reference architectures and a range of pretested network configurations that are optimized to support Internet commerce applications. Cisco's e-commerce reference architecture is fully interoperable with all server, application, and database vendors. Chapter 2, "Internet System Architecture Design Overview," details this architecture, and the technologies that support the architecture are detailed throughout the book.

Supply Chain Management Solution and Architecture

More and more businesses must run at the Internet's speed to satisfy escalating customer demands. To compete in this quickly changing, customer-driven era, companies must move beyond functional World Wide Web sites and e-mail. A networked supply chain is one way that companies are revolutionizing their services. Along with quality, cost, and customer support, responsiveness is also a key characteristic of a company creating "raving fan" customers. A networked supply chain allows an enterprise to best fulfill its promise to customers of consistent, timely delivery, quality products, and lower costs. With a networked supply chain, customers place orders on a World Wide Web-based front end (which could include configuration) and they are promised delivery dates based on supply chain availability. The ability to immediately communicate orders to supply chain constituents who manufacture, test, and deliver products at unprecedented cost and speed drives order fulfillment.

By seamlessly integrating supply chain suppliers, manufacturers, distributors, and retailers into a single virtual enterprise serving the customer, companies achieve huge competitive advantages. Companies such as Ford, Federal Express, Proctor & Gamble, and Wal-Mart have used the networked supply chain to dramatically transform the competitive landscape of their markets. Figure 1-9 demonstrates this architecture.

Figure 1-9 *Networked Supply Chain*

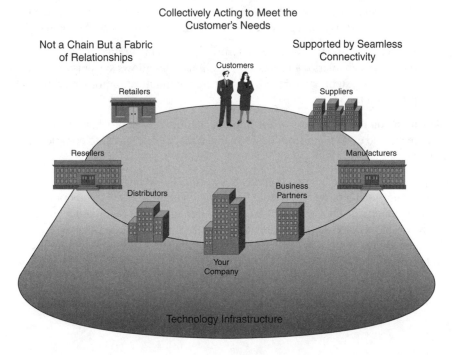

Cisco Supply Chain Management Architecture

Figure 1-10 illustrates Cisco's networked supply chain management architecture.

Figure 1-10 *Cisco Networked Supply Management Architecture*

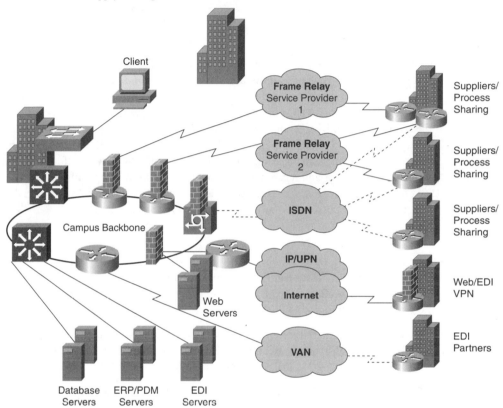

The Cisco extended enterprise is built on a scalable and reliable network and system infrastructure that uses end-to-end connectivity strategies to support each supplier's business requirements. Everything from critical business transactions, product information, test scripts and results to customer demand signals travel over these secure connections.

e-learning Solution

IT professionals face rapid changes in skill requirements. Executives worldwide need to know that their employees are prepared. With e-learning's power, effectiveness, and efficiency, today's learners can turn fast-paced change into a key advantage for themselves and their organizations. IT professionals are not the only professionals who require information to be effective in their job. Virtually every job requires skill enhancement or refinement. It's been said that training for an aspect of every job in the future will be delivered over the Internet. e-learning allows the learner to assimilate the finest content visually and auditorally. The last learning style, kinesthetically (or with hands-on application) is being added to e-learning systems to allow the learner to practice and apply what they learn. With this component in place, every learner can receive content that best fits their individual learning style, whether that is visually, auditorally, or kinesthetically.

Traditional Learning Challenges

With e-learning being the most effective solution to the education challenge, some companies still make use of airlines and individual videotapes to update and train their employees. This type of training is expensive and slow. 8,500 employees from 170 sites (50 employees per site) traveling for training at least once a year for one week will spend 17 million dollars in classroom costs and T&E, compared to 1.7 million dollars online using Cisco Content Delivery Networks (covered later in Chapter 5). Many executives and CEOs now see the benefit of being able to deliver a message in seconds through the corporate network. If the CEO has to make an extremely important announcement, do you think an employee would rather see, hear, and feel the emotion of the CEO's message on video at their desktop or would they rather read the message in an impersonal e-mail?

What e-learning Provides

e-learning provides faster learning at reduced costs, increased access to learning, and clear accountability for all participants in the learning process. Some of the benefits of e-learning include the following:

- Learners can learn through a live feed or are free to study at their own pace 24 hours a day, regardless of location. Because e-learning makes learners accountable through online testing and progress management, employees achieve their predetermined goals.

- Organizations benefit by tracking learner performance to assess workforce preparation.

- Developers of e-learning content receive immediate feedback on the performance of their learning tools and provide continual and timely improvement to their curriculum.

- Organizations build communities of collaboration where multiple learners can meet to cultivate and refine a concept or idea.

The following two media-based delivery technologies provide the backbone for e-learning programs:

- **Scheduled delivery**—Fixed in time and place, this technology includes multicasts (to desktops) and virtual classrooms.

- **On-demand**—Available to individuals when they have particular learning needs, this technology includes World Wide Web-based training, content-on-demand, simulation, and CD-ROM.

On-demand delivery is more flexible and is accessible from anywhere and at any time. Because of the demand for network video, on-demand delivery poses more challenges to a company's existing infrastructure and should be thought about in advance because of the many unicast streams.

Case Study: Genuity

Acquired by GTE in 1997, Genuity needed to train its rapidly expanded sales force on a completely new set of products. The training needed to be available to salespeople located around the world. Bringing salespeople up to speed quickly on new products was a key priority to the success of the organization.

Solution

Using its existing, fully redundant network that employs Cisco routers for a scalable architecture, Genuity deployed Virtual University, an e-learning solution that salespeople across the globe use to learn about company products and offerings. They created World Wide Web-based content to train sales reps as well as a learning management system to track the entire process. The program was augmented by mentoring and short classroom sessions.

Results

Virtual University helps new salespeople get up to speed more quickly on company products. The company found that salespeople trained with the program accomplished their first sale 25 percent faster than those trained in a traditional classroom did, and the size of their first sale was double. A new hire's training period decreased from 18 weeks to 8 weeks with the e-learning solution. The program also helps keep veteran employees up to date with refresher courses.

Cisco's e-learning Architecture

Figure 1-11 illustrates Cisco's e-learning Content Delivery Networks (CDN) architecture for scheduled delivery of e-learning programs.

Figure 1-11 *Cisco's e-learning CDN Architecture*

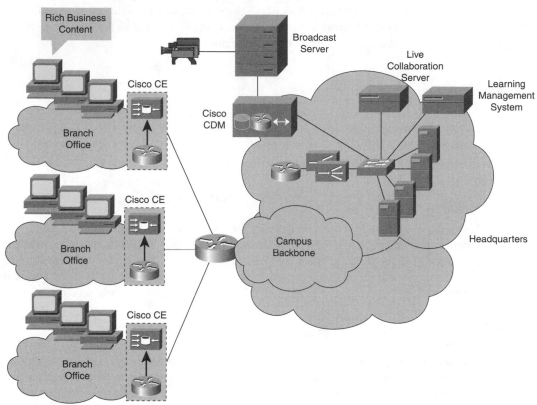

Today, more and more enterprises bring learning online to experience the benefits of increased cost savings, improved revenues, and corporate agility. While e-learning makes knowledge available anywhere, anytime, organizations still struggle with how to deliver a quality experience without causing massive network congestion. Using Cisco Enterprise Content Delivery Networks (e-CDNs) as the e-learning infrastructure, enterprises can finally solve this problem and make rich online learning a reality.

Cisco e-CDNs bring all kinds of learning and communications —live or on-demand—to employees, partners, suppliers, and customers. Content Delivery Networks are covered in more detail in Chapter 5, but the basic premise is to move high-bandwidth content as close as possible to the learner, and enable a highly interactive, engaging experience at the desktop without being constrained by a "skinny" Internet connection. Content is streamed locally using available LAN bandwidth through Cisco Content Engines.

Cisco e-CDNs provide the caching functionality that organizations need to improve World Wide Web application performance, as well as integrate with the industry's leading learning applications for end-to-end solutions that include courseware, testing and assessment, virtual classrooms, knowledge and learning management, publishing, and more.

Workforce Optimization Solution

The Japanese have one word that means gradual, orderly, and continuous improvement. The word is *KAIZEN* and it means *to continually improve in all areas of life—personal life, home life, social life, and working life*. The word KAIZEN when applied to business involves empowering everyone in an organization to work together to make improvements without large capital investments. The philosophy is similar to Cisco's Workforce Optimization Solution. The Workforce Optimization involves having every business unit asking the question, "What are some ways we can add value to the organization by either enhancing productivity or increasing profit contribution?" One proven answer is through World Wide Web-based applications.

The Internet is responsible for a plethora of workforce optimization tools that companies can use to improve employee productivity and satisfaction. Companies now automate administrative tasks and employees step into more responsible roles; these advances dramatically affect the workplace culture. Every new employee adds an incremental burden of tasks, such as processing expenses, benefits, and purchase requisitions. Traditionally, a growing business would add support staff in the finance, procurement, and human resources (HR) departments to handle the increased volume of these manual transactions. To reduce administrative costs and create more agile organizations, companies are incorporating World Wide Web-based tools, rather than more personnel, into their infrastructure design. This process creates a win-win situation—companies save money and existing employees grow from more challenging processes than manually working on rote administrative tasks. These new responsibilities enable a person to become even more empowered to grow and improve productivity contributed to the company.

A productive workforce is now defined by how easily accessible information is—whether it is corporate administrative information that saves an employee time, or market knowledge that improves employee-customer interaction. Today, effective information is dynamic, or real-time, and is "virtually" accessible. World Wide Web-based company systems provide workers with the dynamic information they need to make better decisions in a timely manner. They enable a range of activities, from employees managing their own benefit plans, to business unit managers growing their business divisions. By making information available anytime, anywhere, organizations create the expectation that employees are responsible for making informed decisions. When employees spend less time looking for information, they have more time for making strategic contributions to the business.

The payoff for deploying Internet-powered workforce optimization is impressive:

- Greater employee productivity

- Increased profitability

- Faster growth

- Enhanced employee loyalty

Every penny saved by converting old processes into a streamlined, Internet-powered workforce optimization solution can contribute to cost-cutting efforts or be reinvested in new initiatives and product and service innovation. For example, Cisco saves over 2,500 dollars per employee every year as a direct result of its workforce optimization applications. These savings are reinvested in new programs and services to improve customer satisfaction and retention, and to ensure Cisco's continued market leadership.

The following examples show how Cisco has used workforce optimization to increase profit contribution and enhance productivity:

- **Improved communication and effectiveness**—Cisco Employee Connection is the launching pad for Cisco's workforce optimization applications and communications.

- **Streamlined processes and reduced administrative overhead**—Cisco's Benefits Online application automates paper-intensive procedures and time-consuming administrative tasks.

- **Effective decision-making data**—Cisco's Executive Information System provides booking and backlog information for use in real-time business analysis.

- **Results-oriented, cost-effective recruiting capabilities**—Cisco's HR department actively recruits online 24 hours a day, 7 days a week. Unique World Wide Web applications match candidates to the appropriate job, reducing the cost per hire.

- **Real-time access to employee contact information**—Cisco's online employee directory provides reporting chains and organization charts, in addition to basic employee contact information.

- **Improved effectiveness and reduced travel costs**—Cisco's Distance Learning applications enable employees to learn when, where, and how they want to from their computer.

e-publishing Solution

In this age of Internet ubiquity, an e-business strategy is necessary for a company to sustain its position in the marketplace. A truly agile e-business uses relationships with all its constituents to drive a sustainable competitive advantage. Building a robust World Wide Web foundation provides the platform for all e-business activity. e-publishing is a cornerstone of that infrastructure.

e-publishing is about creating the rich experience that can be used to build valuable relationships with your clients and partners. Without a solid e-publishing plan and processes providing control over the experience, a company will be unable to leverage its e-business efforts to build the advantage it needs to stay competitive.

The way a company's information flows online is directly related to the online experience a customer will have with that company. The following list provides e-publishing strategies that, as implemented, incrementally increase the quality of the online relationship between the company and the customer:

- **Static**—Content that doesn't change until the author manually refreshes it.
- **Dynamic**—Content that changes automatically, but looks the same for every audience.
- **Customized**—Content that is built from predefined components that the audience combines into a customer experience.
- **Adaptive**—Content from predefined components.
- **Relationship-based**—Content that incorporates the audience into the publishing process by creating an environment where users contribute to the process with feedback or subject matter expertise.

The correct e-publishing model can streamline the development of new applications that transform relationships. This agility helps your business provide more services, more quickly and cheaply to a broader audience.

e-publishing is a cornerstone of the World Wide Web foundation model that enables all e-business. This strategic component encompasses the tools, business processes, and systems architecture necessary for an integrated Internet experience.

In addition to the business strategy and process elements of using content to build relationships, an e-publishing solution has three primary components:

- **Content Creation**—The authoring and developing content into structured components
- **Content Management**—Validating, versioning, and deploying the components
- **Content Delivery**—Recombining and distributing the managed components into various media for all audiences

These components provide the building blocks for creating e-publishing systems at all phases of the e-publishing spectrum, from static through relationship-based.

Summary

This chapter explains what Internet-based applications are and that companies use them to move to the next level. Each and every Internet-based application and solution provides significant payback and profit through productivity increases and expense decreases. As you read through the remaining chapters of this book, keep in mind that these Internet-based applications are what drive the specific requirements of the architecture. The next chapter tackles what customers have defined as the absolute musts of an Internet system architecture and what components make up the Internet system architecture.

Review Questions

1 What is an Internet system architecture?

2 What are the six types of Internet business solutions?

3 How does Lands' End apply the principles of the New World Customer Care Architecture?

4 What are some ways that companies can leverage the e-learning solution?

5 What Cisco architecture solution makes up the e-learning architecture?

6 Companies use the IP Contact Center Architecture Solution to improve what part of their business?

7 What solution seamlessly integrates suppliers, manufacturers, and purchasers?

After reading this chapter, you should be able to perform the following tasks:

- Explain the various parts of the Cisco Internet system reference architecture and their functionality.

- List the benefits of the Cisco Internet system reference architecture.

CHAPTER 2

Internet System Architecture Design Overview

Internet system architecture is an infrastructure that supports Internet business. It includes both network and system components.

This chapter discusses the components of Cisco Systems' Internet Reference Architecture and how they fit together. It covers the architecture benefits as well as important considerations to take into account when designing and implementing the reference architecture.

Internet System Architecture Components

An Internet system infrastructure includes the following software components:

- Central database servers
- Application servers
- Web servers
- Clients

An Internet system infrastructure includes the following network components:

- Campus network provides connectivity to all end users on the campus
- Connectivity across a WAN network to remote offices, partners, and suppliers
- Connectivity over switched networks to telecommuters, mobile users, and suppliers
- Connectivity to the Internet to allow extensive access for employees, customers, and partners

You can view Internet system architecture as a set of fundamental technologies that provide secure, manageable, ubiquitous access for all networked applications, enabling technologies and data. Combined, these technologies create a single, connected network and system fabric used as a platform for hosting applications that cross traditional corporate boundaries and enable key constituents to work together. By adding multiple copies of pieces of the architecture for scalability and to separate application functions, you can create multiple tiers to create the classic *n-tier* model.

Cisco Internet System Reference Architecture Components

The Cisco Internet System Reference Architecture was developed by top systems engineers at Cisco, with many years of experience working with real-world customer networks. The resulting architecture scales extremely well, forms a highly available network, and is supported by a group in Cisco's award winning Technical Assistance Center (TAC) that specializes in supporting this architecture.

TAC Internet engineers are trained on and support the reference architecture as a whole. In contrast to technical support individuals who know about a single product, these engineers know how the components interact. This means that as soon as a customer calls the center, the engineers already have a basic understanding of the network and component interactions and as a result, can resolve issues rapidly.

This chapter works progressively, adding to the basic architecture to build the full Cisco Internet System Reference Architecture from the individual pieces. As the chapter progresses, you will see certain terms and definitions used to describe the various pieces and functions in the architecture. These are recapped at the end of this chapter.

Perimeter Routers

The first component in the architecture, the perimeter router, connects the architecture to the Internet.

The perimeter routers, along with the Layer 3 switches, provide the backbone for the reference architecture design, as demonstrated in Figure 2-1.

Figure 2-1   *Perimeter Routers*

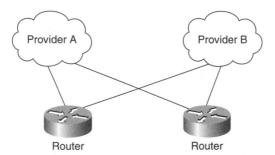

As with all components in the architecture, duplicate routers can be configured for 100 percent redundancy. This avoids single points of failure and allows software and hardware upgrades to be done *hitlessly*. The term *hitlessly* means that no system user notices any outage and no network packets get lost as a result of the changes. This, along with the other component redundancy the architecture supports, dramatically improves the entire architecture's availability.

Availability refers to the amount of time a system is available to users.

For an application or service to be available, all system architecture components—including database servers, storage devices, and the end-to-end network—must provide continuous service.

The perimeter router has many functions. It connects the system to the Internet or extranet. This connection can take many forms, including Ethernet, Fast Ethernet, Gigabit, T1, T3, and many others. As you can imagine, being able to seamlessly take one perimeter router out of service to upgrade or change interface types allows you to seamlessly increase or decrease bandwidth or change transport types as traffic varies, or as different technologies become cheaper.

In addition, this router can be used as a first line of defense from hacking attempts by running the Cisco IOS-based firewall software. This software, different from that used in the PIX firewall, also protects your network from the remote possibility that a bug in the PIX software would allow a hacker to gain access to your network because that bug won't be present in the perimeter router.

The redundant configuration using two or more routers with Border Gateway Protocol Version 4 (BGP-4) running between your network and dual Internet service providers (ISPs) provides fully redundant access to the Internet or extranet. When you set up two separate connections, each connection should be homed to its own perimeter router. If either of the connections or routers fails, connectivity is not lost.

The router's size and speed depends on several factors, including the amount of traffic that will flow through the router and the number of functions the router performs. In its simplest form, the router terminates link and routes packets to the Layer 3 switch in the design. If one of your architecture goals is to connect your network to multiple ISPs, you will most likely need to implement BGP. To add BGP-4 into the solution to add redundant ISPs, you may need to add extra memory to your border routers to support using full Internet routing tables. At the time of this writing, BGP-4 generally requires a minimum of 128 MB of DRAM.

Providing quality of service (QoS) is also an important consideration. If you must drop packets anywhere within your infrastructure, you want to drop the packets that are least important. QoS involves deciding which packets are important and how important they are relative to other packets, and acting on those priorities throughout the infrastructure so that every component is in agreement about which packets are important and which are not. The border router is the primary place where packets enter your network, and at this point they need to be screened and marked with their appropriate importance—this uses CPU power.

If you add BGP-4, firewall software, or QoS, you must take the edge router's CPU requirements into consideration.

Just as the needs of the system impact the memory, processor speed and expansion slot characteristics of the perimeter router, all the components in the architecture need ultimately to be able to accommodate the amount of users to which you wish to provide service. All the architecture components need to be chosen carefully to provide enough system capacity.

When communicating your needs to an ISP or hardware vendor, several terms can be used to describe the type of routers and other components that you need. Because the border router is the first piece of the architecture you'll need to specify, and because you need to use these terms for each component, familiarize yourself with them now.

In network terms, *capacity* is defined as the data-carrying capability of a circuit or network, and is usually measured in bits per second (bps).

To the user, capacity is reflected as a certain level of performance; when there is not enough capacity, performance suffers. An analogy would be a highway traffic jam. When there is too much traffic and too few lanes to accommodate it, the result is congestion and traffic delays.

Capacity is closely related to *utilization*. Utilization is defined as the percent of total available capacity in use.

Another concept that relates to capacity is *scalability*. If a business is growing, an architecture that has enough capacity today might not have enough capacity six months from now. To meet the expanding needs of the organization, architecture must be designed to be scalable. Most of Cisco's products are modular and allow you to switch out components to improve the system. This is closely linked to the redundancy and hitless upgrading previously mentioned.

Capacity is the first consideration in designing Internet system architecture. One strong design requirement is adequate capacity. You do not want to design an architecture that does not have enough capacity to satisfy user requests.

If at any point in the system you don't have enough capacity, be it network or server, bottlenecks appear. A *bottleneck* in a network is the point at which network traffic slows down because of limited bandwidth. When you have bottlenecks in your system, the system might still be available, but it is too slow to be useful. Consequently, users perceive your service to be slow and their opinion of it suffers. For example, if a web page does not paint within a few seconds, users generally abort the connection and go elsewhere. If most of your users are external customers, the result is lost customers and lost business. Capacity is one of the most important considerations in designing Internet system architecture. Capacity, availability, and other design facets for each of the components are explained in further detail later in this chapter.

Layer 3 Switches

The Layer 3 switches form your architecture's Ethernet switching fabric and provide connectivity for all of your network's components—each provides the physical connection points for all the servers and network equipment that plug into the network. Figure 2-2 shows how Layer 3 switches fit into the architecture topology.

Figure 2-2   *Layer 3 Switches*

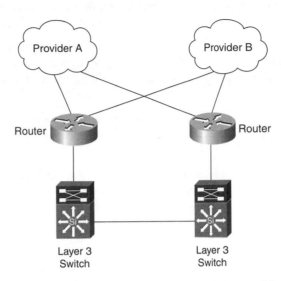

Using Layer 3 switches as opposed to older Layer 2 switches enables you to provide redundancy in the architecture above and beyond physical connectivity. It enables you to use routing protocols to reroute around failures far faster than Layer 2 healing mechanisms can. For example, the Enhanced Interior Gateway Routing Protocol (EIGRP) can reroute around a failed link in fractions of a second, while Spanning Tree, Layer 2's process for this function, is far slower.

Connectivity is the interconnections that get the user from where they are to where the data is. It is the glue between all the components (network and servers) in system architecture.

System architecture with good connectivity allows application users to perform their business tasks from any location across any medium.

Switches must be chosen for the number of hosts you need to plug in, the type of physical connections you need to support, and the amount of traffic that the system needs to sustain on the backplane.

Some types of connectivity within an Internet system follow:

- Intranet (corporate LANs and WANs)
- Extranet
- Internet
- Remote access
- Mobile user access

Networking starts with connectivity. With Internet connectivity, organizations can communicate with customers, employees, partners, suppliers, and prospects over the Internet any time, from anywhere. Conversely, without proper intranet, extranet, Internet, and remote access connectivity, you cannot do Internet business successfully.

Connectivity is especially important for supply chain management, because supply chain management relies on a network that not only reaches into all corners of a single organization, but also links that organization to external trading partners, including suppliers, distributors, and retailers.

If connectivity fails, suppliers are unable to receive orders from customers, manufacturers can't receive orders from suppliers, and billing and payment processes also fail. In short, the supply chain is broken and business stops.

Connectivity is also the foundation for availability. If any connectivity fails, the system or part of the system is no longer available for certain users. Connectivity is a vital dimension in designing Internet systems.

Switch Sizing

In sizing switches, look at the following three main components:

- Queuing model
- Switching implementation
- Switching fabric

Queuing Model

The switch uses the *queuing model* to control traffic when multiple ports are sending data to one destination port. When several ports send more data than the output port can handle, the data must be stored and sent later when the output port has available bandwidth. Buffers (storage space in memory) store these packets in queue, waiting to be sent out the destination port. These buffers can be a fixed size or dynamic. Fixed-size buffers allow easy switch but are not very memory efficient. Using fixed-size buffers produce fewer buffers to hold packets per kilobyte of buffer space available.

Variable-size buffers are more difficult to build into a switch and more expensive, but are far more memory efficient than fixed-size buffers. Using variable-size buffers allows you to queue up more packets per kilobyte of buffer memory than fixed buffers do.

In addition to the types of buffers, the queues themselves can be placed in several places in the switch. You could queue packets before they leave the destination port, or queue them at the source ports where they first arrive. Placing these queues on the input ports is easier but less efficient. Placing them on output ports allows you to avoid "head of line blocking," which is a condition where an output port is too busy to service the input ports and, as a result, the performance on those multiple input ports slows down while waiting for the output port to finish transmitting. With output queuing, the input ports can send data into the buffer available for the queue and do not slow down. Output queuing is preferred over input queuing.

A last approach to assigning buffers for queuing is to use a shared-memory queue. Here there is a central pool of memory and each port does not have its own dedicated buffers. This is even more memory efficient than the other two types of buffering.

Whichever buffering technique is used, make sure that your switch also provides for multiple queues per port and proper QoS. If some traffic needs to be dropped as a result of congestion on a port and lack of buffer space, you want to drop relatively unimportant traffic. This should be done based on the architecture-wide QoS settings used on the perimeter routers to classify traffic, providing end-to-end QoS in the architecture. By using multiple queues per port—each with their own buffers—and assigning specific traffic to specific queues, you can control which traffic is dropped when congestion occurs. Having more queues allows you to do this more granularly. If you specify three levels of QoS packet priority, you should attempt to have three queues per port.

Switching Implementation

The *switching implementation* is how the switch makes decisions on where to send each Ethernet frame. This decision can take place in a centralized fashion where one Central Processing Unit (CPU) or Application Specific Integrated Circuit (ASIC) makes the choice, or it can occur in a distributed fashion where each card or port in a switch makes the choice itself. Distributed switching is generally faster but involves more technology to make sure that all the ports or cards agree on where a packet needs to go. In centralized switching, the CPU or ASIC must be fast enough to make sure that the number of packets per second that need to flow through the switch can be achieved.

As previously mentioned, in addition to basic Ethernet switching, using Layer 3 switching in the architecture achieves faster convergence (convergence is the term that describes how fast a network finds a stable route around a problem, or how long the network takes to adapt to a topology change).

In Layer 3 switching, a routing choice first needs to be made when an IP or other Layer 3 packet enters the switch to determine which port the packet is destined for. This decision directs the Layer 2 portion of the switch to which port to send the packet to. This Layer 3 decision can be made using route caching (also known as *flow-based switching*), where you calculate where a specific network packets flow needs to go when you see the first packet and cache that information for subsequent packets in the flow. The number of new flows per second is important because this decision uses the CPU. If a switch is unable to set up enough flows (create enough cache entries) per second, no matter how fast the switch's Layer 2 portion, or how big the switch's backplane is (backplanes will be discussed in the next section), the switch cannot process those new connections. This is particularly critical in an Internet architecture because there could be tens of thousands of different flows from different endpoints on the Internet. An enterprise has far fewer possible endpoints.

The second method of Layer 3 switching is to use a forwarding information base (FIB) where you precalculate the routing information ahead of time and populate a table that can be consulted quickly because it is not built on the fly. This is a more complicated architecture to build in a switch and, once again, the process that looks up the entries in the FIB table must be fast enough that it doesn't slow the switch down.

Switch Fabric

The final piece of a switch is the *switch fabric*. This fabric is the system of components that actually connects any two ports together when data is flowing between them. It is responsible for delivering a packet from the input port to the output port once a decision has been made as to where to send it.

The first type of switch fabric is a bus architecture fabric that connects to all ports. In this design, the ports themselves are allocated a certain window in which they have unfettered access to the fabric to send their Ethernet frame. In this type of architecture, the method of determining which port is allowed access to the switch fabric is critical.

A crossbar switch fabric is the second type of fabric and essentially uses a mesh within the fabric to connect to all ports or all linecards at high speed. It is efficient for balanced traffic—traffic that is evenly distributed among ports as opposed to traffic being mostly destined for a single or a few ports. These fabrics have to block all ports from transmitting when a multicast or broadcast Ethernet frame is sent, however.

The last type of fabric is a shared-memory fabric where the switching core places the Ethernet frames into memory and the destination card and port retrieve them. Port buffers are built into the switch fabric in this architecture.

When looking at a switch, do not simply look at backplane speeds or any single metric. You must be aware of the architecture, which types of traffic flows you experience, and which architecture and traffic flows the switch handles best.

Redundancy with Layer 3 Switches

As mentioned at the beginning of this section, using Layer 3 switches enables you to create an additional level of fast-acting redundancy. Interconnecting each perimeter router to both of the redundant switches creates a full mesh, as shown in Figure 2-3.

Figure 2-3 Fully Meshed Switches

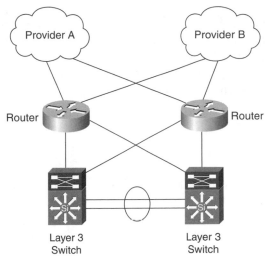

If an entire switch goes down, the traffic from both routers can still terminate onto the remaining switch. Because the switches are also connected to each other, no single connection failure will limit connectivity.

Several other switch features contribute to the overall design and might be features you implement in your network. Of important note is Cisco's EtherChannel software.

EtherChannel software on the Catalyst line of switches allows you to aggregate up to eight FastEthernet or Gigabit links into one virtual connection. The advantages are compelling. You can increase bandwidth on switch-to-switch links, router-to-switch links, and on some server to-switch links up to eightfold. In doing so, you also create multiple redundant paths. If one physical link goes down, seven others remain intact—effectively, you lose only one eighth of the bandwidth and the connection remains up.

Be aware that EtherChannel distributes frames across the links in a channel by reducing part of the binary pattern formed from the addresses in the frame to a numerical value that selects one of the links in the channel. EtherChannel distribution can use MAC addresses, IP addresses, and Layer 4 port numbers, and will, by default, use both source and destination IP address. You can specify source address, destination address, both source and destination addresses, or Layer 4 port numbers. As a result, some configurations do not work well, and the defaults should generally be used. For example, connecting four FastEthernet connections between a perimeter router and a switch using source MAC address usually does not work well. All packets are sourced from the same MAC address (that of the router), so all frames travel over one of the links. Be sure to configure EtherChannel properly.

More information on EtherChannel, as well as other technologies mentioned in this chapter, can be found at www.cisco.com under the documentation section. A similar standards-based protocol, 802.1Q is available as a trunking protocol in addition to EtherChannel should you need it.

When deploying two switches for redundancy, you can use EtherChannel to connect the two switches. The two switches connected together function as one virtual switch, so that putting half of the networking equipment on one and half on another has the effect of reducing single points of failure but in no way functions differently than if you had all equipment on a single switch, aside from the way that spanning tree functions. Spanning Tree is an advanced topic that is outside the scope of this book, but is covered in detail in the documentation section of Cisco Connection Online (CCO) at www.cisco.com.

Chapter 3, "High Availability Overview," covers EtherChannel in more detail.

Content Switches

Content switches are the next generation of load balancers. Traditional load balancers, such as the Cisco LocalDirector, distribute a large amount of traffic among several web, FTP, SMTP, and some other types of servers. This allows you to aggregate servers to gain performance as well as redundancy. Each new user who attempts a connection is sent to a specific server based on server load or a multitude of other parameters. Several algorithms determine which server to send a request to, including Round Robin, Weighted Round Robin, Least Connections, and some proprietary methods. Figure 2-4 shows an example of a typical packet flow from the user to the final destination—the server.

Figure 2-4 *Content Switches*

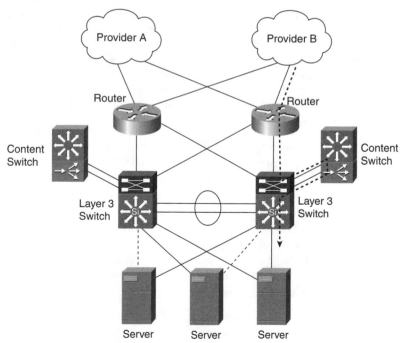

Simple load balancers are all software based. Each and every packet that goes to or from a server typically passes through the load balancer. This is because each pool of servers has a virtual IP address associated with it. Each client requests a page or network resource from the virtual server address. When the load balancer sees a packet destined for the virtual address, it decides which server to send the packet to, and from that point performs address translation or port translation on the initial and all subsequent packets in the connection flow.

For example, assume that you have three web servers in a server farm, as shown in Figure 2-5.

Figure 2-5   *Simple Load Balancing*

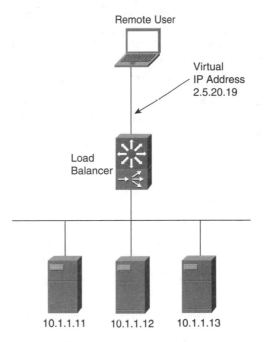

The remote user attempts to connect to the 2.5.20.19 server that actually does not exist. Instead, the load balancer sees the packet destined for 2.5.20.19 and decides which of the three servers to send the packet to. If it chooses to send the packet to the 10.1.1.11 server, it needs to rewrite the packet's destination IP address as 10.1.1.11 so that the server will receive and process it. When a return packet comes back from the server, the load balancer needs to change the source IP address in that packet to 2.5.20.19 so that the receiving remote user machine thinks it is getting a return packet from the server it was communicating with in the first place (2.5.20.19) and not a new server—10.1.1.11. In addition to simple IP address mapping, TCP sequence numbers are also mapped in the same way in the Cisco line of content switches to enable some important features. A significant amount of mapping gets done to each and every packet that passes through a load-balancing device.

All this dynamic changing of every packet by a program running in a software-based load balancer slows the packets down because the CPU must inspect each one. Generally, this adds a significant amount of latency to the connection.

The solution to this basic latency problem was to design hardware application-specific integrated circuits (ASICs), or chips, to do handle dynamic packet changes much faster. In the same way, as switches are the hardware equivalent of the old bridges that ran software, content switches do load balancing in hardware that used to happen in software. With content switches, the CPU decision on which server to load balance to happens only for the very first packet. All subsequent packets in the flow are switched by hardware. The CPU decides which server to send the packet to because this decision is fairly complex and can't be put onboard a simple chip. The CPU then reprograms the ASICs attached to the Ethernet ports on the fly to remap both addresses and sequence numbers. Once again, this is a good example of control versus forwarding planes on switches. The CPU, in this case, is the control plane. It has to reprogram the ASICs for each connection setup (the first packet in a flow). The ASICs take care of the rest of the packets (they comprise the forwarding plane). No matter how fast you move the data once a connection is set up, if you can't set up connections fast enough, the traffic gets bottlenecked by the CPU decision process itself.

In addition to regular load balancing based on a connection coming in and assigning that to a server based on an arbitrary algorithm, the Cisco Content Smart Switches (CSS) allow you to do far more.

Figure 2-6 shows a simplified example of a regular client requesting the page www.cisco.com from a server.

Figure 2-6 *A Simple HTTP Request*

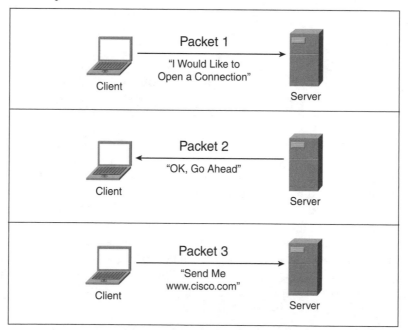

After an initial handshake between a client and a server, a client usually sends an HTTP request in a packet to the server requesting a particular URL. This can be a web page, a graphic, a movie, a sound, and so on. Along with the request, the client also sends the server cookie information, as well as basic information about the type of browser, language used, and various other client properties.

Older load balancers made their decision on which server to send the client to as soon as the first handshake packet arrived because they needed to pass that packet to the correct server for the server to set up the connection, as shown in Figure 2-7.

Figure 2-7   *Simple Load Balancing of an HTTP Request*

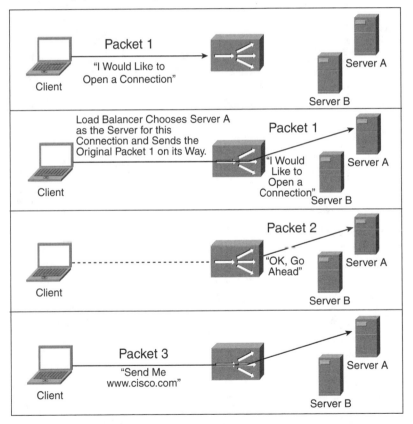

The issue with this type of load balancing is that it is particularly unintelligent. The load balancer is unaware of anything about the request except the source and destination IP addresses. The next step was to look at ports and be able to load balance based on port numbers. For example, if multiple users were connecting to 209.233.130.37, one using Telnet, another using FTP, and a third using HTTP, each of those requests could be sent to a completely different set of servers on the backend, despite trying to get to the same IP address.

With Cisco's Content Switch line you can do something even more sophisticated. When a connection is requested, the content switch itself replies to the connection, as shown in Figure 2-8.

Figure 2-8 *Spoofing of an HTTP Response*

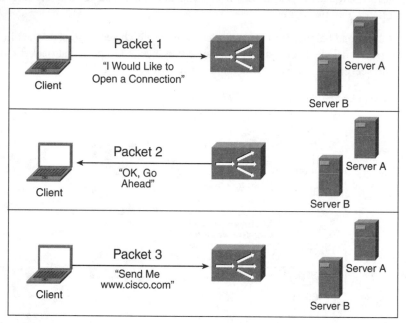

After the content switch, or CSS, sees the actual HTTP request, it requests the server it picks to send this user to. This basically produces two separate connections, one from the user to the CSS, and one from the CSS to the server. In hardware (the data plane), the CSS appliance now translates IP addresses, port numbers, and TCP/IP sequence numbers, as shown in Figure 2-9.

Figure 2-9 *Connecting an HTTP Server to an Existing Request*

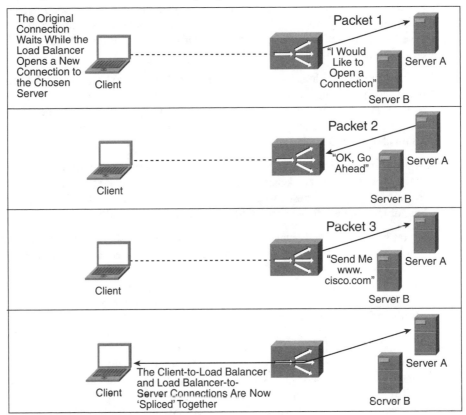

This scenario demonstrates several benefits. You can make choices about which server to send the user to based on anything in the HTTP request, such as load balancing choices based on URL, cookies, browser type, language, and so on. For example, suppose that you have a web site with news pictures on it. You might have ten servers with copies of all the pictures on the site resident on all of them; no matter which server you send a person to he gets the image. The issue with this is that most people hitting the web site are looking for recent images. You could move older images to a separate server and, based on URL, you could automatically move users who look for old pictures to that "old image" server. This has saved some of Cisco's customers hundreds of thousands of dollars in disk storage and CPU power. In addition, several servers for different languages or browsers can be set up and users can automatically be routed to the correct server pool.

Another advantage presents itself in the form of a security feature. A significant number of World Wide Web-based attacks use SYN attacks. The Step 1 packets in the requests shown in the preceding figures are SYN requests. Each time a request comes into a server, it must allocate a small amount of memory to remember that it is setting up a connection and wait for the HTTP request. In SYN attacks, the attacker never sends the HTTP request and keeps sending SYN packets, overwhelming the server and depleting its memory resources. Because the CSS opens a connection to the server only when a legitimate request is received, it avoids this problem. To save the CSS itself from being overrun, sophisticated algorithms that run on the CSS drop connections that never send an HTTP request.

Aside from regular load balancing, you might also need to keep users who request multiple pages, such as in any HTTP application, coming back to the same server. Once again, you can achieve this *stickiness* using several methods, including based on source IP address, and SSL secure connection ID number. Because the CSS has visibility into HTTP headers, you can even do this based on a URL or cookie.

The preferred method of maintaining this "session state"—maintaining a record of which server a user is working on and keeping the user there—is to use the tools available at the application layer. These tools are best implemented on the database server, but in the event that they are not available in the application, the CSS switches can provide this functionality.

If you were to correctly make load-balancing choices based on what users want to see, you would send the users to the server that serves up the content fastest and not necessarily which server has the most memory, is next in rotation, has the least connections, and so on. The issue with previous load-balancing technologies was that while they knew how long the session lasted, that was not a good indication of speed. For example, you may have had a user get a 200-kB file from server A, while another user retrieved a 20-kB page from server B that had backend database interactions. If they both took the same amount of time, it stands to reason that server A seems to outperform server B because it transferred ten times the data. To get a real-world basis for your choice, you really need to measure the time it takes for both servers to serve the same exact piece of content. Because the CSS sees the URLs themselves, it can compute realistically which server serves best by comparing the time it takes in a real-world connection to serve the same URL from different servers. No matter what type of algorithm—round robin, CPU, least connections, or any other basic load-balancing choice you make—you will never be as accurate as the CSS because the CSS load balances based on what makes the difference for your user—which server is currently serving up the content fastest.

The CSS also provides a way to handle flash crowds. Suppose, for example that there is a new music video available on a prominent web site. Visitors to the web site are clamoring to download the file. This one piece of content is being requested far more than any other on the servers, yet the servers each still have to process other requests. Wouldn't it be convenient to have the CSS automatically see that this *hot* content is being requested and copy that content to backup servers whose sole purpose is to serve only the hottest items at any particular time and bring those servers into the load-balancing pool for that specific piece of content only? The CSS appliances will do exactly that—automatically. ISPs might also have servers available for you to use as hot content servers for usage fees, avoiding the need for you to buy expensive servers for those few times when your site is overwhelmed. These backup servers can also be located around the globe so you can automatically stage hot content near the target audience. Far more CSS switch features exist, such as caching features and SLA hooks, and there is more depth to each feature mentioned thus far. More information is available online on CCO www.cisco.com under the documentation section.

Firewalls

Security is the process by which a company's information assets are protected. The goals of security are as follows:

- Maintain integrity

- Protect confidentiality

- Assure availability

Firewalls are the first line of defense used in networks to protect one segment from another and provide security. Other security pieces of the architecture, including hardware and security policies, are discussed further in Chapter 4, "Security Concepts and Design."

In the case of the Internet architecture, firewalls make sure that users or hackers on the extranet or Internet are unable to gain access to servers or network equipment that they should not have access to. In essence, firewalls are filters that keep unauthorized traffic from reaching sensitive parts of your network. Figure 2-10 shows the placement of the PIX firewalls between edge routers and the CSS switches.

Figure 2-10 *Placement of PIX Firewalls*

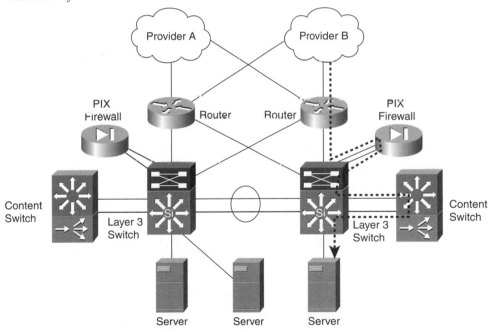

The packets from the Internet are forced to follow the path of the arrows on the diagram by the switch's configuration. The next few figures show this flow in a more logical way, as opposed to the physical connectivity shown in Figure 2-10.

As an example of a firewall operation, assume that you have a simple web site that provides information to users. Anyone from the Internet need only connect to your servers using the World Wide Web. Because HTTP (Standard WWW traffic) uses specific TCP port numbers to communicate with a server, you could put a firewall between the users and the server and only allow packets destined for the servers on port 80 to pass through the firewall, as shown in Figure 2-11.

Figure 2-11 *A Simple Firewall to Allow Port 80 Only*

With proper configuration, any other machines on the internal side of the firewall can still have unfettered access to any applications outside the firewall if they initiate the connections.

Firewalls allow you to do more than simply allow traffic in to specific ports on specific machines. They also make sure that only properly set-up connections pass through the firewall so that another machine on the network can't "butt in" on a conversation between a client and server masquerading as the original participant. Maintaining a list of active connections and keeping track of this information is characteristic of a *stateful* firewall. Firewalls without this stateful function do not keep track of which conversations are in progress and allow any packets matching TCP ports that have been allowed in the firewall to pass through.

Firewalls inspect each and every packet that passes through them to make sure that no hack attempts are allowed. As a result, a firewall can affect the speed at which an architecture functions. As with any network component, the firewall can potentially slow down the overall infrastructure by adding latency if the firewall becomes too busy, but also by adding a certain amount of latency because of regular operation.

A firewall will slow down all packets passing though it as it inspects each packet. If it takes the firewall 15 milliseconds to inspect a packet and sends it on its way, packets entering the firewall will leave the other side of the firewall 15 milliseconds later.

Each device on the network adds a certain amount of *latency* to the packet as it travels. The faster the firewall's CPU, the less time it takes to inspect each packet, and the faster the packet travels through the firewall. The actual process consists of the packet being received on the ingress interface and copied into a buffer in RAM. The CPU compares what is in the buffer (the packet itself) to tables to determine if the packet meets the criteria to pass through the firewall. The packet can also be altered here to support Network Address Translation (NAT). When the firewall's CPU is done looking at the packet in RAM, it is sent out the egress interface and on its way.

Throughput is another issue with all networking equipment—how many megabits of traffic the box can transfer per second. As with your content switch you must size the firewall to handle a certain number of connection setups per second and, in addition, the firewall (because it is stateful and keeps track of all active connections) needs to be sized for the number of simultaneous connections at any one time.

At the high end and as of this writing, the PIX 535 can handle one Gigabit of throughput, 500,000 concurrent sessions, and handles new sessions at a rate of 7,000 per second.

Firewalls can also have multiple interfaces, as shown in Figure 2-12.

Figure 2-12 *Firewall with Multiple Interfaces*

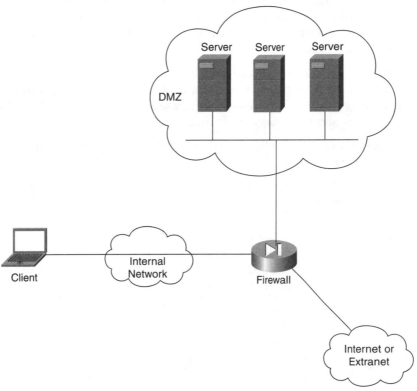

Usually one interface connects the firewall to the Internet or extranet, while another connects to a demilitarized zone (DMZ) where the servers reside. Yet another interface might connect to the company internal network (intranet) so that data can be transferred to and from the internal network.

Using a DMZ, the traffic destined for a web, FTP, or e-mail server can be localized and additional layers of security can be built between internal hosts, external hosts, and the servers themselves, each with different policies to match.

PIX firewalls support many interfaces and can support up to six-Gigabit Ethernet interfaces simultaneously.

Chapter 4 covers firewalls in greater detail.

CiscoSecure IDS Sensors and Directors

Cisco's intrusion detection portfolio includes stand-alone Intrusion Detection System (IDS) devices, IDS blades for chassis-based switches, as well as IDS software for routers. The CiscoSecure Intrusion Detection System is a set of devices that add yet another type of security to your network. They are passive devices for the most part. They do not sit in-line in an information flow like the firewalls do and do not introduce any latency into the network packet flow. Instead, they watch traffic on the network looking for hacking attempts. Within the each sensor's software is the intelligence to actually recognize a number of hacking techniques. Although firewalls stop most hacks, they generally do not provide a very comprehensive picture of who is attempting to hack the network, where the hackers are, or how they are attempting to hack your network.

With IDS, you add an additional layer of visibility to not only see that nobody is getting in, but also to be alerted to the real threats that exist on your network. This information is invaluable in keeping your security tight—proactively seeing attempts and avoiding them is far better than finding out about an attempt by discovering a security breach.

To get a better understanding of the kinds of defense that the IDS system provides, consider the example that follows.

Most firewalls provide a firewall log of security exceptions similar (although not as simplified) to that shown in Table 2-1.

Table 2-1   *Firewall Log*

Time	Exception	Src	Dst	Action
22:34:01	ICMP PING REQUEST	209.2.23.4	208.233.43.1	Denied
22:34:23	FTP	173.45.24.5	208.233.43.1	Denied
22:34:30	ICMP PING REQUEST	23.65.43.45	208.233.43.3	Denied
22:34:45	ICMP PING REQUEST	209.2.23.4	208.233.43.5	Denied
22:34:48	SMTP	65.77.124.23	208.233.43.1	Denied
22:34:55	ICMP REDIRECT	16.23.45.132	208.233.43.3	Denied
22:35:04	HTTP	191.23.145.6	208.233.43.3	Denied
22:35:10	FTP	65.77.124.23	208.233.43.1	Denied
22:35:12	ICMP PING REQUEST	209.2.23.4	208.233.43.3	Denied

Table 2-1   *Firewall Log (Continued)*

Time	Exception	Src	Dst	Action
22:35:18	SMTP	64.83.6.1	208.233.43.1	Denied
22:35:30	SMTP	61.77.65.1	208.233.43.1	Denied
22:35:43	FTP	71.2.45.66	208.233.43.1	Denied
22:35:55	ICMP PING REQUEST	209.2.23.4	208.233.43.2	Denied
22:35:58	FTP	85.66.74.21	208.233.43.1	Denied

Normally, the ping requests from 209.2.23.4, which in this case are denied, might not raise a flag. In fact, you might even have decided not to block ping attempts because some users use ping tests to see if your site is available, in which case you would never see the ping attempts in your log. If you do see them, as shown in Table 2-1, you might not be aware that a ping sweep of your IP addresses is in progress because that ping sweep might not be executed in address order (209.2.23.4, 209.2.23.5, 209.2.23.6, 209.2.23.7, and so on). The ping sweep might take place over a long period of time, and the pinging machine's source address might vary. At any rate, it is difficult for a user to decipher even this, the simplest of hacks, let alone do anything about it in real-time.

Enter the CiscoSecure IDS system. The IDS sensors deployed on various segments watch those segments for hack attempts. When spotting attempts, the sensors send messages to the IDS director console that produces alerts. The systems can generate reports, send alerts, stop attempts by dynamically creating access lists on routers (called *shunning*), or even by sending TCP resets to close the active hack connections, depending on the type of IDS device you use.

An active update notification system notifies you of updates to the list of hack signatures that the sensors can detect and, because the sensors are not intrusive to the network, they can be upgraded without any network outages. This allows you to keep your network security up to date with no downtime.

Because you might want to watch several segments on your network, you might want to deploy several sensors at strategic points on the network. Each sensor has two interfaces—one for the segment to monitor and one for the connectivity to the security administration segment, as shown in Figure 2-13. This segment is set aside for management and is an example of an out-of-band management segment, where management happens without impacting the production network segments.

Figure 2-13 *IDS System Components*

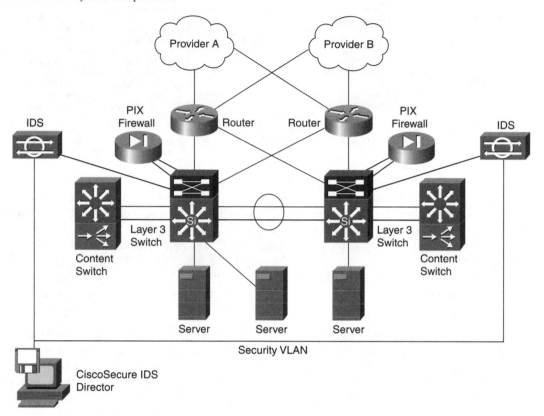

The CiscoSecure IDS Director is the management station that is located on the security VLAN where it can push new configurations to the sensors or receive hack logs from the sensors. It handles alerting, reporting, and sensor configuration.

Content Engines

The vast majority of data that is served up by any web server consists of images, sounds, video files, or other data scattered throughout a page. The server usually generates the actual HTML dynamically when it talks to a back-end database. Take a look at an example and see how the Cisco Connection Online (CCO) web site at www.cisco.com is created. If you look at the main page, you can identify several static images on the page, as shown in Figure 2-14.

Figure 2-14 *Static Web Page Images*

In contrast, the items highlighted in Figure 2-15 are all text-based HTML items that have been pulled from a database that contains a list of product categories, latest news, services, and so on.

Figure 2-15 *Dynamic Web Content*

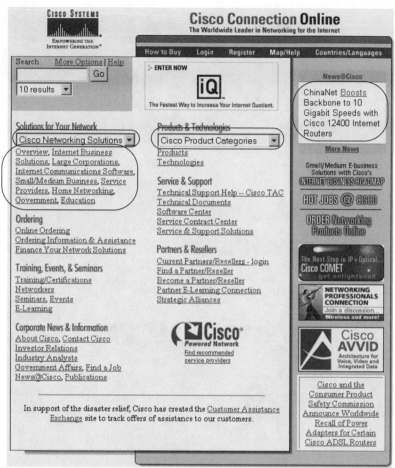

The servers are, therefore, doing two distinctly different types of serving. The first involves receiving a request from the user and, based on the request, retrieving the correct information from a database or application server and returning the data to the user in a formatted way. The second involves simply serving up data without manipulating it.

For example, the CCO database contains a list of news items in a table. When I visited the main web page, the latest piece of news was retrieved from the database and displayed on the top right of the page: "ChinaNet Boosts Backbone to 10 Gigabit Speeds with Cisco 12400 Internet Routers." By using a database or application, Cisco has created an easy management page so that the correct department can post a new news item without access to the web server and without any required HTML knowledge.

The amount of effort that goes into retrieving the headline from the database is relatively high. The server has to open a connection to the database. It then sends a request to the database, retrieves the data, and paints the result to the screen. Database security, connection pooling setups, and such are involved in doing this. As a result, you must have sophisticated software running on the server to do this, and that software is expensive. A typical server can easily cost tens of thousands of dollars.

In contrast, the images served by the same server could easily be served by just about anything. Serving images does not require any sophistication. A simple device, such as a PDA, can even act as a basic web server and fulfill this function. The amount of data in these connections is generally far larger than that in the HTML page itself. For example, the total text size served up on the main CCO page is 19 kilobytes (KB). Each of the graphics is larger than four KB a piece—at eight graphics on a page, that's larger than the size of the database driven text. Cisco does extremely well at keeping image size down. On a site with rich content, such as MTV, the HTML page contains 88 KB of text, whereas a large image might be hundreds of kilobytes in size.

Content Engines are devices that can serve up static content far faster and cheaper than servers can. Because they do not need to run the software that talks to databases, run large operating systems, handle pointing devices, keyboards, or other non-necessary elements, these devices can also be far smaller and easier to manage than any server can.

The Content Engines can be used in several different ways. They can function as simple caches. In this scenario, the content engines sit next to a router in the network and use Web Cache Communication Protocol (WCCP) to talk to the router. Figure 2-16 shows this type of arrangement.

Figure 2-16 *Using a Content Engine as a Cache*

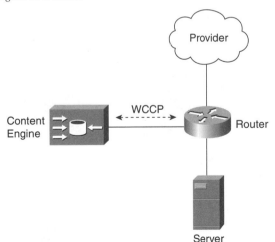

The router watches for requests coming into the site and redirects them to the Cache Engine. When a request for a static piece of content is seen coming in for the first time and the cache has been configured to cache the item, the cache requests the information from the origin server and fulfills future requests from its own copy, as shown in Figure 2-17.

Figure 2-17 *Web content Is Requested by the Cache Engine*

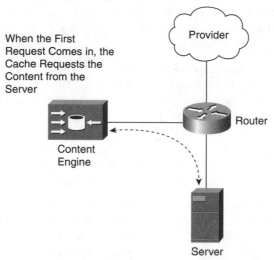

The next time someone tries to get the same data, the client retrieves the information from the cache instead of requesting it from the web server, as shown in Figure 2-18. This offloads the web server, makes management practically transparent, and improves the site's throughput.

Figure 2-18 *Requests Are Fulfilled by the Cache Engine if the Content Is Found in the Cache*

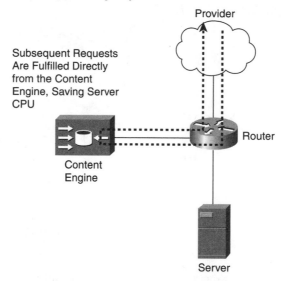

The caches in this scenario are configured for aging so that images or static data will be refreshed from the servers at regular intervals.

The Content Engines' deployment method most commonly found in the Internet Systems Architecture is to use the Content Engine as a cache in conjunction with the CSS switch. As previously mentioned, the CSS is extremely intelligent. As a result, it enables you to perform functions related to caching based on the actual URL. The Content Engine works the same way with a CSS as it does with the router, as shown in Figure 2-19.

Figure 2-19 *Content Switches Redirect Requests to Caches Intelligently*

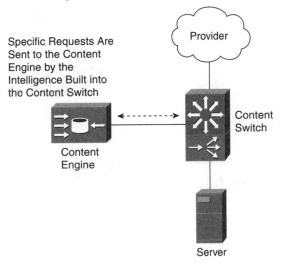

The CSS can route requests to the Content Engine based on URL, cookie, browser type, and so on, in much the same way as the WCCP router-to-content engine scenario worked.

In serving up content to users, a great deal of work goes into server scaling as well as caching at the data center, but companies such as Akamai began to offer file hosting services in the 1990s that allowed a company with a single data center to host files on servers throughout the network. Cisco Systems and several other companies have taken this concept to a new level with the introduction of Content Delivery Networks (CDNs). These are networks of Content Engines, Content Routers, and Content Switches that bring content (files, images, videos, and so on) to users faster and more efficiently. The Cisco Content Engines were actually developed with these networks in mind.

CDNs try to bring content as close to the end user as possible without incurring management and scaling overhead. The figures that follow show a few basic CDN types.

Figure 2-20 shows a datacenter scenario where you have a few content engines hanging off of a content switch. You are simply redirecting web or other requests to the content switches in the same manner as simple caching.

Figure 2-20 *Enterprise Network Without CDN*

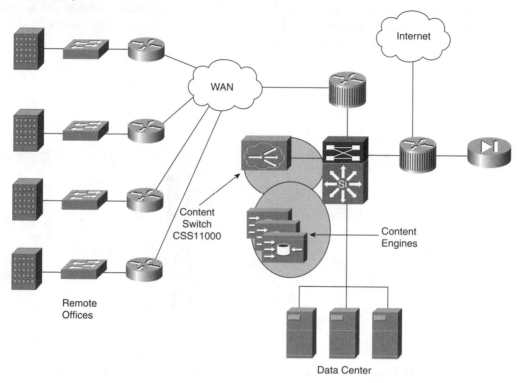

Figure 2-21 shows a remote office scenario where you push specific content out to remote sites.

Figure 2-21 *Enterprise Network with CDN Components Added to Boost Remote Performance*

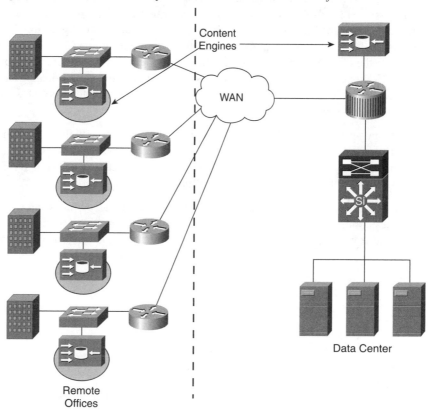

Here, you can use a Content Distribution Manager (CDM) server to schedule what content to populate in the remote content engines, as well as when to populate it. In this manner you could, for example, push out a video file at 3:00 am to each of the remote sites when the bandwidth is not saturated. When users log on in the morning, the video is available locally for them to use. The CDM allows an administrator to not only populate Content Engines on a timed basis, but also control how much bandwidth is used while populating them. In remote stores or locations where bandwidth is at a premium, you could tell the CDM to send over the new files at any data rate—20 kBps, for example. This allows you to avoid saturating small links. After the content is available, users who would normally have slow performance and would never be able to play high bandwidth content or view large files can now do so because the files are stored locally. This concept allows you to prestage video, audio, HTML, installation files, .pdf files, and just about anything else. The Content Engines can even stream Real Video or Audio formats, as well as provide a video connector for connections to kiosk TV monitors, video walls, and so forth, as in the case of the Hard Rock Café chain who uses Content Engines to play all the videos at their sites.

Using this same concept, Content Engines can be deployed at remote datacenters to speed up access to specific content. If I have a single data center in New York, I might want to rent a small amount of space in Los Angeles and place a single Content Engine there. This way I can purchase a single unit of rack space and accelerate my own content easily for users in Los Angeles. Content Engines can even be sent out without any configuration, because they use Dynamic Host Configuration Protocol (DHCP) to get an address. After this, you can simply add them to the CDM database and start configuring them by remote. Because you could populate these Content Engines based on the CSS switch's flash crowd functionality previously covered, you can see that this makes for a very scalable and simple system to vastly improve the performance of your applications.

When a user tries to download a particular file, he or she is actually sent to the Content Distribution Manager. The manager then makes a choice as to which Content Engine to send the user to based on which engine will serve the user best. The CDM then redirects the user's browser to use the best working Content Engine on the network.

Figure 2-22 shows a full Content Router scenario where a Content Router actually makes choices about where to send users. In addition to allowing video-on-demand or audio-on-demand from pre-stored content, you can also add live broadcasts to your architecture.

Figure 2-22 *A Fully Content-Enabled Network with Live Video Broadcasting*

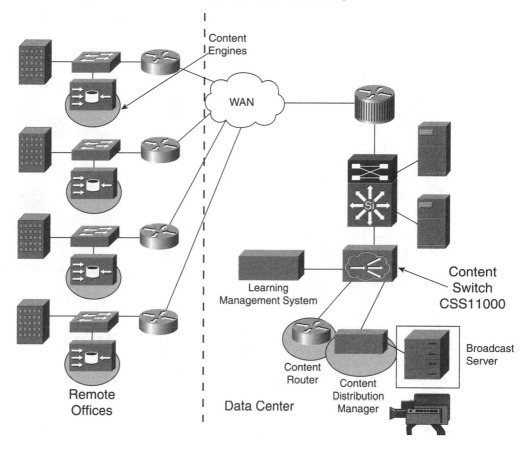

Content Routers

The Content Router was mentioned briefly with regards to Content Engines, but this particular piece of the reference architecture deserves a little more scrutiny.

Content Routers provide DNS-based redirection. This solves distributed server site selection problems and uses DNS to redirect a client to the best site on the Internet based on network delay. As a result, using DNS, the Content Router works with any IP application as opposed to the Content Distribution Manager implementation by itself, which only works with HTTP requests.

Figure 2-23 shows the placement of Content Routers in the architecture.

Figure 2-23 *Content Router Placement in the Cisco Internet System Reference Architecture*

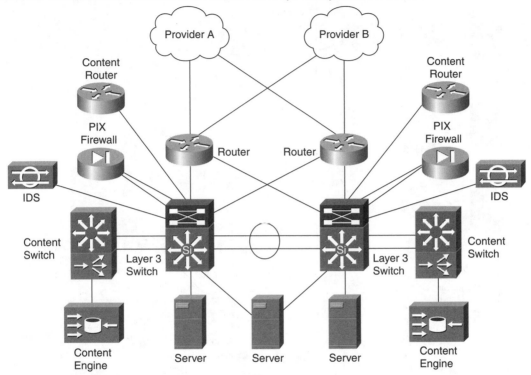

The DNS mode is transparent to the end user and can use a Domain Name System (DNS) Race to make sure that the client is sent to the closest system.

Assume that you have five Content Engines placed throughout the country, as shown in Figure 2-24.

Figure 2-24 *National Network with Content Routers*

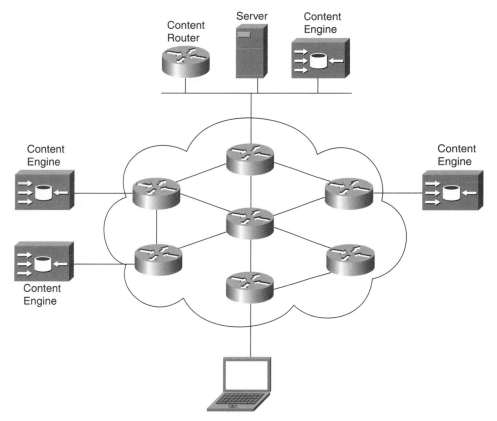

The client sends a DNS request to the Content Router for the address of the server to which it needs to connect. The Content Router forwards that request to the top couple of load balancers, Content Switches, or Content Engines. The first reply to get back to the user is the fastest candidate and the one used. This system has very good performance characteristics.

Take a look at exactly how this works. First, a user sends a DNS request to the Content Router, which is set up as the authoritative DNS for the domain, as shown in Figure 2-25.

Figure 2-25 *DNS Request Is Sent to the Content Router*

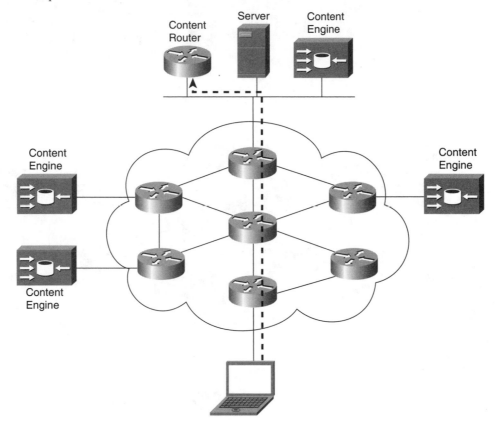

The DNS query is forwarded to the top candidate sites or Content Engines, as shown in Figure 2-26.

Figure 2-26   *DNS Requests Are Forwarded to the Top Candidates Who Have the Content*

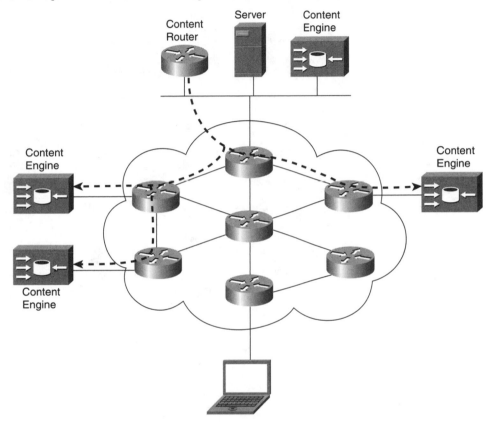

Each candidate replies with its own information to the original DNS request, but only the fastest response is actually received and processed by the client, as shown in Figure 2-27.

Figure 2-27 *The Closest Site's DNS Response Is Received First and Used by the Client*

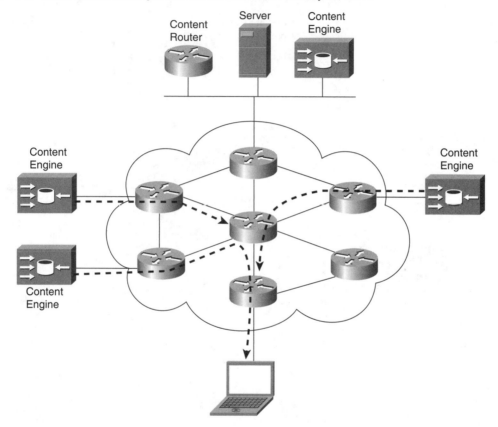

Server Placement for Web, Databases, and Application Servers

Almost all applications architectures in production today use a multitiered approach. They include web servers, as well as applications and database servers that are not yet in our design. In addition, most sites' servers are not attached to a single switch, but might be attached to both Layer 3 switches so that if any switch fails, the site does not lose 50 percent of its serving power. These applications and database servers are usually protected by firewalls and, in some cases, might be load balanced themselves—meaning that connections from the web servers back to the database or applications servers might well be load balanced across the backend servers too. For the most part, firewalls protect the sensitive data in the backend servers. Figure 2-28 shows the full basic design for the Internet Systems Architecture including these additional layers and redundant connections. It includes IDS sensors on the backend networks as well as CiscoSecure

Scanners, which are products that actively go out on your LAN and detect things, such as internal machines with unauthorized modems, copies of remote control software, and so on.

Figure 2-28 *The Complete Internet Architecture*

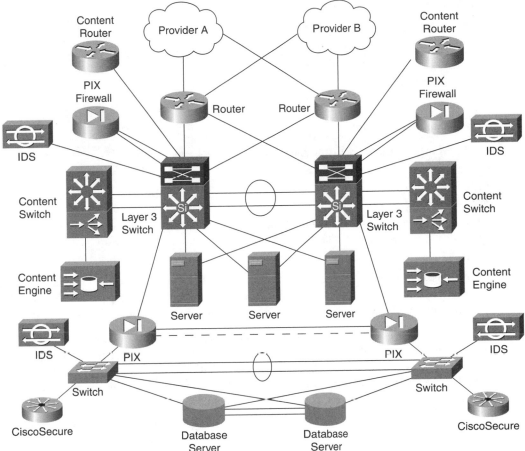

Benefits Realized After Implementing the Internet Systems Architecture

By implementing the Internet Systems Architecture, you are implementing a solution that has been worked on for years by Cisco and other engineers. Aside from the obvious benefits and features covered so far, there are several subtle benefits to the system. Many mistakes have been made implementing different network designs in the past. By using this architecture you avoid pitfalls that have cost companies money and achieve some additional benefits.

As you built up the architecture progressively throughout the chapter, the chapter also introduced and educated you on most of the considerations and explained how they affect your choice of hardware components. The next sections examine the following refresher list of those considerations along with a few more, their definitions, and some notes on why they are important:

- Capacity

- Connectivity

- Availability

- Security

- Quality of Service

- Manageability—Network and System Management

Capacity

Capacity is the network and servers' capability to handle user requests. In network terms, capacity is defined as the data-carrying capability of a circuit or network, usually measured in bits per second.

To the user, capacity is reflected as a certain level of performance; when there is not enough capacity, performance suffers. An analogy would be a highway traffic jam. When there is too much traffic and too few lanes to accommodate it, the result is congestion and traffic delays.

Capacity is one of the primary concerns when sizing most of the architecture's network components. You need to consider the equipment's life cycle and determine the capacity that the architecture will need to support at peak usage during that lifetime. Fortunately, Cisco produces a large range of equipment, most of which can be scaled by replacing processor cards or adding switch fabric cards, providing investment protection.

Connectivity

Connectivity is the interconnections that get the user from where they are to where the data is. It is the glue between all the components (network and servers) in a system architecture.

A system architecture with good connectivity allows application users to perform their business tasks from any location across any medium.

Some components of the architecture come in several varieties. Certain switches, for example, take certain types of blades supporting anything from Fast Ethernet to Gigabit Ethernet, ATM, T1s, and almost anything in between. In addition, you need to consider the number of ports you might want to support. Chassis solutions work best because they can be populated as the architecture grows.

Availability

Availability refers to the amount of time a system is available to users.

For an application or service to be available, all system architecture components, including database servers, storage devices, and the end-to-end network, need to provide continuous service.

Availability and how to achieve it has been briefly covered in some sections in this chapter, but is explained in more detail in the next chapter.

Security

Security is the process by which a company's information assets are protected. Security's goals are to maintain integrity, protect confidentiality, and assure availability.

Security to assure availability is covered in a later Chapter 4. However a standard security analogy is good to keep in mind and is worth repeating.

Consider a customer visiting a bank. He must first pass by the lobby guard and be authorized to enter the bank. Similarly, for information security, authentication refers to the process of checking a user's credentials (such as ID and password) to allow him access to the network.

After the customer is allowed in, he can access account information (restricted to his accounts). In information security, authorization allows an authorized user to access only those data portions to which he is entitled.

Finally, as the customer leaves the bank, a record is maintained of his bank visit through a variety of mechanisms, including surveillance cameras and logs maintained by the bank. Similarly, in information security, accounting records are maintained for every successful (or unsuccessful) user attempt to enter the network.

Quality of Service

QoS is a set of technologies and configurations that allow a network to provide differentiated services to different network traffic.

With QoS, you can increase bandwidth for critical traffic, limit bandwidth for non-critical traffic, and provide consistent network response, among other things. This allows you to use expensive network connections more efficiently. Primary QoS goals include managed bandwidth, controlled jitter and latency (required by some real-time and interactive traffic, such as VoIP and video), and improved loss characteristics.

QoS functionality guarantees that network resources are available for mission-critical, interactive, and time-sensitive Internet business applications. You can protect your mission-critical applications, such as Enterprise Resource Planning (ERP), data warehousing, and sales force automation, which are closely linked to various Internet business solutions. You can prioritize different user groups, such as finance, sales, or suppliers. For example, in a supply chain management solution, you can classify your suppliers into three different groups: gold, silver, and bronze, and you can provide differentiated services to these different suppliers with proper QoS implementation. You can also enable multimedia applications, such as distance learning and desktop video conferencing, which are essential parts of e-learning. In short, QoS is an important consideration in designing Internet system architecture.

Manageability—Network and System Management

Network and system management is the art and science of managing network equipment, such as switches, routers, hubs, and other communications equipment composing a network infrastructure, as well as system components, such as servers and clients.

Network and system management activities can be classified into five functional areas that are important for you to know:

- Fault management
- Configuration management
- Accounting management
- Performance management
- Security management

Network and system management is a proactive tool to ensure that the network stays up. Cisco views network and system management as an ongoing process of planning and designing, deploying and implementing, operating and monitoring network equipment, and ensuring the network is secure from outside attack. All of these areas must be performed with downtime being kept to an absolute minimum. Network management shouldn't be a passive process.

In today's Internet economy, networks have become a critical piece of the business process because efficient networks mean additional revenue and downtime costs money. The need for proactive network management has become a critical element in most organizations.

With network and system management tools, you can measure and monitor aspects of the system's health, such as capacity, availability, performance, security, and connectivity. By monitoring your system, you can adjust it to avoid disasters. Network and system management has a direct tie to enforcement of the Service Level Agreement.

The Internet system architecture must be designed to facilitate proactive network monitoring and management to ensure ongoing operation stability and resource availability. Network and system management is an essential consideration in Internet system architecture design.

Summary

You should now be able to do the following:

- Explain the various parts of the Cisco Internet System Reference Architecture and their functionality.

- Define capacity and explain why it is important in Internet system architecture design.

- Define connectivity and explain why it is important in Internet system architecture design.

- Define availability and explain why it is important in Internet system architecture design.

- Define security and explain why it is important in Internet system architecture design.

- Define QoS and explain why it is important in Internet system architecture design.

- Define network and system management and explain why it is important in Internet system architecture design.

Glossary of Key Terms in This Chapter

Application-specific integrated circuit (ASIC) is a chip specifically designed to perform a function usually done with software.

Availability refers to the amount of time a system is available to users.

Border Gateway Protocol is a routing protocol that routers in the Internet use to communicate route paths to each other. It is the standard protocol that allows different sets of routers owned by different companies to communicate effectively with each other.

Capacity is the data-carrying capability of a circuit or network, and is usually measured in bits per second (bps).

Connectivity is the interconnections that get users from where they are to where the data is.

Congestion refers to traffic in excess of network capacity.

Convergence, in routing, refers to the time it takes for all routers to update their routing tables and agree on the routing topology.

Dynamic Host Configuration Protocol (DHCP) provides a mechanism for allocating IP addresses dynamically so that addresses can be reused when hosts no longer need them.

Dynamic random-access memory (DRAM) is RAM that stores information in capacitors that must be refreshed periodically.

DeMilitarized Zone (DMZ) is a network segment that lies between the Internet and an internal network and hosts Web, FTP, and other servers providing services to clients on the Internet.

Ethernet is a LAN technology capable of ten-Mbps transmission rates.

Extranet is an intranet that is partially accessible to authorized outsiders.

FastEthernet is a LAN technology capable of 100-Mbps transmission rates at full duplex.

File Transfer Protocol (FTP) is an application protocol that is part of the TCP/IP protocol stack and transfers files between network nodes.

Full duplex refers to the capability of being able to send data and receive data simultaneously.

Gigabit Ethernet is a LAN technology capable of 1000-Mbps transmission rates at full duplex.

Intranet is a network based on TCP/IP protocols (an internet) belonging to an organization, usually a corporation, accessible only by the organization's members, employees, or others internal to that organization.

Latency is the delay between the time a device requests access to a network and the time permission is granted to transmit, or the delay between the time a device receives a frame and the time that frame is forwarded out the destination port.

Layer 2 is the OSI layer at which packets are encoded and decoded into bits for transmission on a physical wire or optical cable.

Layer 3 is the OSI layer at which routing operates, creating logical paths for transmitting data from node to node. Routing and forwarding are functions of this layer, as well as addressing, internetworking, error handling, congestion control, and packet sequencing.

Layer 3 switching is a technology that integrates routing with switching to yield high routing throughput rates in the millions-of-packets-per-second range. The movement to Layer 3 switching is designed to address the downsides of the current generation of Layer 2 switches, which are functionally equivalent to bridges.

Media Access Control (MAC) address is a hardware address that uniquely identifies each node of a network at Layer 2.

Network Address Translation (NAT) is a mechanism for reducing the need for globally unique IP addresses. NAT allows an organization with addresses that are not globally unique to connect to the Internet by translating those addresses into globally routable address space.

Quality of service (QoS) is a set of technologies and configurations that allow a network to provide differentiated services to different network traffic.

Security is the process by which a company's information assets are protected.

Spanning-Tree Protocol is a bridge protocol that uses the Spanning-Tree algorithm, enabling a learning bridge to dynamically work around loops in a network topology by creating a spanning tree. Bridges exchange BPDU messages with other bridges to detect loops, and remove the loops by shutting down selected bridge interfaces.

Session is a related set of communications transactions between two or more network devices.

Simple Mail Transfer Protocol (SMTP) is an Internet protocol providing e-mail services.

T1 is a WAN technology capable of 1.536-Mbps transmission rates.

T3 is a WAN technology capable of approximately 45-Mbps transmission rates.

Trunk is a physical and logical connection between two switches across which network traffic travels. A backbone is composed of a number of trunks.

For any other terms, you can refer to Cisco's online Terms and Glossary page:

www.cisco.com/univercd/cc/td/doc/cisintwk/ita/index.htm

Or consult other third-party web sites, such as Webopedia at:

www.webopedia.com/

Review Questions

1 Name the four major types of network connectivity in an Internet infrastructure.

_____

_____

_____

2 What does "hitless" mean in terms of the Internet Systems Architecture?

_____

_____

_____

3 Define availability.

_____

_____

_____

4 Define capacity.

_____

_____

_____

5 Define utilization.

_____

_____

_____

6 What three pieces of a switch should you consider when choosing a switch?

_____

_____

_____

7 What does the term "stickiness" mean?

_____

_____

_____

8 What are the three goals of security?

_____

_____

_____

9 What does a "stateful" firewall do?

_____

_____

_____

10 What is out-of-band management?

_____

_____

_____

11 Define QoS.

_____

_____

_____

After reading this chapter, you should be able to perform the following tasks:

- Define high availability.

- Explain high-availability objectives and the trade-offs between high-availability design and cost.

- Explain why high-availability design is important and its benefits.

- Explain the two high-availability design types.

- Explain the process of failure analysis and recovery.

- Explain the technologies that enable high availability.

- Explain how to design a high-availability architecture.

CHAPTER 3

High Availability Overview

High availability is defined as the continuous operation of computing systems. Applications require different availability levels depending on the business impact of down time. For an application to be available, all components, including application and database servers, storage devices, and the end-to-end network, must provide continuous service.

Availability is the probability that a product will operate when needed or, for mature communications equipment in a steady state, the average fraction of connection time that the product is expected to be ready in operating condition. For a communications system that can have partial as well as total system outages, availability is typically expressed as connection availability.

Application availability deals with the entire application's availability to the users and not simply the individual pieces.

As businesses begin to rely more and more on the network systems for e-commerce, supply chain, and so on, availability becomes more important. With the current move to put voice, video, and data on the same system, this high availability requirement is becoming even more important. Users are used to having voice communications available all the time—when you pick up a phone, it simply works. As voice is moved onto the network you will see even greater demands for high availability.

Consider the following three facets of high availability when developing a highly available design:

- **Uptime**—A network or system can fail to be available if its device or its connectivity has failed.

- **Proper performance**—Users see a network and system as unavailable if they are too slow to handle practical processing.

- **Accessibility**—Users can reach and use destination services for which they are authorized.

Typically, you only think about uptime when designing highly available systems but performance and accessibility should not be overlooked because they affect the client's experience and directly impact the network's effectiveness.

This chapter touches on several factors affecting availability. These include the impact of redundant devices, service contracts, and equipment replacement times.

Benefits of Highly Available Systems

The benefits of a highly available system are fairly simple but you should be able to communicate to customers or management the importance of availability with respect to the multiple benefits it provides. Highly available systems do the following:

- Minimize financial loss resulting from network and system downtime.

- Minimize lost productivity resulting from network and system downtime.

- Improve external customer satisfaction and loyalty.

- Improve internal user satisfaction.

- Protect company brand names.

- Reduce reactive information technology (IT) support costs.

In general, high availability is seen as a major requirement for at least part of every company's network because computers are used ubiquitously to place orders, ship products, balance books, and generally conduct business.

Total Cost of Ownership Model

All companies would choose to have a system that is up 100 percent of the time. Unfortunately, this can be costly and, as a result, each company must evaluate how much money it needs to invest in a high availability design. For stock trading companies, where downtime could cost millions per minute, this might be an extremely high priority. A company that sells items in retail stores might have a system that can fail for a while because users can still transact business.

A difference exists between the total cost of ownership of a non-redundant design and a redundant one. In a redundant design you pay for double the amount of equipment, maintenance contracts, and circuits. Keep in mind that you might decrease the cost of your annual recurring support contract because you no longer need replacement parts as quickly and a lower level of support contract can be used. Over time, lower maintenance and savings in potentially lost revenue could pay for the difference in capital costs.

The differences in up-front costs must be weighed against the business's cost of downtime and the savings associated with a highly available system with regards to support contracts.

In addition to simple redundancy, components such as the IDS sensors and PIX firewalls reduce downtime and improve availability by avoiding software vulnerabilities. For example, security holes on operating systems are found on an almost daily basis. Hackers use these flaws to gain access to systems, or simply overpower them causing the systems to crash. As the software running on servers is upgraded, new breaches in security will inevitably occur.

These soft costs are usually not incorporated into the total cost of ownership models because they are overlooked but they remain an important consideration when choosing the components that affect a system's availability.

Different pieces in the design can cause differing amounts of downtime. For example, a switch with ten users that fails might cause only ten users downtime, as shown in Figure 3-1. A core switch that fails would cause all users to experience an outage, as shown in Figure 3-2. Carefully plan which components to make redundant.

Figure 3-1   *Failure Affecting a Small Group of Endpoints*

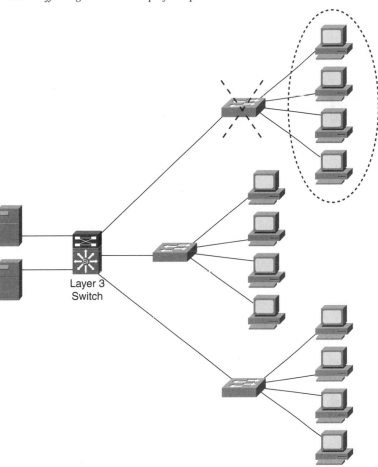

Figure 3-2   *Failure Affecting a Large Group of Endpoints*

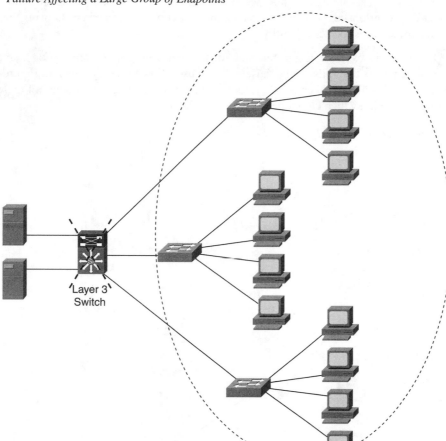

In addition, several components in the architecture are available in different forms to improve availability. For example, servers, switches, and routers can provide a certain amount of redundancy internally—at an additional cost—in terms of redundant power supplies, hard drives, and so on.

Ultimately, the more available a system becomes, the more costly it becomes to purchase upfront. The primary focus of designing a highly available system should be to maximize availability with currently available funds.

owntime and Availability

Downtime is typically expressed in minutes per year and is the expected time that a system is not operational per unit of in-service time. Downtime expresses unavailability.

For a mature system, downtime is related to availability, as indicated here:

Downtime (in minutes per year) = (1 - Availability) * 525,600

The number 525,600 comes from (365 days) * (24 hours) * (60 minutes). Downtime is a more convenient variable to evaluate compared to availability because of the linear and additive nature of downtime. You can specify individual downtime numbers for the different system functions; the sum of these numbers constitutes the entire network's downtime. A system that has twice the downtime of another system implies that it is twice as "bad." Availability lacks these convenient mathematical features.

If a single component experiences a failure and the system is designed so that there is no impact to the user, this downtime should not be added to the total system downtime because the system was available. In this case, the component downtime increases but the system downtime does not.

Most people are comfortable with downtime and have less of a grasp on availability.

A system that is 99.999 percent available (a "five nines" system) is a system that will be down for five minutes or less per year. Is this feasible?

Table 3-1 shows a table of availability and the related number of minutes per year that the system can be down to achieve this availability.

ble 3-1   *Network Availability Table*

Availability	Downtime		
	Days	Hours	Minutes
99.0000%	3	15	36
99.500%	1	19	48
99.900%	0	8	46
99.9500%	0	4	23
99.9900%	0	0	53
99.9990%	0	0	5
99.9999%	0	0	0.5

Note that in the telephony world the five nines reliability clause does not necessarily pertain to the entire system. For example, if a private branch exchange (PBX) experiences an outage that affects 24 users or less, the outage is not considered in the downtime calculation. Planned downtime is also not included.

A system that is 99.9 percent available is considered a reliable system, but achieving 99.99 percent or higher availability results in a truly highly available network. This corresponds to 53 or fewer minutes of downtime a year. After IP Telephony is deployed on a network, the requirements jump up to 99.999 percent because those are the kinds of uptimes that are expected of telephony systems.

You should also consider the human implications of trying to achieve high availability. The following section covers the process of achieving a highly available system. This process involves people looking at technology and business, and evaluating the two pieces. As you approach a 99.999 percent architecture, making sure that people are correctly trained, that they adhere to policies, and that those policies are well defined and make both business and technical sense is critical.

Thorough, well-documented policies for emergency situations, change control, and operations can dramatically reduce downtime and accelerate the learning curve of new staff members. A well-documented network is also easier to troubleshoot because it is generally more organized, and passing that information on to a third-party technical assistance group becomes far easier.

Designing High Availability Architecture

Cisco follows these steps for designing or customizing high-availability solutions for customers:

Step 1 Define an up-front availability objective based on business requirements.

Step 2 Follow a top-down approach beginning with overall high-availability goals.

Step 3 Develop an availability model.

Step 4 Compose a development road map.

Step 5 Perform design verification.

These steps address the development phase of designing availability, which is the most critical phase of the high-availability design process. However, the effort to ensure high availability does not end here.

The sections that follow drill down further into each step.

Defining Objectives

Defining objectives enables you to do several things. You need to design the system based on the client's expectations. Because the client drives the entire business, it stands to reason that the design must be built around the client's needs. This also allows you to communicate to the client what they can realistically expect from the system when you are done.

Define what constitutes a failure or outage with the client. This leads to a service level agreement (SLA), discussed later in the book. In addition, define criticality levels for each component or function. For example, you might need to clarify that losing ten administrators' connections is not as critical as losing ten sales agents' connections. These factors must be made clear because your design can change based on these weights. A risk assessment should be done to determine how likely a failure is based on the particular piece of the design and the impact of such an outage in terms of downtime cost and tolerance for loss.

A highly available system's cost should also be weighed against the costs of other disaster recovery plans where geographic diversity might be used. If you were to forgo a highly available system and place a complete back-up system at a remote location, how much more does it cost to perform data replication between the two systems, and what are the logistical implications of that remote site? What are the other operational costs, such as the costs of space, power, and the management of a disaster recovery site? How does the software cope with duplicate systems?

Following a Top-Down Approach

As previously mentioned, your high availability strategy should begin with a business availability requirement and the overall outage and recovery goals and progress of specific design implementations. Because you are building this network to support a business, it is important that it be designed with that business goal in mind. A miscommunication frequently occurs between the network technicians and management regarding what is actually important or critical to business and this needs to be addressed early.

Developing an Availability Model

The availability model should provide a visual representation to help translate overall objectives into prioritized design requirements.

While designing for high availability, you might need to make trade-offs among various elements and costs. The effects of various design parameters on availability need to be quantified, and their relative weights on availability must be assessed at an early stage so that you can make design trade-offs intelligently, while meeting the availability goal based on business needs. A top-down availability model constructed before development and refined during development serves this purpose. In addition, the availability model assigns budgets to each system component and specifies the levels of improvement planned for the future. This can also assist in making tradeoffs during the design process and helping management fully understand design decision ramifications.

Composing a Development Road Map

The development road map helps achieve availability objectives and should include the following:

- Step-by-step availability improvement
- Plans to minimize service outages
- Provisions for maintenance and upgrades without downtime
- Plans to minimize recovery time
- Plans to minimize high-availability environment restoration time
- Contingent recovery plan

Not only does this provide a structured way of achieving initial goals, but it also allows you to improve the system on an ongoing basis. In addition, if any outages do occur that could have been avoided, this roadmap distinctly shows that a specific piece was deemed less important but that it was considered in the overall design. Although a fully redundant system might never be achieved, you should always have a roadmap to achieve that goal so that the system's current state can be compared to what is optimal. Too often the business decision makers are simply not aware of all options, and a roadmap clears this up.

Another factor to consider is the cause of outages. Figure 3-3 shows a breakdown of the causes of an outage for typical phone systems. As you can see, several factors influence downtime and several different solutions can be applied to each. Determining what typically causes outages should be part of the availability architecture-planning phase.

Figure 3-3 *Causes of failures*

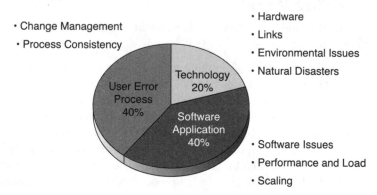

Source: Garner Group

Performing Design Verification

After a design has been implemented, it needs to be tested. Document these tests including effects, failure, and restoration times, as well as solutions to potential problems. This allows you to avoid potential issues and provides a real-life baseline for client expectations. Each critical component should be tested and various types of failures should be tested for each. The vast majority of outages occur because of an unforeseen failure type. For example, powering down a component can cause a fail-over to occur because the Ethernet link has gone down. You might assume this is a good test, however, what would happen if someone were to unplug an Ethernet port from the same component and plug it into a different switch? The link would show as up, but the failover software on the device might not be smart enough to trigger a failover event.

Testing should be done on a regular basis from a test plan that is updated as components or requirements change. Having planned outages in off-peak hours is far better than experiencing them at critical times. For example, most hospitals run on backup systems once a week because they provide such a critical function. The frequency of the testing is determined by the risk involved. Testing along with test plan revision should naturally be done when new components are added or components are changed.

The Two Design Approaches to Availability

There are two basic models to building high-availability networks and systems:

- Based on fault tolerant devices
- Based on redundant topologies

Network and systems elements are not standalone devices, but components of a network system. Each system component also resides in a physical environment that requires electrical power, environmental control, and human operators.

Imperfections in any of these "softer" or "facility" aspects of the network and system can potentially cause failures that cannot be offset solely through device-level hardware redundancy or network topology redundancy.

Some examples of the factors contributing to these aspects follow:

- Lack of proper procedures and documentation
- Lack of training for operators leading to misconfiguration or lack of understanding of a technology
- Lack of proper upgrade and system patch procedures
- Lack of regular testing of critical components, such as UPS systems

Networks and Systems Based on Fault Tolerant Devices

Systems based on fault tolerant devices rely on the devices to internally provide redundancy without providing redundant devices themselves. For example, the Catalyst switch used in the design in Chapter 2, "Internet System Architecture Design Overview," could be provisioned with redundant power supplies, backplanes, fans, processors, and so forth. They also allow you to connect to other devices using multiple ports to provide link redundancy. In the Catalyst 6000 series, with this degree of internal redundancy, you can achieve calculated device-level meantime between failure (MTBF) of up to 100,000 hours. Assuming a meantime to repair (MTTR) of one hour, this MTBF would correspond to a theoretical device-level availability of 99.999 percent—five nines.

Although an availability of 99.999 percent sounds impressive and would be a great advantage, trying to achieve high availability solely through device-level fault tolerance has a number of drawbacks:

- Massive redundancy within devices adds significantly to the cost, while at the same time reducing physical capacity that could otherwise house network interfaces or provide useful network services.

- Redundant subsystems within devices are often maintained in a hot standby mode where they cannot contribute additional performance because they are fully activated only when the primary component fails.

- Focusing on device-level hardware reliability can result in a number of other failure mechanisms being overlooked, such as those outlined in the preceding list.

You should also be aware of how long it can take to troubleshoot a problem. If a port fails on a switch, for example, and you spend an hour troubleshooting the issue and narrowing down the error to that particular port, you can well exceed your downtime limits.

Putting policies in place determining how long systems can be down before they are replaced is critical. In doing this, be aware of MTTR for each component. A document or database, including issues and their MTTR, should be maintained and possibly expanded to produce a Knowledge Base—a tool that technicians use to refer to previously experienced problems and quickly resolve them. MTTR for a component gives you a very strong indication of how long the problems for each component is likely to affect the system, and will allow you to determine which components to look at first in your high-availability architecture.

Networks and Systems with Redundant Topologies

One approach to building high-availability networks is to provide most of the reliability through redundancy in the network topology rather than primarily within the network devices themselves. With this design approach, the network would be designed as you saw in Chapter 2.

A backup exists for every link and for every network device in the path between the client and the server. In addition, you could provide a certain amount of device-level redundancy within some of the key devices, such as the core switches.

With proper configuration, the software controlling all the devices that make up the architecture can automatically reroute traffic around failures by using other links or devices. The proper configuration along with redundancy makes any outage invisible to the end-user.

Figure 3-4 and Figure 3-5 illustrate the differences between a non-redundant topology and a redundant one.

Figure 3-4　*Non-Redundant Topology*

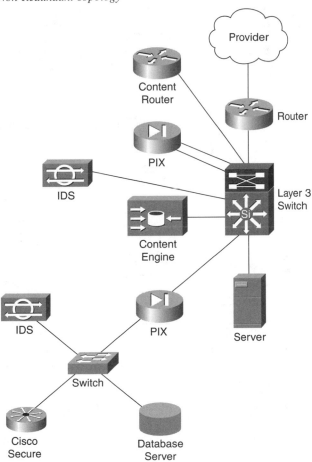

Figure 3-5 *Redundant Topology*

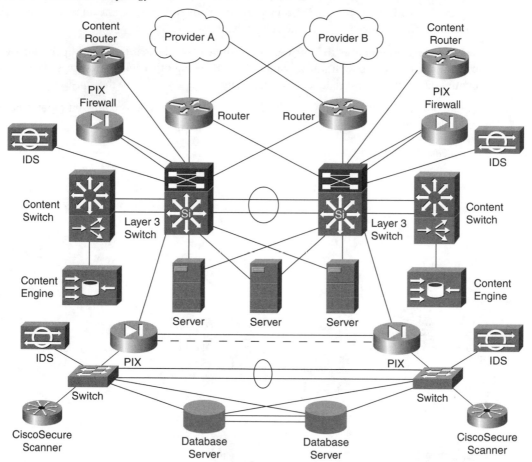

Several advantages exist to using a redundant topology:

- The network and system elements providing redundancy do not need to be at the same location as the primary network and system elements. This reduces the probability that problems with the physical environment will interrupt service.

- Problems with software bugs, upgrades, or configuration errors or changes can often be dealt with separately in the primary and secondary forwarding paths without completely interrupting service. Therefore, network-level redundancy also reduces the effect of non-hardware-failure mechanisms.

- With the redundancy provided by the network, each network device no longer needs to be configured for the ultimate in standalone fault tolerance. By partially relaxing the requirements for device-level fault tolerance, you can reduce the cost per network device while offsetting the requirement for more devices.

- With appropriate resiliency features and careful design and configuration, the traffic load between the respective network topology layers can be shared between the primary and secondary forwarding paths. Therefore, network-level redundancy also provides increased aggregate performance and capacity, which in turn helps to reduce the incremental cost of a redundant network. Because it uses the redundant links, you are also assured that those links are operational at all times without testing.

- Redundant networks and systems can be configured to failover from primary to secondary facilities automatically without operator intervention.

The main disadvantage of building availability through topology redundancy is the additional cost involved in having two or more of each network element and server. Additionally, synchronization between redundant systems requires stringent management control, especially in terms of server software.

E-Commerce Architecture

The E-Commerce architecture discussed in Chapter 2 is used as a basis for sound network designs. This architecture encompasses several factors, the primary being that of high availability.

Non-Redundant Design

Figure 3-4 showed a basic E-Commerce architecture design with no redundancy. All the basic building blocks described in Chapter 2 are present in this design, but you will notice that they all constitute a single point of failure. If any one device or connection fails or needs to be reinitialized, the entire system will fail. In addition to hardware failures, software failures can also result in downtime. For example, if a server crashes the entire system is rendered useless. Very few companies would choose to deploy non-redundant production environments because the availability of such a solution is terribly low.

Redundant Design

By contrast, Figure 3-5—the architecture built in Chapter 2—provides a fully redundant system. If an ISP link fails, there is a backup. If a switch fails, you have a backup path to every type of device in the network. In all cases, each component is redundant and each redundant device is connected to a switch fabric on a second, redundant switch. Some of the devices, such as the Catalyst switches, might have redundant components built in to minimize the likelihood of failure in the system itself.

Notice in Figure 3-2 that a packet from any user on the Internet or extranet that is destined for any server has several paths it can take to reach the destination server. If any path fails, the packet is simply rerouted around the failure.

High Availability Design Enabling Technologies

To ensure high availability, Cisco, as well as other networking and OS companies, have developed several technologies. The upcoming sections highlight a few of these technologies, because you need to be aware of them. New technologies are being developed all the time

Within the high-availability design, you use the following:

- Load balancing to reroute requests to available servers when existing ones fail

- Spanning Tree to provide backup physical paths

- Etherchannel to aggregate multiple physical paths together

- Hot Standby Router Protocol (HSRP) or Virtual Router Redundancy Protocol (VRRP) to allow physical routers and other network devices to appear as one virtual device

- Routing to quickly reroute around failures

In some cases, custom failover mechanisms have even been developed for specific components. A good high-availability design usually involves many of these technologies working together.

Load Balancers

As mentioned in Chapter 2, load-balancing devices provide a huge advantage for building scalable, redundant networks. Cisco provides several models of load balancers including the CSS, Local Directors, Load Balancing blades for the Catalyst 6000 series, and IOS software-based load balancers. Depending on the application, one or more of these might be used. By providing redundant servers or network hardware behind a load balancer, you can build redundancy into almost any network components and load balance over those components for additional performance while none of the components are in a failed state. If any server or component fails, the load balancer detects the failure and sends the user to an operational server, as shown in Figure 3-6.

Figure 3-6   *Load Balancing Redirecting a Broken Connection*

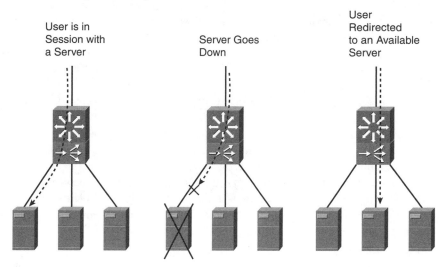

Ethernet Spanning Tree

One of the inherent features of Ethernet is its capability of maintaining multiple redundant connections between switches and bridges. When multiple paths between two pieces of equipment are found, the switches use the Spanning-Tree Algorithm to disable one of the links. In this way, dual links are placed in the network so that if a single link fails, Spanning Tree enables a backup link. Careful tuning of Spanning Tree, in conjunction with your Layer 3 Protocol, should be done so that the correct links are put into backup state and traffic flows properly in the system before and after a failure. Spanning Tree backup links are inactive while the primary links are in operation. The disadvantage to using Spanning Tree to provide link redundancy is that the redundant links are not used. Cisco's EtherChannel, as well as some other technologies, solve this.

NOTE   For more information on Spanning Tree, visit www.cisco.com and type "understanding spanning tree" into the search box.

In addition to basic Spanning Tree tuning, you can also configure Cisco switches to use PortFast, UplinkFast, and BackBoneFast. These commands make sure that ports enable quickly. By default, an Ethernet port does not start transmitting as soon as a cable is plugged in and the link is established. It spends an average of 30 seconds making sure that it is not causing a loop in the network. The PortFast, BackBoneFast, and UplinkFast commands reduce this delay.

NOTE	For more information on UplinkFast, BackboneFast, and PortFast, visit www.cisco.com and type "configuring uplinkfast portfast backbonefast" into the search box.

EtherChannel

Fast- and Gigabit-EtherChannel technology allows two pieces of network equipment to be connected using multiple physical connections. For example, the two main switches in the E-Commerce design can be connected by between two and eight Gigabit connections. While they are operational, traffic is load balanced between all of them. If one fails, traffic is rerouted and redistributed among the working connections. The aggregate connections in the higher-end Cisco switches can be connections from different cards, so that if an entire card fails, the connection is not dropped. This feature is almost exclusively available on Cisco switches. You should know how EtherChannel works because it can lead to problems if you do not. Here again is the quote on how it works from Chapter 2:

> Be aware that EtherChannel distributes frames across the links in a channel by reducing part of the binary pattern formed from the addresses in the frame to a numerical value that selects one of the links in the channel. EtherChannel distribution can use MAC addresses, IP addresses, and Layer 4 port numbers. You can specify source or destination address, both source and destination addresses, or Layer 4 port numbers. The default is to use source and destination IP address. Be aware that some configurations do not work well. For example, connecting four FastEthernet connections between a perimeter router and a switch using MAC usually does not work well. All packets are sourced from the router's MAC address so all frames travel over one of the links. Be sure to configure Etherchannel properly.

NOTE	For more information on Fast and Gigabit Etherchannel, visit www.cisco.com and type "configuring fast and gigabit etherchannel" into the search box.

Hot Standby Routing Protocol (HSRP) and Virtual Router Redundancy Protocol (VRRP)

HSRP and VRRP protocols allow two pieces of network equipment to act as one virtual piece. In both implementations, one of the two or more redundant pieces is designated as a primary and assumes the IP and MAC addresses to which packets are sent. When the primary fails, the secondary piece of equipment no longer sees update packets and assumes the primary role. Cisco's proprietary HSRP adds significant functionality that reduces failover times and errors. HSRP is frequently used to make two routers look like a single IP address to equipment on the network. Figure 3-7 illustrates this.

Figure 3-7 *HSRP Failover*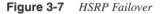

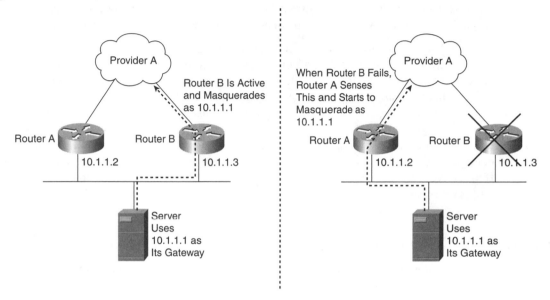

NOTE   For more information on HSRP, visit www.cisco.com and type "configuring HSRP" into the search box.

Device-dependant Failover Mechanisms

Devices such a PIX firewall and LocalDirector also support proprietary failover mechanisms. These proprietary mechanisms are available for almost all network components, including servers in some fashion or another. Typically, they use a similar function as HSRP—where one of the boxes at any given time has a specific IP address and MAC address. When the primary fails, the secondary activates and answers requests to those addresses. In effect, the secondary unit is configured the same way as the primary, but remains dormant until the primary fails.

For example, in a LocalDirector/PIX failover configuration, one LocalDirector/PIX is the primary unit (default active), and the other LocalDirector/PIX is the backup unit (default standby). The primary unit performs normal network functions. The backup unit monitors the primary unit operation and is ready to take control if the primary unit fails.

When a failure occurs, the backup unit becomes the active unit and assumes control by using the primary unit's MAC address and IP address instead of its own (which it uses at all other times). The units, however, do not give up their primary or backup designations. The currently active unit (whether primary or backup) always uses the primary system IP and MAC addresses.

The standby unit (whether primary or backup) uses the backup IP address and MAC address. Because the currently active unit always uses the same IP and MAC addresses, Address Resolution Protocol (ARP) entries do not need to change or time out anywhere on the network.

The standby unit monitors failover communications, active unit power status, interface line status, and received hello packets. A failure of any of these parameters on the active unit causes the standby unit to take control. A failure or switch generates syslog messages regarding the cause of the failover. By default, the standby unit does not keep state information on each connection; all active connections are dropped and must be reestablished by the clients. However, if you configure stateful failover on the primary and secondary LocalDirector/PIX units, the standby LocalDirector/PIX not only has copies of the active LocalDirector/PIX configuration but also has copies of the tables that show the active connections and their states. If the active unit fails, these connections are still valid and users continue an active session with the server.

Non-network Considerations

In addition to network changes you can make to cause your system to be more available, a few other topics warrant mention that can greatly improve the system's availability. The sections that follow outline these topics.

Operational Best Practices

You can minimize the non-hardware failure rate by adopting best industry practices to reduce the frequency of other common causes of failures. Applying best practices in software version control, device configuration control, user access privileges and security, wiring closet and computer room cabling, physical plant maintenance, and so on can significantly contribute to reducing the overall failure rate. Additionally, support staff awareness, notification procedures, and user education offer non-hardware availability advantages.

Cisco provides several White Papers on best practices available online on the www.cisco.com web site, including the following:

- Best Practices for Catalyst 4000, 5000, and 6000 Series Switch Configuration and Management

- Baseline Process: Best Practices White Paper

- Network Management System: Best Practices White Paper

- Performance Management: Best Practices White Paper

- Service Level Management: Best Practices White Paper

- Capacity and Performance Management: Best Practices White Paper

- Configuration Management: Best Practices White Paper

- New Solution Deployment: Best Practices White Paper
- Network Security Policy: Best Practices White Paper
- Change Management: Best Practices White Paper
- Disaster Recovery: Best Practices White Paper

Searching on www.cisco.com for "Best Practices White Papers" will yield links to these. Downloading and reading each of them is highly recommended if you want to increase your knowledge on these topics. The Best Practices pages are continually being updated and all the papers are free of charge.

Server Fault Tolerance

The network system's availability cannot exceed that of the servers used to deliver critical applications, data, and key network services. Therefore, server fault tolerance strategies such as dual homing, clustered systems, or networked backup servers, cannot be overlooked. The availability tracking mechanism employed should be able to distinguish between network and server failures.

Power Considerations

In planning for redundant World Wide Web sites, plan for power failures so that equipment affected is backed up by other equipment that is not on the same power circuit.

Do not provide power in such a way that multiple failovers occur at the same time; for example, having a gateway router and a switch served by the same power circuit or supply. The switch and router would both try to converge their routes at the same time which would cause problems in a heavily loaded network.

Failure Analysis and Recovery

Inevitably, equipment fails. A critical part of designing a highly available system is to plan for the time when something fails. High quality equipment, placed in a controlled environment, maintained consistently and regularly, and configured appropriately to the expected demand, will minimize incidents and failure severity. However, components wear out, external factors influence component life cycles, and mistakes are made. The goal for failure analysis, recovery, and restoration in a high-availability architecture environment is to recover the business process with minimal impact and restore the high-availability architecture environment as quickly as possible.

Early in hardware and software development cycles, architectures are constructed to handle essential high-availability element such as fault detection and containment, fault management, and fast, reliable recovery, online-failure isolation and repair, online repair verification, and reintegration of repaired equipment back into the environment. To ensure that any necessary recovery procedures are completed as quickly, safely, and automatically as possible, human intervention requirements should be minimized.

The general elements to failure analysis, recovery, and restoration follow:

- Error/degradation/failure detection
- Failover to alternate component
- Functional process recovery
- Notification of failure
- Isolation/removal of failed component
- Analysis/repair/replacement
- Test/verification of repair
- Reintegration into the configuration
- Restoration of high-availability architecture environment

Figure 3-8 illustrates how this process is continuous.

Figure 3-8   *The Failure and Recovery Cycle*

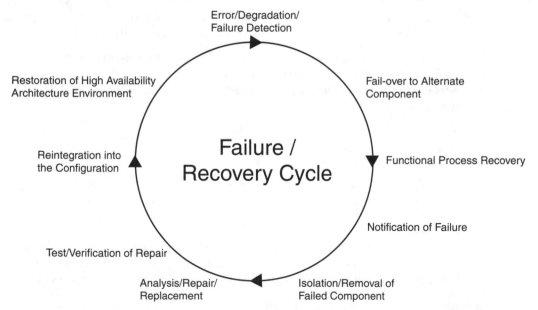

Failure detection is usually best accomplished with monitoring tools. At the first indication of a less than optimal condition, monitoring tools generate alert messages that often include the specific component that is struggling and the specific cause. Occasionally, a component will not fail outright or cleanly. Components often show signs of pending doom prior to complete failure. On these occasions, you have ample time to perform a planned and controlled failure analysis, recovery, and restoration process. However, this condition can also create severe performance degradation until the ailing component actually fails. When a component is no longer performing its commissioned duty it must be decommissioned due to failure. Packet storms, alert message floods, or retransmits can effectively cause a denial of service if the failing component is not quickly and effectively isolated from the configuration.

Whether through automatic detection with tools or human observation, in a redundant or fault tolerant environment, a failed or failing component should failover to an alternate component. With proper configuration, the alternate component will fulfill the failed component's responsibility with minimal (or no) transaction loss and minimal performance degradation. In a non-redundant or non-fault-tolerant environment, the functional business process will halt until the primary component is restored to a satisfactory performance condition.

Elimination of single points of failure through redundant, fault-tolerant design drastically decreases downtime and improves availability.

Summary

You should now be able to perform the following tasks:

- Define high availability.

- Explain high-availability objectives and the trade-offs between high-availability design and cost.

- Explain why high-availability design is important and its benefits.

- Explain the two types of high-availability designs.

- Explain the process of failure analysis and recovery.

- Explain the technologies that enable high availability.

- Explain how to design a high-availability architecture.

Review Questions

1 Define high availability.

_____

_____

_____

2 What are the three facets of high availability that need to be considered when designing a highly available system?

_____

_____

_____

3 How many minutes per year is a "five nines" system down for at the very most?

_____

_____

_____

4 What are the five steps for designing or customizing high-availability solutions?

_____

_____

_____

5 What are the two design approaches to high availability?

_____

_____

_____

6 What objectives should be met when composing a development roadmap?

_____

_____

_____

7 What are MTBF and MTTR?

_____

_____

_____

8 What Layer 2 technologies can be used to provide automatic recovery of lost connections?

_____

_____

_____

9 What is the standards based version of Cisco's HSRP?

_____

_____

_____

After reading this chapter, you will be able to perform the following tasks:

- Explain why security is needed.
- Explain why security is important.
- Explain what a security policy is.
- Explain the Security Life Cycle Model.
- Explain some common network attacks.
- Understand the different Cisco Security Solutions.
- Define the Cisco SAFE Architecture and its purpose.
- Explain the modules within the SAFE Architecture.

CHAPTER 4

Security Concepts and Design

Chapter 1, "Internet System Architecture Overview," discussed how the Internet and, more specifically, Internet-based applications are changing the way people work, shop, live, play, and learn. These changes are occurring both in ways that we currently experience (e-commerce, real-time information access, e-learning, expanded communication options, and so forth), and in ways not yet experienced. For example, imagine a day when your enterprise can make all its telephone calls over the Internet for free. On a more personal note, picture logging on to a daycare provider's web site to check how your child is doing throughout the day.

Society is just beginning to unlock the potential of the Internet. Over the next decade, Internet access will conservatively reach one-fifth of the planet, but with the Internet's unparalleled growth comes unprecedented exposure of personal data, critical enterprise resources, government secrets, and so forth. Every day hackers pose an increasing threat to these entities with several different types of attacks.

This chapter's purpose is to outline why security is necessary, what steps an enterprise must take to implement a sound security policy, and how an enterprise can equip itself with the resources necessary to mitigate risk. A blueprint, called the Cisco SAFE Architecture, which is introduced throughout this chapter, brings those resources together. The SAFE Architecture is composed of Cisco's best-in-class security products brought together in individual modules or reference architectures to provide an end-to-end, secure infrastructure. The individual modules and how they are applied are discussed later in this chapter.

Internet applications are transforming continuous access to information and the benefits that it provides. As the Internet grows and companies rely more on the Internet and its inherent benefits for their effectiveness, more and more importance is placed on having a functional, always-on architecture.

Unfortunately, some people want to take those benefits from others to become instantaneously significant. It's been said that tearing something down is easier than building it up, and that's exactly what a hacker is does; he tears down what so many have spent so much time building. So what is the goal of security? To protect what so many have spent so much time, effort, and energy building and maintaining as well as protect what is most important to a company—its customers' and employees' privacy, assets, resources, and, ultimately, the purest indicator of valuation, the stock price.

Securing a network is a continuous process. It's an ongoing effort to protect a company's information assets.

Figure 4-1 shows that as the Internet becomes more viable to larger groups of people, and as Internet-based applications serve more and more people, the risk of a security breach increases even more.

Figure 4-1   *The Security Challenge*

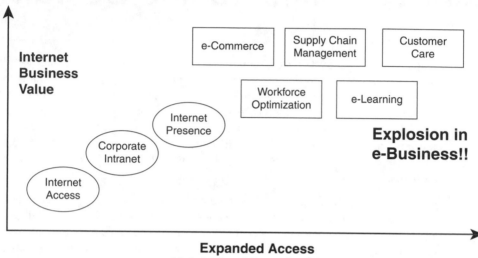

You need to know the following three goals of security:

- Maintain integrity
- Protect confidentiality
- Assure availability

What is *integrity*? In security terms, integrity refers to the assurance that data is not altered or destroyed in an unauthorized manner. Integrity is maintained when the message sent is identical to the message received. Even for data that is not confidential, measures must be taken to ensure data integrity.

For example, many banks would certainly care if a business transaction were modified. This could positively or negatively impact their bottom line.

Confidentiality is the protection of data from unauthorized disclosure to a third party. Whether it is customer data or internal company data, a business is responsible for protecting the privacy of its data. Customers have the right to have their private information protected. This protection might very well be a legal requirement. It behooves a business to maintain a trustworthy relationship with its customers by respecting their right to privacy. Company proprietary information that is sensitive in nature also needs to remain confidential. Only authorized parties should be granted access to information that has been identified as confidential. Many companies today specifically mark their internal documents with "Company Confidential" to reduce the occurrence of inadvertent transmission to third parties.

The third goal of security is to ensure that services are available and useful to all intended parties on a consistent basis. In an enterprise, if a resource is unavailable it costs the organization money. Security should protect those assets from becoming compromised and being controlled by parties other than the enterprise.

How Important Is Security?

So how important is security really? Well, how important is a company's earnings per share, price/earnings ratio, revenue, consumer confidence, and a company's stock price? You'd probably say that all these are important. A company's performance indicators are protected by the organizing principle of keeping a secure infrastructure.

Many companies have been hit significantly in their bottom line because of security breaches and downtime caused by those breaches. Table 4-1 displays how heavy a hit a company takes for every minute of downtime. The numbers are very conservative and are based on 20 percent revenue loss per hour.

Table 4-1   *Revenue Lost Cost of Downtime*

Company	Daily Internal Revenue in Dollars	Lost Revenue per Hour of Downtime in Dollars (Assume 20 percent Revenue Loss)
Company A	$2,700,000	$22,500
Company B	$10,000,000	$91,320
Company C	$20,000,000	$182,640
Company D	$33,000,000	$274,980

What Is a Security Policy?

The first and probably the most important step to building a long-term, secure architecture is to generate a security policy. This security policy is your outcome and purpose rolled into one document that stands as the standard for your corporation's secure architecture. A security policy can be as simple as an acceptable user policy for network resources, or can be several hundred pages in length and detail every element of connectivity and associated policies. Although somewhat narrow in scope, RFC 2196 suitably defines a security policy as follows:

"A security policy is a formal statement of the rules by which people who are given access to an organization's technology and information assets must abide."

This book does not attempt to go into detail on developing a security policy. RFC 2196 has some good information available on the subject, and numerous locations on the World Wide Web have example policies and guidelines. The following web pages might assist the interested reader:

- RFC 2196 "Site Security Handbook" www.ietf.org/rfc/rfc2196.txt
- www.cert.org/
- www.cisco.com/warp/public/126/secpol.html

The Need for a Security Policy

By defining a security policy before choosing security methods, organizations can avoid redesigning security processes after they are implemented. True network security comes from a combination of products and services, combined with a comprehensive security policy and a commitment to adhere to that policy from the top of the organization down. A properly implemented security policy without dedicated security hardware can be more effective at mitigating the threat to enterprise resources than a comprehensive security product implementation without an associated policy. No one product can make an organization "secure." The security policy should not determine how a business operates; the nature of the business should dictate the policy. Security policies should be living documents.

Network security is an area where Constant and Neverending Improvement (CANI) needs to be practiced . Because organizations are constantly subject to change, security policies must be systematically updated to reflect new business directions, technological changes, and resource allocations.

The first step to building a secure infrastructure is clearly defining a security policy. After the policy has been put in place, the next step is to maintain the security policy with continual testing, managing, monitoring, responding, and improving. Maintaining a secure infrastructure is much like maintaining a garden. This process results in security policies that significantly improve information availability, integrity, and privacy. A properly executed information policy also encourages buy-in across the organization.

To develop an effective security policy, organizations need to do the following:

- **Identify the assets to protect**—An organization must understand what they want to protect, what access is needed, and how these considerations work together.

- **Determine points of network access**—An organization must understand how potential intruders can enter its network. Special areas of consideration are network connections, dial-up access points, and misconfigured hosts.

- **Limit the scope of access**—Organizations can create multiple barriers within networks so that unlawful entry to one part of the system does not automatically allow entry to the entire infrastructure.

- **Identify assumptions**—Examine and justify assumptions. Any hidden assumption is a potential security hole.

- **Determine the cost of security measures**—When an organization decides which security measures to implement, it must understand the costs and weigh these against potential benefits. If security costs are out of proportion to actual dangers, the organization should not implement security measures.

- **Consider human factors**—Define human factors and any corresponding policies as a formal part of a complete security policy.

- **Keep a limited number of secrets**—The more secrets there are, the harder it is to keep all of them.

- **Implement pervasive security**—Any security policy's goal is to create an environment that is not susceptible to every minor change.

- **Understand the network environment**—This kind of awareness helps an organization detect security problems.

- **Remember physical security**—Software security measures can often be circumvented when access to the hardware is not controlled.

- **Remember host security and patches**—Continually stay informed on the holes in software and become familiar with the ways that hackers have gotten into similar sites to prevent the same from happening to your organization.

After a security policy is in place, it needs to be tested and implemented. Because of budget, time, or resource constraints, testing procedures are often reduced to a "quick-fix" type of implementation. However, inadequate testing usually results in a disastrous implementation or reactive conditions in a disrupted production environment. The rule of thumb is to always exercise due diligence when determining the required minimum levels of testing. Figure 4-2 describes the process that includes implementing a security policy and then testing, monitoring, and improving it.

Figure 4-2 *Security Life Cycle Model*

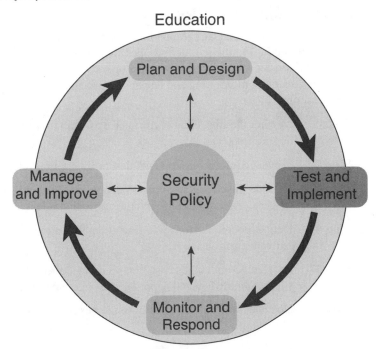

Test and Implementation Considerations

Testing is necessary to ensure that the solution is reliable. Take the following steps to ensure that testing is performed effectively:

Step 1   Define test scripts and scenarios that validate configured security rules. Where applicable, include metrics for test results.

Step 2   Set up a test environment that closely reflects the production environment.

Step 3   Repeat the process until desired test results are achieved and validated.

Step 4   Consider the impact on overall performance.

Step 5   Stage the promotion of the tested solution into production. Ensure that the production environment is prepared to receive the promotion. For example, verify that the latest software versions or patches are applied across all affected components.

Step 6   If possible, begin the implementation in a pilot mode. After satisfactory results are attained, phase in the remainder of the implementation.

Monitor and Respond Considerations

A primary objective of monitoring and responding is to ensure that an implementation does not cause any major disruptions to the production-operating environment. In other words, an implementation should not disrupt normal business operations. To achieve minimal disruption, you must establish adequate monitoring and responsive procedures. Take the following steps to ensure proper response times:

Step 1   Monitor the impact on performance as changes occur in systems, applications, and the network.

Step 2   Enable required warning and alert notification levels.

Step 3   Consider installing an intrusion detection system to support real-time alerts and to simplify monitoring and incident response tasks.

Step 4   Define procedures for reviewing anomalies and approving corrective actions.

Step 5   Respond to anomalies based on predefined procedures that support the review and approval of corrective actions.

Step 6   Document responses for input to the next phase of managing and improving.

The desired outcome of implementing security is the successful attainment of security goals with minimal disruption to business operations. To ensure that this is accomplished over the long-term, a company must review and refine all security implementations to insure their constant improvement.

Manage and Improve Considerations

Take the following the steps to improve what is in place:

Step 1   Gather input from the monitoring and responding phase for review.

Step 2   Identify opportunities to improve system performance or security, and identify any unforeseen roadblocks that might have arisen.

Step 3   Determine whether security policies are being enforced and refine policies, standards, and procedures as required.

Step 4   Begin new plans and designs based on refinements and continue the cycle.

Part of a security management life cycle is the need for an ongoing effort to raise security awareness at all levels of the organization, including at the executive, management, administrator, and end-user levels. This educational process cuts across all other steps, and includes both administrator training for emerging threats to their systems, and awareness among end-users of the benefits of working within the security architecture.

Two interrelated items come to the forefront when thinking about education and security:

- The IT people need education in how the end-users feel about security.

- The end-user needs to be educated about what could happen to his business, or to him, if security is breached.

Many in the workplace, from senior management to customers and suppliers, view security as a necessary evil. At worst, they think it is an expensive and unwanted intrusion into normal business operations. This inappropriate view must be overcome because, no matter how strong an Internet architecture is, without end-user commitment to using the security resources in place, a company will have many security challenges. One person leaving their passwords stuck on their computer because they can't remember them all is enough to compromise an entire network. But how can these challenges be overcome if IT professionals make the systems difficult and time-consuming to use?

The truth is that a single security breach in the Internet world can be far more damaging than it would be in the physical world in terms of strategic information lost, bad publicity, loss of customer and partner confidence, and stakeholder liability. Many organization leaders and other individuals within an organization do not realize this. After this is understood, through education and examples of what could happen, information security quickly becomes a priority for all concerned. Education of both end-users and IT professionals must permeate every part of a security management life cycle.

Types of Attacks

This section discusses the different types of hacks or attacks possible, and later in this chapter you'll learn about the Cisco security solutions and architectures that help to prevent the challenges discussed here.

Network attacks can be as varied as the systems that they attempt to penetrate. Some attacks are elaborately complex, while well-intentioned device operators perform others unknowingly. You should understand some of the TCP/IP protocol's inherent functionality when evaluating attack types. When the Internet was formed, it linked various government entities and universities to one another to facilitate learning and research. The original Internet architects never anticipated the kind of widespread adoption the Internet has achieved today. As a result, in the early days of the Internet Protocol (IP), security was not a specification in the design. For this reason, most IP implementations are inherently insecure. Only after many years and thousands of Requests for Comments (RFCs) are the tools available to begin to deploy IP securely. Because specific provisions for IP security were not designed from the onset, it is important to augment IP implementations with network security practices, services, and products to mitigate inherent IP risks. The sections that follow offer brief coverage of the types of attacks commonly seen on IP networks and how these attacks can be mitigated.

Packet Sniffers

A *packet sniffer* is a software application that uses a network adapter card in promiscuous mode (a mode in which the network adapter card sends all packets received on the physical network wire to an application for processing) to capture all network packets that are sent across a particular collision domain. Sniffers are used legitimately in networks today to aid in troubleshooting and traffic analysis. However, because several network applications send data in clear text (Telnet, FTP, SMTP, POP3, and so forth), a packet sniffer can provide meaningful and sensitive information, such as usernames and passwords.

One serious problem with acquiring usernames and passwords is that users often reuse their login names and passwords across multiple applications and systems. In fact, many users employ a single password for access to all their accounts and applications. If an application is run in client-server mode and authentication information is sent across the network in clear text, this same authentication information can likely be used to gain access to other corporate or external resources. Because hackers know and use human characteristics (attack methods known collectively as social engineering attacks), such as using a single password for multiple accounts, they often successfully gain access to sensitive information. In a worst-case scenario, a hacker gains access to a system-level user account, which the hacker uses to create a new account that can be employed at any time as a back door to break into a network and its resources.

You can mitigate the threat of packet sniffers in several ways:

- **Authentication**—Using strong authentication is a first option for defense against packet sniffers. Strong authentication can be broadly defined as a method of authenticating users that cannot easily be circumvented. A common example of strong authentication is one-time passwords (OTPs). An OTP is a two-factor authentication. Two-factor authentication involves using something you have combined with something you know. For example, automated teller machines (ATMs) use two-factor authentication. A customer needs both an ATM card and a personal identification number (PIN) to make transactions. OTP requires a PIN and your token card to authenticate to a device or software application. A token card is a hardware or software device that generates new, seemingly random passwords at specified intervals (usually 60 seconds). A user combines that random password with a PIN to create a unique password that only works for one instance of authentication. If a hacker learns that password by using a packet sniffer, the information is useless because the password has already expired. Note that this mitigation technique is effective only against a sniffer implementation that is designed to grab passwords. Sniffers deployed to learn sensitive information (such as mail messages) will still be effective.

- **Switched infrastructure**—Another method to counter the use of packet sniffers in your environment is to deploy a switched infrastructure. For example, if an entire organization deploys switched Ethernet, hackers can only gain access to the traffic that flows on the specific port to which they connect. A switched infrastructure does not eliminate the threat of packet sniffers, but it can greatly reduce their effectiveness.

- **Cryptography**—The most effective method for countering packet sniffers does not prevent or detect packet sniffers, but renders them irrelevant. If a communication channel is cryptographically secure, the only data a packet sniffer can detect is cipher text (a seemingly random string of bits) and not the original message. Cisco's network-level cryptography deployment is based on IP Security (IPSec). IPSec is a standard method for networking devices to communicate privately using IP. Other cryptographic protocols for network management include Secure Shell (SSH) and Secure Sockets Layer (SSL).

IP Spoofing

An IP spoofing attack occurs when a hacker inside or outside a network pretends to be a trusted computer. A hacker can do this in one of two ways. The hacker either uses an IP address that is within the range of trusted IP addresses for a network, or an authorized external IP address that is trusted and to which access is provided to specified resources on a network. IP spoofing attacks are often a launch point for other attacks. The classic example is to launch a DoS attack using spoofed source addresses to hide a hacker's identity.

Normally, an IP spoofing attack is limited to the injection of malicious data or commands into an existing stream of data that is passed between a client and server application or a peer-to-peer network connection. To enable bi-directional communication, the hacker must change all routing tables to point to the spoofed IP address. Another approach hackers sometimes take is to not worry about receiving any response from the applications. If a hacker tries to obtain a sensitive file from a system, application responses are unimportant.

The threat of IP spoofing can be reduced, but not eliminated, through the following measures:

- **Access control**—The most common method for preventing IP spoofing is to properly configure access control. To reduce IP spoofing's effectiveness, configure access control to deny any traffic from the external network that has a source address that should reside on the internal network. Note that this only helps prevent spoofing attacks if the internal addresses are the only trusted addresses. If external addresses are trusted, this method is not effective.

- **RFC 2827 filtering**—You can also prevent a network's users from spoofing other networks (and be a good 'Net citizen at the same time) by preventing any outbound traffic on your network that does not have a source address in your organization's own IP range. Your Internet service provider (ISP) can also implement this type of filtering, which is collectively referred to as RFC 2827 filtering. This filtering denies any traffic that does not have the expected source address on a particular interface. For example, if an ISP provides a connection to the IP address 15.1.1.0/24, the ISP could filter traffic so that only traffic sourced from address 15.1.1.0/24 can enter the ISP router from that interface. Unless all ISPs implement this type of filtering, its effectiveness is significantly reduced. Now that access control lists (ACLs) are configured in hardware on many Cisco platforms, ISPs now implement ACLs with more comfort because of increased performance. Also, the further you get from the devices you want to filter, the more difficult filtering becomes at a granular level. For example, performing RFC 2827 filtering at the access router to the Internet requires that you allow your entire major network number (that is, 10.0.0.0/8) to traverse the access router. If you perform filtering at the distribution layer, as in this architecture, you can achieve more specific filtering (that is, 10.1.5.0/24).

The most effective method for mitigating the threat of IP spoofing is the same as that for mitigating the threat of packet sniffers: eliminating its effectiveness. IP spoofing can function correctly only when devices use IP address-based authentication. If you use additional authentication methods, IP spoofing attacks are irrelevant. Cryptographic authentication is the best form of additional authentication, but when that is not possible, strong two-factor authentication using OTP is also effective.

Denial of Service

The most publicized form of attack, denial-of-service (DoS) attacks, are also among the most difficult to completely eliminate. Even among the hacker community, DoS attacks are regarded as trivial and considered bad form because they require so little effort to execute. Still, because of their ease of implementation and potentially significant damage, DoS attacks deserve special attention from security administrators. If you are interested in learning more about DoS attacks, researching the methods employed by some of the better-known attacks can be useful. These attacks include the following:

- TCP SYN Flood

- Ping of Death

- Tribe Flood Network (TFN) and Tribe Flood Network 2000 (TFN2K)

- Trinco

- Stacheldraht

- Trinity

Another excellent source on the topic of security is the Computer Emergency Response Team (CERT). CERT has published an excellent paper on dealing with DoS attacks, which you can find at the following URL: www.cert.org/tech_tips/denial_of_service.html

DoS attacks are different from most other attacks because they are generally not targeted at gaining access to your network or the information on your network. These attacks focus on making a service unavailable for normal use, which is typically accomplished by exhausting a resource limitation on the network, or within an operating system or application.

When involving specific network server applications, such as a World Wide Web server or an FTP server, these attacks can focus on acquiring and keeping all the available connections supported by that server open, effectively locking out valid users of the server or service. DoS attacks can also be implemented using common Internet protocols, such as TCP and Internet Control Message Protocol (ICMP). Most DoS attacks exploit a weakness in the overall architecture of the system being attacked rather than a software bug or security hole. However, some attacks compromise your network's performance by flooding the network with undesired, and often useless, network packets, and by providing false information about the status of network resources. This type of attack is often the most difficult to prevent because it requires coordination with your upstream network provider. If traffic meant to consume your available bandwidth is not stopped there, denying it at the point of entry into your network will do little good because your available bandwidth has already been consumed. When this type of attack is launched from many different systems at the same time, it is often referred to as a distributed denial-of-service attack (DDoS). Figure 4-3 illustrates a DDoS attack.

Figure 4-3 *DDoS Attack*

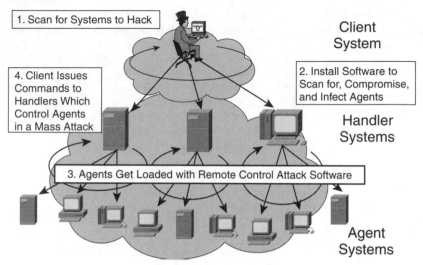

The threat of denial-of-service attacks can be reduced through the following four methods:

- **A network-based intrusion detection system**—For example, Cisco Secure Intrusion Detection System. Intrusion detection systems are discussed later in this chapter.

- **Anti-spoof features**—Proper configuration of anti-spoof features on your routers and firewalls can reduce your risk. This includes RFC 2827 filtering at a minimum. If hackers can't mask their identities, they might not attack.

- **Anti-DoS features**—Proper configuration of anti-DoS features on routers and firewalls can help limit an attack's effectiveness. These features often involve limits on the amount of half-open connections that a system allows open at any given time.

- **Traffic rate limiting**—You can implement traffic rate limiting with your ISP. This type of filtering limits the amount of nonessential traffic that crosses network segments to a certain rate. A common example is to limit the amount of ICMP traffic allowed into a network because it is used only for diagnostic purposes. ICMP-based DoS attacks are common.

Password Attacks

Hackers can implement password attacks using several different methods, including brute-force attacks, Trojan horse programs, IP spoofing, and packet sniffers. Although packet sniffers and IP spoofing can yield user accounts and passwords, password attacks usually refer to repeated attempts to identify a user account and/or password. These repeated attempts are called brute-force attacks.

A brute-force attack is often performed using a program that runs across the network and attempts to log in to a shared resource, such as a server. When hackers successfully gain access to resources, they have the same rights as the users whose accounts have been compromised to gain access to those resources. If the compromised accounts have sufficient privileges, the hackers can create back doors for future access without concern for any status or password changes to the compromised user accounts.

Another problem exists when users have the same (possibly strong) password on every system they connect to. This often includes personal systems, corporate systems, and Internet systems. Because that password is only as secure as the weakest administered host that contains it, if that host is compromised, hackers have a whole range of hosts on which they can try the same password.

You can most easily eliminate password attacks by not relying on plain-text passwords in the first place. Using OTP and/or cryptographic authentication can virtually eliminate the threat of password attacks. Unfortunately, not all applications, hosts, or devices support these authentication methods. When standard passwords are used, choose a password that is difficult to guess. Passwords should be at least eight characters long and contain uppercase letters, lowercase letters, numbers, and special characters (#%$ and so forth). The best passwords are randomly generated but are difficult to remember, often leading users to write their passwords down.

Several advances have been made relative to password maintenance—both for the user and the administrator. Software applications are now available that encrypt a list of passwords to be stored on a handheld computer. This allows the user to remember only one complex password and have the remaining passwords stored securely within the application.

Man-in-the-Middle Attacks

A man-in-the-middle attack requires the hacker to have access to network packets that come across a network. An example of such a configuration could be someone who is working for an ISP and has access to all network packets transferred between his employer's network and any other network. Such attacks are often implemented using network packet sniffers and routing and transport protocols. Such attacks can be used to steal information, hijack an ongoing session to gain access to private network resources, analyze traffic to derive information about a network and its users, to deny service, corrupt transmitted data, and introduce new information into network sessions.

Man-in-the-middle attacks can be effectively mitigated only through the use of cryptography. If someone hijacks data in the middle of a cryptographically private session, all the hacker will see is cipher text and not the original message. If a hacker can learn information about the cryptographic session (such as the session key), man-in-the-middle attacks are still possible.

Application Layer Attacks

Application layer attacks can be implemented using several different methods, including exploiting well-known weaknesses in software that are commonly found on servers such as sendmail, HTTP, and FTP. By exploiting these weaknesses, hackers can gain access to a computer with the permissions of the account running the application, which is usually a privileged system-level account. These application-layer attacks are often widely publicized in an effort to allow administrators to rectify the problem with a patch. Unfortunately, many hackers also subscribe to these same mailing lists so they learn about the attack at the same time (if they haven't discovered it already).

The primary problem with application-layer attacks is that they often use ports that are allowed through a firewall. For example, a hacker executing a known vulnerability against a World Wide Web server often uses TCP port 80 in the attack. Because the World Wide Web server serves pages to users, a firewall must allow access on that port. From a firewall's perspective, it is merely standard port 80 traffic.

Application-layer attacks can never be completely eliminated. New vulnerabilities are always being discovered and publicized to the Internet community. The best way to reduce your risk is by practicing good system administration. The following are a few measures you can take to reduce your risks:

- Read OS and network log files and/or have them analyzed by log analysis applications.

- Subscribe to mailing lists that publicize vulnerabilities, such as Bugtraq (www.securityfocus.com) and the CERT (www.cert.org).

- Keep your OS and applications current with the latest patches.

- In addition to proper system administration, using intrusion detection systems (IDSs) can help. There are two complementary IDS technologies:

  — Network-based IDS (NIDS) operates by watching all packets traversing a particular collision domain. When NIDS sees a packet or series of packets that match a known or suspect attack, it flags an alarm and/or terminates the session.

  — Host-based IDS (HIDS) operates by inserting agents into the protected host. HIDS concerns itself only with attacks generated against that one host.

IDS systems operate by using attack signatures. Attack signatures are the profile for a particular attack. They specify certain conditions that must be met before traffic is deemed to be an attack. In the physical world, IDS can be most closely compared to an alarm system or security camera.

Network Reconnaissance

Network reconnaissance refers to the overall act of learning information about a target network by using publicly available information and applications. When hackers attempt to penetrate a particular network, they often need to learn as much information as possible about the network before launching attacks. This can take the form of DNS queries, ping sweeps, and port scans. DNS queries can reveal such information as who owns a particular domain and what addresses have been assigned to that domain. Ping sweeps of the addresses revealed by the DNS queries can present a picture of the live hosts in a particular environment. After such a list is generated, port-scanning tools can cycle through all well-known ports to provide a complete list of all services running on the hosts discovered by the ping sweep. Finally, the hackers can examine the characteristics of the applications running on the hosts. This can lead to specific information that is useful when the hacker attempts to compromise that service.

Network reconnaissance cannot be completely prevented. If ICMP echo and echo-reply is turned off on edge routers, for example, ping sweeps can be stopped, but at the expense of network diagnostic data. However, port scans can easily be run without full ping sweeps; they simply take longer because they have to scan IP addresses that might not be live. At the network and host levels, IDS can usually notify an administrator when a reconnaissance gathering attack is underway. This allows the administrator to better prepare for the coming attack or to notify the ISP who is hosting the system that is launching the reconnaissance probe.

The best defense against network reconnaissance is to render it irrelevant by filtering all traffic except that to the addresses and ports where you actually want to offer services to the public. Depending on your security policy, you might want to allow network reconnaissance to monitor who is trying to get more information on your network.

Trust Exploitation

Although not an attack in and of itself, trust exploitation refers to an attack where an individual takes advantage of a trust relationship within a network. The classic example is a perimeter network connection from a corporation. These network segments often house DNS, SMTP, and HTTP servers. Because they all reside on the same segment, compromising one system can lead to compromising other systems because they might trust other systems attached to their same network. Another example is a system on the outside of a firewall that has a trust relationship with a system on the inside of a firewall. When the outside system is compromised, it can leverage that trust relationship to attack the inside network.

Port Redirection

Port Redirection attacks are a trust exploitation that uses a compromised host to pass traffic through a firewall that would otherwise be dropped. Consider a firewall with three interfaces and a host on each interface. The host on the outside can reach the host on the public services segment (commonly referred to as a DMZ), but not the host on the inside. The host on the public services segment can reach the host on both the outside and the inside. If hackers compromised the public services segment host, they could install software to redirect traffic from the outside host directly to the inside host. Although neither communication violates the rules implemented in the firewall, the outside host has now achieved connectivity to the inside host through the port redirection process on the public services host.

Port redirection can primarily be mitigated through the use of proper trust models (as previously mentioned). Assuming a system is under attack, host-based IDS can help detect and prevent a hacker installing such utilities on a host.

Unauthorized Access

Although not a specific type of attack, unauthorized access refers to the majority of attacks executed in networks today. For someone to brute-force a telnet login, he must first get the telnet prompt on a system. Upon connection to the telnet port, a message might indicate: "authorization required to use this resource." If the hacker continues to attempt access, his actions become "unauthorized." These kinds of attacks can be initiated both on the outside and inside of a network.

Mitigation techniques for unauthorized access attacks are very simple. They involve reducing or eliminating a hacker's ability to gain access to a system using an unauthorized protocol. An example is preventing hackers from having access to the telnet port on a server that needs to provide World Wide Web services to the outside. If a hacker cannot reach that port, attacking it is very difficult. The recommendation is to disable all unused services on the server or at the firewall/security level to allow only authorized machines telnet access. The primary function of a firewall in a network is to prevent simple unauthorized access attacks.

Virus and Trojan Horse Applications

The primary vulnerabilities for end-user workstations are viruses and Trojan horses. Viruses refer to malicious software that is attached to another program to execute an unwanted function on a user's workstation. For example, a program that is attached to command.com (the primary interpreter for windows systems) that deletes certain files and infects any other versions of command.com that it can find is a virus. A Trojan horse is different only in that the entire application is written to look like something else when, in fact, it is an attack tool. An example of a Trojan horse is a software application that runs a simple game on the user's workstation. While the user is occupied with the game, the Trojan horse mails a copy of itself to every user in the user's address book. Then other users get the game and play it, spreading the Trojan horse.

These kinds of applications can be contained through the effective use of antivirus software at the user level and potentially at the network level. Antivirus software can detect most viruses and many Trojan horse applications and prevent them from spreading in the network. Keeping up –to date with the latest developments in attacks leads to a more effective posture against them. As new virus or Trojan horse applications are released, enterprises need to keep up –to date with the latest antivirus software and application versions.

Conclusions About Attacks

The previous sections covered the major attacks that are perpetrated against organizations daily. The next sections focus on potential solutions to the challenges addressed by these types of attacks. As previously discussed, the first step is the security policy, and the second is building the secure architecture. All of the following sections discuss building a secure architecture and the components that make up the architecture.

The immediate sections that follow address the primary components of the SAFE architecture:

- Firewalls

- VPNs

- Network- and Host-based intrusion detection

Firewalls

In the physical security analogy a *firewall* is the equivalent of a door lock on the perimeter or inside of a building—it permits only an authorized user (such as those with a key or badge) to enter. A firewall is one or more devices that control the authorized flow of network traffic and services to and from a particular network. It protects internal resources from outside intruders. A firewall serves as a buffer between any connected public networks and a private network. A firewall enforces a comprehensive policy (authorized traffic flows and services) put together by its security organization in conjunction with business needs. In general, there are two types of policies:

- That which is not specifically authorized is denied.

- That which is not specifically denied is authorized.

The first type of policy is by far the most prevalent, but it requires that the customer know the risks involved before authorizing services to pass through the firewall. For example, if the firewall allows web traffic to pass, an attacker can send a command that exercises a buffer overflow in the web browser application. The firewall will not stop these packets from reaching the victim system, however, the Cisco Secure IDS would be able to identify that attack. The Intrusion Detection system is further explained later in this chapter.

There are three types of firewalls:

- Packet filtering

- Application proxy

- Stateful inspection

Packet filtering controls the inbound and outbound IP network traffic. Perimeter routers are the most ideal devices to perform packet filtering because they are the first line of defense to external connections. However, this does not preclude dedicated firewall devices from performing this granular filtering.

Packet filtering should be performed on the following elements:

- Source and destination IP address

- Protocols used

- Source and destination ports

- SYN/ACK bits, which allow the filter to determine which session partner initiated a TCP/IP connection

From a security perspective, the purpose of application proxy servers is to protect (or hide) internal devices from external devices during connections that are made from the internal to the external.

For example, internal browsers connect to the proxy for any external web access. Subsequent replies from external sources are directed to the proxy server. An external source is prevented from having direct access to any internal devices. Proxy servers can reside behind or function as part of a dedicated firewall.

Stateful inspection, or filtering, is a feature in dedicated firewall devices that provides a secure method of analyzing data packets by placing detailed information about data packets into a table.

Cisco PIX Firewalls

Cisco PIX (Private Internet Exchange) firewalls have many advanced features and have set the standard for years for security, reliability, and speed. Today, there are six PIX models that make up the PIX firewall line—the 501, 506, 515,525, 535, and the PIX Firewall Blade. The firewall line serves the home user's need with the 501, to the large enterprise with the five-Gbps PIX Firewall Blade. The sections that follow cover the features that distinguish the PIX from other firewalls.

Proprietary Hardened OS

Many attacks try to exploit the weaknesses in operating systems of host machines or network devices. As such, you need to ensure that your firewall architecture isn't vulnerable. Attacks can compromise not only general-purpose operating systems, but also the firewall applications that run on top of them.

The Cisco PIX Firewall is a purpose-built firewall appliance that offers an unprecedented level of protection. This is tightly integrated with the PIX Operating System (OS), which is a proprietary, hardened system that eliminates security holes and performance degrading overhead. Because the OS is a proprietary OS, PIX does not experience any of the many security holes present in either UNIX or Windows NT.

Stateful Inspection

The Cisco PIX Firewall's Adaptive Security Algorithm (ASA) is a stateful, connection-oriented design that creates session flows based on source and destination addresses, randomized TCP sequence numbers, port numbers, and additional TCP flags. This granular inspection provides robust security policy enforcement on both inbound and outbound traffic.

Application Awareness

The **fixup protocol** command performs the Adaptive Security Algorithm based on different port numbers other than the defaults The **fixup protocol** commands enable you to view, change, enable, or disable the use of a service or protocol through the PIX Firewall. The ports you specify are those that the PIX Firewall listens at for each respective service. This command is global and changes things for both inbound and outbound connections.

Denial-of-Service Guards

PIX Firewalls thwart many types of DoS attacks through the use of Guard features. Examples of PIX Guards include the following:

- Flood Guard prevents denial-of-service attacks on authentication, authorization, and accounting (AAA) services in particular. Controlling the AAA service's tolerance for unanswered login attempts optimizes AAA system use.

- The PIX Firewall DNS Guard feature identifies each outbound DNS resolve request, and only allows a single DNS response. A host might query several servers for a response (if the first server is slow in responding), but only the first answer to the specific question will be allowed. All the additional answers from other servers will be dropped.

- The Flood Defender feature protects systems on an internal network from denial-of-service attacks by setting a maximum number of available embryonic connections for NAT and static commands. The connection limit allows you to set the maximum number of outbound connections that can be started with IP address criteria you specify. This prevents attacks where processes are started without being completed.

FragGuard and Virtual Reassembly Features

The PIX Firewall can be configured to detect and reject large (as used in the Ping of Death) or fragmented ICMP packets by using the FragGuard and Virtual Reassembly features. FragGuard provides IP fragment protection that fully reassembles all ICMP error messages and virtually reassembles the remaining IP fragments that are routed through the PIX Firewall. This feature uses syslog to notify of any overlapping fragment and small fragment offset anomalies, especially those caused by a teardrop attack. PIX Firewall enforces two additional security checks to those recommended by RFC 1858 against IP fragment style attacks. First, each non-initial IP fragment is required to be associated with an already seen, valid initial IP fragment. Second, IP fragments are rated to 100 full IP fragmented packets per second to each internal host.

TCP Intercept Feature

PIX Firewall's TCP intercept feature helps prevent SYN-flooding attacks by intercepting and validating TCP connection requests. After the optional embryonic connection limit is reached, and until the embryonic connection count falls below this threshold, every SYN bound for the affected server is intercepted. For each SYN, PIX responds on the server's behalf with an empty SYN/ACK segment. PIX Firewall retains pertinent state information, drops the packet, and waits for the client's acknowledgment. This protects destination servers while still allowing valid requests. If the ACK is received, a copy of the client's SYN segment is sent to the server and the TCP three-way handshake is performed between PIX Firewall and the server. If this three-way handshake is successfully completed, the connection resumes as normal. If the client does not respond during any part of the connection phase, PIX Firewall retransmits the necessary segment using exponential back-offs. Connection attempts from unreachable hosts will never reach the server. PIX Firewall handles UDP data transfers in a manner similar to TCP. The PIX creates UDP connection state information when a UDP packet is sent from the inside network. Response packets resulting from this traffic are only accepted if they match the connection state information.

Intrusion Detection

Intrusion Detection provides another layered of defense against denial-of-service attacks. The PIX Firewall includes intrusion-detection technology, based on the Cisco Intrusion Detection System (IDS). It identifies 53 common attacks (including packet fragments, ping-of-death, floods, echo replies, and so on) using single-packet (atomic) signatures to detect patterns of misuse in network traffic. When suspicious activity is detected, PIX responds immediately and can be configured to do the following:

- Send an alarm to a syslog server

- Drop the packet

- Reset the Transmission Control Protocol (TCP) connection

NAT Options

RFC 1918 (1597, 1627) specifies that networks that are reserved for private use should never be seen on the public Internet. Furthermore, to minimize risk, an organization using private IP addresses should choose randomly from the reserved pool of private addresses when allocating sub-blocks for its internal allocation. One or more types of Network Address Translation (NAT), as outlined in RFC 1631, typically perform this function.

NAT means that when a host starts an outbound connection, the IP addresses in the internal network are translated into global addresses. This allows your network to have any IP addressing scheme while protecting these addresses from visibility on the external network. The Cisco PIX Firewall allows you to enable or disable address translation for one or more internal addresses using the following methods:

- **Dynamic NAT**—Dynamic translation is useful for desktop machines that do not need constant addresses on the Internet. By enabling dynamic address translation, inside network hosts with IP addresses not registered with the Network Information Center (NIC) can directly access the Internet with standard TCP/IP software on the desktop. No special client software is needed.

- **Static NAT**—Static translation effectively moves an internal, unregistered host into the virtual network in the PIX Firewall. This is useful for internal machines that need to be addressed from the outside Internet gateways; for example, an SMTP server.

- **Port Address Translation (PAT)**—PAT lets multiple outbound sessions appear to originate from a single IP address. With it enabled, the PIX Firewall chooses a unique port number from the PAT IP address for each outbound xlate (translation slot). This feature allows you to share a single, globally unique address for up to 64,000 hosts simultaneously, and is valuable when an Internet service provider cannot allocate enough unique IP addresses for your outbound connections.

Standards-based IPsec

IPSec encryption is an IETF standard that supports 56-bit and 168-bit encryption algorithms in IPSec client software. With IPSec, data can be transmitted across a public network without fear of observation, modification, or spoofing. As part of its security functions, the PIX Firewall provides IPSec standards-based VPN capability. VPNs maintain the same security and management policies as a private network. With a VPN, customers, business partners, and remote users can access enterprise-computing resources securely.

Site-to-Site/Remote Access

Site-to-site and remote-access VPNs are the two main types of VPN. The PIX Firewall supports both. Site-to-site VPNs are an alternative WAN infrastructure that replace and augment existing private networks that use leased lines, Frame Relay, or ATM to connect remote and branch offices and central site(s). Access VPNs use analog, dial, ISDN, DSL, mobile IP, and cable technologies to securely connect mobile users, telecommuters, and branch offices. The PIX Firewall supports mixed VPN deployments, with both site-to-site and remote-access traffic. For site-to-site VPNs, the PIX Firewall can interoperate with any Cisco VPN-enabled network device, such as a Cisco VPN router. For remote-access VPNs, you must currently use one of the following Cisco remote-access VPN applications to gain access to a PIX Firewall-protected network:

- Cisco Secure VPN Client

- Cisco VPN 3000 Client

- Cisco VPN Client, version 3.0

- Windows 2000 L2TP withIPsec

VPN Acceleration

The VPN Accelerator Card (VAC) for the Cisco Secure PIX Firewall series provides high-performance tunneling and encryption services suitable for site-to-site and remote access applications. This hardware-based VPN accelerator is optimized to handle the repetitive, but voluminous, mathematical functions required for IPsec. Offloading encryption functions to the card not only improves IPsec encryption processing, but also maintains high-end firewall performance. As an integral component of the Cisco virtual private network (VPN) solution, the VPN Accelerator Card provides platform scalability and security while working seamlessly with services necessary for successful VPN deployments—encryption, tunneling, and firewall. VPN acceleration is also available on many Cisco routers.

Firewall Redundancy

Firewall redundancy is critical for those organizations whose Internet, intranet, or extranet connections are their corporate lifeline. Every minute a firewall is down means lost revenue, opportunity, or critical information. Cisco offers a fail-over bundle package, enabling firewall redundancy to be met simply and inexpensively. This package provides organizations with a second firewall, especially designed to run exclusively in fail-over mode, for a fraction of the cost. PIX supports a hot standby model (one firewall is active, one is in standby). If you use stateful failover, you can maintain operating state for the TCP connection during the failover from the primary unit to the standby unit.

There are two primary types of failover:

- Stateful failover—Existing sessions should not be dropped.

- Stateless failover—Sessions are dropped, but connections can be re-established.

When a stateful failover occurs, each unit changes state. The unit that activates assumes the IP and MAC addresses of the previously active unit and begins accepting traffic. The new standby unit assumes the failover IP and MAC addresses of the unit that was previously the active unit. Because network devices see no change in these addresses, no ARP entries change or time out anywhere on the network. This failover option maintains concurrent connections through automatic stateful synchronization. This insures that even in the event of a system failure, sessions are maintained, and the transition is completely transparent to network users.

For more detailed information on the Cisco PIX Firewall, refer to the book, *Cisco Secure PIX Firewalls*, by Dave Chapman and Andy Fox.

Virtual Private Networks

A *virtual private network (VPN)* is a network that extends remote access to users over a shared infrastructure. In the physical security analogy, VPNs are like secured tunnels between buildings or armored transport cars that permit secure, confidential transit between two locations.

VPNs maintain the same security, prioritizing, manageability, and reliability as a private network. They are the most cost-effective method of establishing a connection between remote users and an enterprise customer's network. VPNs based on IP meet business customers' requirements to extend intranets to remote offices, mobile users, and telecommuters. They also enable extranet links to business partners, suppliers, and key customers for greater customer satisfaction and reduced business costs.

VPNs are used to connect remote offices and remote users through the Internet. Enterprises can also use VPNs for connecting with customers, partners, and suppliers.

Typically, external access into a network is made either through the public Internet or through dialup lines, both of which are insecure channels. A VPN allows a company to have secure and private external connections into the internal network by leveraging the public Internet or dialup lines.

In order to create a private and secure (encrypted) connection, the clients must be configured to handle the VPN communication protocol. The industry-standard VPN protocol is IP Security (IPSec). Each client desiring a secure connection must first be VPN enabled. In conjunction, the network devices providing this service must also be VPN enabled. This provides a secure connection between the client and the network devices. All the data in the connection is now encrypted. This type of connection is often referred to as tunneling. VPNs use public- and private-key technology to establish the secure tunnel for each client connection.

The three types of VPNs follow:

- **Access VPNs**—Provide secure connections for remote access for individuals (for example, mobile users or telecommuters), a corporate intranet, or an extranet over a shared service provider network with the same policies as a private network.

- **Intranet VPNs**—Connect corporate headquarters, remote offices, and branch offices over a shared infrastructure using dedicated connections. Intranets are networks for businesses that are internal to the companies. In intranets, a business benefits from the same policies as private networks, including security, (QoS, manageability, and reliability. Intranets deliver the most current information and services available to networked employees. Intranets also increase employee productivity by allowing a reliable connection to consistent information. With an intranet VPN, you get the same security and connectivity for corporate headquarters, remote offices, and branch offices as you would with a private network.

- **Extranet VPNs**—Link customers, suppliers, partners, or communities of interest to a corporate intranet over a shared infrastructure using dedicated connections. Extranets are intranets that extend limited access to customers, suppliers, and partners while providing authorized access for telecommuters and remote offices.

VPNs and Data Encryption

VPNs allow a more mobile workforce and for more connectivity options. What also makes VPNs great is that the data is encrypted while transferred over the public Internet. Encryption refers to the conversion of data into a form not easily understood by unauthorized personnel, providing point-to-point data confidentiality. The points involved can be client-to-client, client-to-server, or router-to-router. The data on any given network segment can be bulk encrypted; in other words, every packet between the end points is encrypted. For example, a web server on an e-commerce site can be configured to allow customers to enter confidential information (credit card numbers and other personal data) using a Secure Sockets Layer (SSL) session.

Encryption is the process of applying a specific mathematical algorithm to data to alter its appearance, making it incomprehensible to those who are not authorized to see the information. Decryption is the process of converting that data back into its original form so the authorized receiver can understand it.

The three types of encryption algorithms follow:

- Symmetric-key encryption

- Public-key encryption

- Hash functions

Symmetric-key encryption uses a secret code as a key in the encryption process. This same secret code is used to decrypt the encrypted data. The longer the key length, the more difficult it is to guess the key. Examples of symmetric-key encryption follow:

- **Data Encryption Standard (DES) and 3DES**—These two algorithms are most commonly used in the industry. The encryption key length is 56 bits. Triple DES applies DES three times in succession, using either two or three different keys.

- **RC2, RC4, RC5, RC6**—These algorithms, from RSA Data Security, Inc., are alternatives that offer the advantage of a faster encryption process along with the choice of a range of key sizes.

- **International Data Encryption Algorithm (IDEA)**—IDEA is similar to DES, but uses a 128-bit encryption key, making breaking it more difficult than breaking DES.

Public-key encryption is a form of asymmetric encryption. It uses two mathematically related keys, one public and one private. One key is used to encrypt, while the other key decrypts.

Unfortunately, asymmetric encryption is relatively slow compared to symmetric encryption. As a result, the trend today is to use the two together. Generally, the asymmetric key performs the authentication function while the symmetric key is used to encrypt the data or communication session. One of the most common asymmetric algorithms is Rivest-Shamir-Adelman (RSA).

Hash algorithms are also known as *message digest algorithms*. The primary purpose of these algorithms is to perform a one-way encryption that produces a hashed result or message digest. In other words, the hashed result cannot be decrypted to produce the original data. Hash algorithms are commonly used to ensure a message's integrity. A message's hashed result is sent along with the original message. The recipient then executes the same hash function on the original message, producing a hashed result. This hashed result should match the hashed result that was sent with the original message. If it doesn't, the original message has been tampered with or altered. Examples of hash algorithms include Message Digest 2/ Message Digest 5 (MD2/MD5), a 128-bit digest, and a 160-bit digest.

Public Key Infrastructure allows a neutral, trusted third party—commonly known as the certification authority (CA)—to authorize and manage the distribution of public and private keys in the form of digital certificates. Private keys are either assigned to or generated by an end user when PKI software or hardware is assigned to them. Private keys are not shared, but are mathematically related to the users public key.

Public keys are bound to their owners by public key certificates, also called Digital IDs. These certificates serve the same purpose as a driver's license or passport—that of identification. Digital certificates can be used not only to identify people, but also to identify World Wide Web sites. This ability to identify World Wide Web sites is crucial to secure e-business.

Figure 4-4 shows how Digital IDs, or public key certificates, work.

Figure 4-4 *Public Key Certificate Operation*

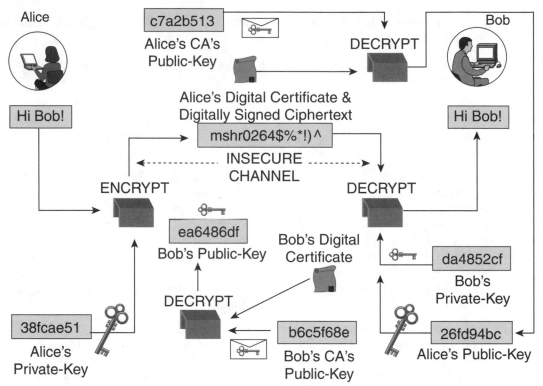

1 Alice sends e-mail to Bob.

2 Alice's plaintext message gets encrypted with Bob's public key derived from his digital certificate using his CA public key (Bob's public key was encrypted in his digital certificate with his CA's private key).

3 Alice signs the encrypted message with her private key.

4 Alice's encrypted and digitally signed e-mail gets transmitted to Bob over an insecure channel (that is, the Internet).

5 Bob decrypts the message with Alice's public key, which is derived from Alice's digital certificate using Alice's CA's public key (Alice's public key was encrypted in her digital certificate with her CA's private key).

6 Bob decrypts the message with his own private key.

Successful process proves authenticity of both parties, the sent message's integrity, and nonrepudiation of the message sent.

In addition to persons, public and private keys are also used for authentication between devices. For example, the Secure Sockets Layer (SSL) protocol uses public and private keys to establish a secure connection between the requesting device and the server. When you look at an Internet address, if the address starts with https, the s stands for a secure connection between your Internet device and the server to which you are connected.

Digital signatures increase an enterprise's confidence in electronic transactions. Using digital signature allows a seller to prove that a particular buyer requested the goods or services and demand payment.

Figure 4-5 shows an example of public-key encryption with digital signature.

Figure 4-5   *Public-Key Encryption with Digital Signature*

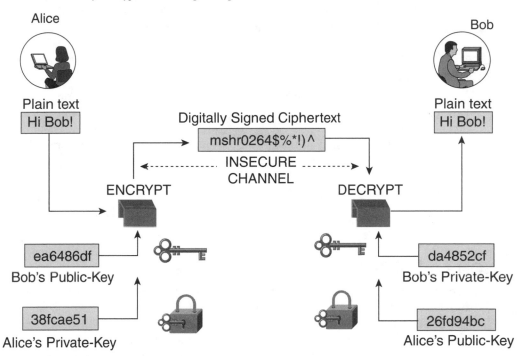

 1 Alice sends e-mail to Bob.

 2 Alice's plaintext message gets encrypted with Bob's public key and with her own private key.

 3 Alice's encrypted and digitally signed e-mail gets transmitted to Bob over an insecure channel (the Internet).

 4 Bob decrypts the message with Alice's public key and with his own private key.

Successful process proves authenticity of both parties and the sent message's integrity.

Cisco Devices that Support Encrypted VPN Access

The sections that follow describe some of the Cisco devices that support encrypted VPN functionality.

Cisco IOS Routers

Utilizing Cisco IOS Software, Cisco VPN Routers also provide a comprehensive feature set to meet the most diverse networking requirements, including support for routing, multiprotocol, and multicast across the VPN, as well as enhanced features like firewall and QoS. The Cisco VPN Router portfolio provides solutions for small office/home office (SOHO) access through central-site VPN aggregation, including platforms for fast-emerging cable and digital subscriber line (DSL) access technologies. VPN Routers also provide scalability through optional encryption acceleration, which comes in an add-on module.

Cisco VPN 3000 Series Concentrators

The Cisco VPN 3000 Series Concentrators are a family of purpose-built, remote access VPN platforms and client software that incorporates high availability, high performance, and scalability with the most advanced encryption and authentication techniques available today. The VPN 3000 is designed to terminate VPN connections for the small enterprise or the large organization through scalable add-on modules that provide increased throughput and connection capacity.

For more information on VPNs, refer to the Cisco Press title, *Cisco Secure Virtual Private Networks*, by Andrew Mason, which you can find described at ciscopress.com.

Intrusion Detection

In comparison to physical security, Intrusion Detection Systems are equivalent to video cameras and motion sensors; they detect unauthorized or suspicious activity and are combined with an automated response system, such as a watchguard, to stop the activity. Later in the chapter several hacks are discussed, and many of those can be stopped with an IDS. Some of those hacks have been perpetrated against high-profile targets, including newspapers, telephone companies, Internet startups, computer hardware manufacturers, and government agencies. Other cases have involved disgruntled employees inflicting major damage to their former employer's proprietary data and hardware. To counter these security threats, various commercial vendors have brought security products to the market such as firewalls, encryption and authentication, and access control mechanisms. Although these products serve effectively as preventive measures, they are not capable of monitoring, detecting, or responding to intrusive security incidents. This is where IDSs come into play.

Complex security threats require complex security countermeasures, so there is a definite need for a complementary security technology that accomplishes the following:

- Intelligently monitor the network for ongoing, real-time intrusion
- Be reconfigured easily and dynamically in response to intrusions
- Respond to intrusions in a variety of user-configurable ways

This technology is known as intrusion detection. *Intrusion detection* is the ability to analyze data in real time to detect, log, and stop misuse or attacks as they occur. In practice, intrusion detection is more complex than this simple definition, and various types of IDSs.

Network-based IDSs monitor activity on a specific network segment.

Network-based systems are usually dedicated platforms with two components: a sensor, which passively analyzes network traffic, and a management system, which displays alarm information from the sensor and allows security personnel to configure the sensors. Cisco offers an integrated Sensor Manager on the sensor, as well as an external application known as Cisco Secure Policy Manager for managing the sensor.

The sensors in a network-based IDS capture network traffic in the monitored segment and perform rules-based or expert system analysis of the traffic using configured parameters. The sensors analyze packet headers to determine the following:

- Source and destination addresses
- Type of data being transmitted

In addition, the sensors analyze the packet payload to discover information in the data being transmitted. If the sensor detects misuse, it can perform various security-related actions including the following:

- Logging the event
- Sending an alarm to the management console
- Resetting the data connection
- Instructing a router to deny any future traffic from that host or network

On a very basic level, you can compare signature-based detection to virus-checking programs. Vendors produce a list of signatures that the IDS uses to compare against activity on the network or host. When a match is found, the IDS takes some action such as logging the event or sending an alarm to a management console. Although many vendors allow users to configure existing signatures and create new ones, for the most part customers are dependent on vendors to provide the latest signatures to keep the IDS up to date with the latest attacks.

Placing a sensor behind a firewall shields the sensor from any policy violations that the firewall rejects. For example, if the firewall were configured to deny passage of ping sweeps, the sensor would not detect this activity or generate any alarms.

The solution is to take advantage of the sensor's two interfaces: place the sensor's monitoring interface (which runs in promiscuous mode without an Internet Protocol [IP] address) directly in front of the firewall, and use the second sensor interface to communicate with the director or router through the firewall.

The firewall implements policy filtering. The sensor captures packets between the Cisco router and the firewall, and can dynamically update the Cisco router's access control lists to deny unauthorized activity. Because the sensor's monitoring network interface card (NIC) has no IP address, it cannot be detected, nor can packets be sent to it.

Now that you know what an IDS is, you need to know where to place the sensors in the network. Many network locations could benefit from an IDS. One of the most popular places to put the Cisco Secure IDS Sensor is in the E-Commerce Architecture to allow traffic monitoring between the Internet and the internal web servers, application servers, and database servers. Many customers now implement intrusion detection at every layer of their e-commerce application for additional security. An IDS is most often deployed with a firewall. Because many companies use a firewall to help protect a network perimeter, there are several options for placing a sensor in relation to that firewall. Placing a sensor in front of a firewall allows the sensor to monitor all incoming and outgoing network traffic. However, when deployed in this manner, the sensor will not normally detect traffic that is internal to the network because this traffic is behind the firewall. An internal attacker taking advantage of vulnerabilities in network services would remain undetected by the external sensor.

Figure 4-6 depicts from what points a network is vulnerable and how vulnerable those points are.

Figure 4-6   *Network Vulnerability Locations*

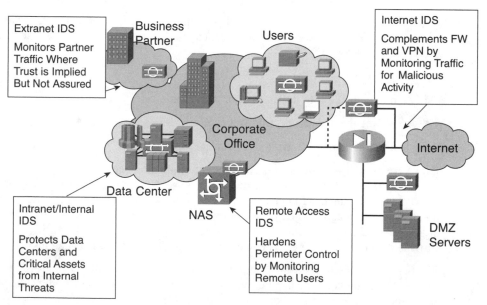

In extranet locations, the sensor monitors an extranet connection with a business partner. More and more companies are connecting to partners via extranets for fast, reliable, and secure network access. Companies must remember that when they connect to a partnering company they inherit the security policy, or lack thereof, of their partnering company. Some unfortunate incidents have occurred involving a hacker jumping from partner to partner using the main company as the proxy. This extraordinary risk can be mitigated by an IDS and a firewall, which disallow access at a higher level in the IP stack. Although most companies have defined policies on the use and security of this type of connection, no guarantee exists that the partner's network is adequately protected. To ensure the strong integrity of partner relationships, individual companies now take responsibility themselves to secure their partner connections to ensure their mission-critical business data isn't compromised.

In another ideal location, the sensor monitors the network side of a remote access server. Although this connection might be only for employee use, it could be vulnerable to external attack by a war dialer, or a company might find it necessary to monitor the activity of its remote users. Once again, depending on the security policy and what has been defined, this location might or might not be conducive to an IDS.

The FBI reported that 80 percent of all security breaches come from the internal network. Many companies put IDS sensors in place to monitor their internal network to utilize an IDS, and take advantage of Cisco's IDS platform custom signature feature. Imagine the benefit of being able to write a custom signature looking for mail exiting the network containing "Company Confidential" anywhere in the body, or monitoring access to financial servers.

Cisco Intrusion Detection Solutions: Network-Based

The Cisco Intrusion Detection System family—consisting of Cisco Intrusion Detection System 4200 network security appliances, an IDS Catalyst 6000 security module, and an IDS Host-based sensor—delivers a family of high-performance, security surveillance solutions for both enterprise and service-provider networks. Designed to address the increased requirements for security visibility, denial-of-service (DoS) protection, antihacking detection, and e-commerce business defenses, the Cisco IDS family leads the market in innovative security monitoring solutions. Together, the Cisco IDS family delivers a wide range of sensing solutions, enabling corporate Internets, intranets, extranets, and critical web servers to operate without security interruptions.

- The list that follows describes some Cisco IDS family features.
- Comprehensive network-based protection
- Easy installation and setup
- Real-time intrusion detection
- Real-time response to unauthorized activity
- Detailed intrusion alarms

- Scalability

- High-speed performance

- Remote configuration capability

- Flexible deployment

- Interoperability with other Cisco products for performing shuns

- Fault-tolerant communications

- Comprehensive attack database

- Custom user-defined signatures

- Notification actions

- Automatic signature updates

- Ability to monitor 802.1q (trunked) traffic

Cisco Intrusion Detection Solutions: Host-Based

Cisco IDS Host Sensor 2.0 delivers breakthrough software technology that provides real-time analysis and reaction to hacking attempts. Cisco IDS Host Sensor 2.0 is able to identify the attack and prevents access to critical server resources before any unauthorized transactions occur. Unlike traditional detection products, Host Sensor 2.0 proactively protects the host by evaluating requests to the operating system and the application-programming interface (API) before they are processed. Using a blend of "signature" and resource access control techniques, Host Sensor 2.0 is able to stop both known and unknown attacks. Straightforward and quickly understood, Host Sensor 2.0 is easy to deploy and offers significant timesavings in security management.

How Host Sensor Works

Host Sensor 2.0 installs adjacent to the operating system and can intercept and validate software calls made to the OS and kernel. Calls are matched to a constantly updated database of both defined and generic attack behaviors. If an attack is found, pre-emptive action is automatically taken to protect the system by referencing a policy customized to the environment.

Actions ranging from "Log Event" to "Prevent" are taken. Key to Host Sensor 2.0's value is the fact that all activity on the host is seen and is not impaired by encryption, switched data, or reliance on system log information. The attack database consists of the following types of attack recognition capability:

- **Individual attack**—Gives protection against single hacking exploits by matching known attack behaviors to activity in the system OS or applications (for example, MDAC, GetAdmin).

- **Generic attack**—Protects against a whole category of hacking exploits directed against the OS and applications, giving coverage for unknown as well as known attacks (for example, Buffer Overflow exploits).

- **Resource protection**—Prevents malicious access to system resources, including processes, services, Registry keys, password files, authentication mechanisms, and so on.

- **Shielding and HTTP protocol protection**—Offered as additional protection for specific applications, such as web servers (requires additional license).

The policy database ships with a fully configured default template incorporating powerful customization ability for the Administrator, allowing false positives to be virtually eliminated. The default policy ensures rapid deployment. Agents are deployed per server, and are controlled and updated from a central management console.

Agents are completely self-contained, protective units and are not reliant on the Console to function. This approach is used because it prevents any communication ports from being left open and provides Fail Safe operation. Agents pull updates from the Console, including code updates and new attack definitions. Triple DES encryption is used for all communications.

The Console provides full management reporting, including exportable log data. The Agent updates are downloaded from the Cisco CCO Web site to the Console and are distributed to the Agents using fully encrypted communication. Agents are available for the following platforms:

- Microsoft Windows NT Server

- Microsoft Windows 2000

- Solaris SPARC Ultra10, running Solaris 2.6, 2.7, and 2.8

The next section covers how to secure access to the network and system components within the architecture.

Access Control

In physical security analogy, access control servers are equivalent to the access card, keys, and the gatekeeper who oversees security. In the networking world, the acronym AAA is used often to abbreviate the most important components of access control—authentication, authorization, and accounting. Essentially, they are the processes that identify the user, give the user permission on what to access, and account for what the user did while he was logged in. The technical definition of Authentication is the process of verifying the identity of a user. For example, to authenticate a remote host or person, a local host requests a username and password (from the other host or person), and verifies the username and password by comparing them to values stored on an authentication server.

The three methods of authentication follow:

- Username and password
- One-time passwords
- Biometrics

The username and password method is the traditional authentication method. It combines the use of a unique identifier and its associated secret password. This method depends on how well the identifier's owner can keep the password a secret (the element of "what you know"). Other vulnerabilities include transmission of the password in cleartext, making it susceptible to network sniffers. Weak passwords can be easily guessed, particularly by password-cracking tools.

Some guidelines for generally accepted password rules include the following:

- Has a minimum of six characters
- Uses a mix of letters and numbers
- Expires when new account is issued or when password is reset
- Expires in 45 days
- Cannot be the same as any previously used password

The second authentication method, the one-time password (OTP) method, is considered stronger than the username and password method.

Common OTP implementations use a challenge-response prompt. Most solutions use a hardware or software token or card, which requires a personal identification number (PIN), similar to a password, before it can be activated to generate the OTP. The token or card adds the element of "what you have" to the PIN's "what you know" element, making one-time passwords a stronger authentication method. Because the generated OTP is good only for the session, it is useless if stolen and replayed.

The latest authentication method is called biometrics. This method is even stronger than the one-time passport method. Biometrics introduces the element of "what you are." This technology uses devices that scan or read physiological characteristic of a person.

Some examples of biometrics technology include identification based on the following:

- Voice recognition
- Fingerprint scan
- Retinal scan
- Palm scan
- Hand geometry
- Facial recognition

Authorization is another security measure that has a few requirements to consider to make it effective. Authorization is a security measure based on restricting a user's access in various ways through policies and procedures.

Authorization is the process of granting system access for a particular user or set of users within certain parameters. Authorization levels can be assigned to give different users and groups different levels of service. For example, standard dialup customers might not have the same access privileges as premium customers. Levels of security, access times, and services might differentiate Service. Authorization profiles should be defined based on established security policies.

The keys to effective authorization are well-defined approval procedures and processes that ensure the validity of a request for authorization. Authorization policies and procedures guide the access control systems' administration. Careful planning and analysis ensure that access to resources, services, and functions are granted only based on a need-to-know or need-to-use basis.

Review the following types of decisions that need to be made when defining an access request process:

- **Who is allowed to request or approve access?** Can end users request access for themselves? Usually, another person must approve the request, depending on the privilege level of the access being requested. For example, access requests for end users should be submitted and approved by the responsible supervisor or manager.

- **How can an access request be validated?** If customers request access to services, they should be able to register and apply for the access. Sufficient information should be collected during the registration process to allow the requestor's identity to be authenticated.

Cisco SAFE Architecture

This section discusses what components are necessary to build a safe and secure network infrastructure. It has also been pointed out many times just how important it is to combine the components together to protect from what are now common hacking techniques. By putting end-to-end security solutions in place the network administrator can give the executive team more certainty that they are protected. The modules discussed within the SAFE Architecture as well as the technologies that make up the architecture can accomplish all this. The next several sections discuss the types of attacks that are common to organizations, and how the SAFE architecture mitigates them.

To provide the foundational security for an enterprise and to complement the security policy put forth by the organization, an architecture for every major part of the network has been created. It is known as the Cisco SAFE Architecture and provides end-to-end security methodology needed by organizations to mitigate attempted attacks.

The Cisco SAFE (Secure Architecture for E-Business) architecture is a flexible, comprehensive security blueprint that enables organizations to safely engage in business today and to help prevent the attacks mentioned earlier. The SAFE architecture combines leading Cisco security solutions with a rich ecosystem of complementary programs, products, partners, and services. The architecture is a layered design built on Cisco's AVVID (Architecture for Voice Video and Integrated Data) Architecture to secure the converged and non-converged network. It uses the organizing principle that no one security component can classify a network as being secure. Instead, the SAFE secure infrastructure is built with layered complementary components. The goal of complementary components is to avoid the trap of building an architecture with a "hard solid outer shell and a soft chewy middle." To simplify the architecture, it is chunked into smaller modules that encapsulate all the Cisco security solutions available to individual end-to-end solutions. The sections that follow document the modules and the Cisco Security solutions offered by those modules. These modules are reference architectures in and of themselves for each solution. The first three sections of each of the following modules describe the traffic flows, key devices, and expected threats with basic mitigation diagrams.

NOTE   To find more information on Cisco SAFE, visit www.cisco.com/go/safe.

Cisco SAFE Architecture Main Module

The Enterprise module in Figure 4-7 is the main module that depicts all of the other modules.

Figure 4-7 *Cisco SAFE Architecture Main Module*

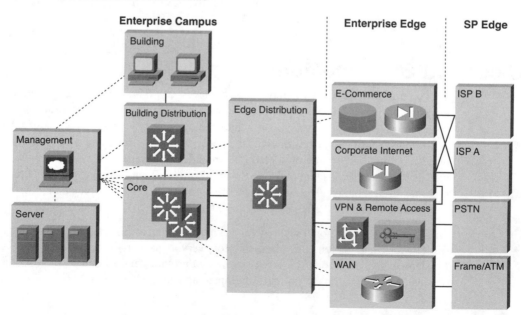

You can see how each module works with the other modules to create a security solution for the entire network. For example, you can see here how the Corporate Internet Architecture module interacts with the Distribution Layer Module and the core layer. The sections that follow show and describe the Enterprise, Management, Server, Corporate Internet, VPN and Remote Access, and E-Commerce modules.

Management Module

The Management Module's primary goal is to facilitate the secure management of all devices within the Enterprise SAFE Architecture. Logging and reporting information flows from the devices to the management hosts, while content, configurations, and new software flow to the devices from the management hosts. Threats to the management network are very real and were explained earlier in the chapter. A One-Time Password server, network-based IDS, Access Control, Management Host, Private VLANs and a PIX firewall work together to prevent the management network from being hacked. Figure 4-8 illustrates the key devices in the Management Module.

Figure 4- 8   *Management Module Key Devices*

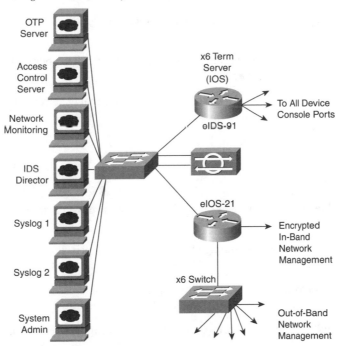

The sections that follow document the SAFE components to the management network, common attacks on the Management Module, and how the SAFE components mitigate those attacks.

Key Devices

The key devices are as follows:

- **SNMP management host**—Provides SNMP management for devices

- **NIDS host**—Provides alarm aggregation for all NIDS devices in the network

- **Syslog host(s)**—Aggregates log information for Firewall and NIDS hosts

- **Access control server**—Delivers one-time, two-factor authentication services to the network devices

- **One-time password (OTP) server**—Authorizes one-time password information relayed from the access control server

- **System admin host**—Provides configuration, software, and content changes on devices

- **NIDS appliance**—Provides Layer 4 to Layer 7 monitoring of key network segments in the module

- **Cisco IOS firewall**—Allows fine-grained control for traffic flows between the management hosts and the managed devices

- **Layer 2 switch (with private VLAN support)**—Ensures that data from managed devices can only cross directly to the IOS firewall

Threats Mitigated

The threats mitigated are as follows:

- **Unauthorized access**—Filtering at the IOS firewall stops most unauthorized traffic in both directions.

- **Man-in-the-middle attacks**—Management data crosses a private network making man-in-the-middle attacks difficult.

- **Network reconnaissance**—Because all management traffic crosses this network, it does not cross the production network where it could be intercepted.

- **Password attacks**—The access control server allows strong two-factor authentication at each device.

- **IP spoofing**—Spoofed traffic is stopped in both directions at the IOS firewall.

- **Packet sniffers**—A switched infrastructure limits the effectiveness of sniffing.

- **Trust exploitation**—Private VLANs prevent a compromised device from masquerading as a management host.

Server Module

The server module describes how to secure one of the most important assets of an IT organization, its corporate servers. The business-critical applications that organizations rely on to run their businesses reside on these servers. Figure 4-9 reflects the common components of the server architecture with the security that protects them.

Figure 4-9   *Server Architecture Components/Security*

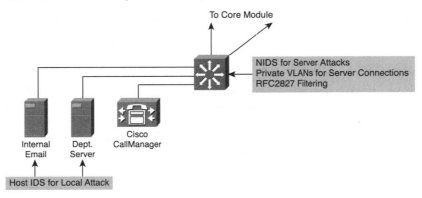

Key Devices

The key devices (as shown in Figure 4-8) are as follows:

- **Layer 3 switch**—Provides Layer 3 services to the servers and inspects data crossing the Server Module with a network-based IDS in the Catalyst 6500.

    All of the servers in Figure 4-8 should contain host-based intrusion detection for buffer overflow and other attack mitigation.

- **Call manager**—Performs call routing functions for IP telephony devices in the enterprise.

- **Corporate and department servers**—Delivers file, print, and DNS services to workstations in the building module.

- **E-Mail server**—Provide SMTP and POP3 services to internal users.

Threats Mitigated by the SAFE Server Module

The threats mitigated are as follows:

- **Unauthorized access**—Mitigated through the use of host-based intrusion detection and access control.

- **Application layer attacks**—Operating systems, devices, and applications are kept up to date with the latest security fixes and protected by host-based IDS.

- **IP spoofing**—RFC 2827 filtering prevents source address spoofing.

- **Packet sniffers**—A switched infrastructure limits the effectiveness of sniffing.

- **Trust exploitation**—Trust arrangements are very explicit; private VLANs prevent hosts on the same subnet from communicating unless necessary.

- **Port redirection**—Host-based IDS prevents port redirection agents from being installed.

Corporate Internet Module

Every organization now needs a connection to the Internet to conduct their business. A Mail, DNS, and HTTP server are often needed to conduct an organization's basic business. How should a company protect these servers and their internal assets? The SAFE Corporate Internet Module, depicted in Figure 4-10, presents the architecture that is recommended to protect the external and internal network and shows how the devices protect the network.

Figure 4-10 *SAFE Corporate Internet Module*

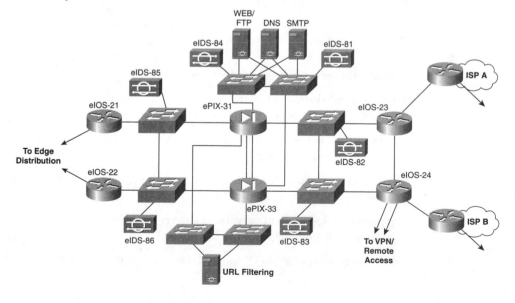

Key Devices

The key devices of the Corporate Internet Module are as follows:

- **SMTP server**—Acts as a relay between the Internet and the Internet mail servers, inspecting content.

- **DNS server**—Serves as an authoritative external DNS server for the enterprise, relaying internal requests to the Internet.

- **FTP/HTTP server**—Provides public information about the organization.

- **Firewall**—Provides network-level protection of resources and stateful traffic filtering.

- **NIDS appliance**—Provides Layer 4 to Layer 7 monitoring of key network segments in the module.

- **URL filtering server**—Filters unauthorized URL requests from the enterprise.

Threats Mitigated

The threats mitigated by the Corporate Internet Module are as follows:

- **Unauthorized access**—Mitigated through filtering at the ISP, edge router, and corporate firewall.

- **Application layer attacks**—Mitigated through IDS at the host and network levels.

- **Virus and trojan horse**—Mitigated through e-mail content filtering and host IDS.

- **Password attacks**—Limited services available to brute force, OS, and IDS can detect the threat.

- **Denial of service**—CAR (Committed Access Rate) or Packet Rate Limiting at the ISP edge and TCP setup controls at firewall. The CAR or Rate Limiting implementation will reclassify or drop all packets that exceed a predefined threshold. The TCP Setup controls implemented at the firewall will prevent SYN flooding and other attacks.

- **IP spoofing**—RFC 2827 and 1918 filtering at ISP edge and enterprise edge router.

- **Packet sniffers**—Switched infrastructure and host IDS limits exposure.

- **Network reconnaissance**—IDS detects recon and protocols are filtered to limit effectiveness.

- **Trust exploitation**—Restrictive trust model and private VLANs limit trust-based attacks.

- **Port redirection**—Restrictive filtering and host IDS limit attack.

Remote Access VPN Module

As organizations realize the benefits of mobilizing their workforce, many corporate users are becoming less confined to one location. They now need to do their work from multiple locations around the world. Thanks to first dialup and now dedicated user VPN access, users can access all corporate resources from a remote location of their choice. The devices in Figure 4-11 and listed in the "Key Devices" section that follows make up the SAFE Remote Access Module. The devices mitigate the common remote access threats explained in the "Threats Mitigated" section.

Figure 4-11   *The SAFE Remote Access VPN Module*

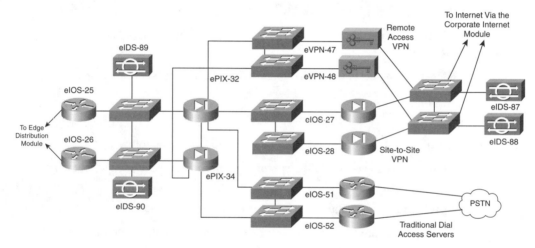

Key Devices

The VPN Module's key devices are as follows:

- **VPN concentrator**—Authenticate individual remote users using Extended Authentication (XAUTH) and terminate their IPSec tunnels.

- **VPN router**—Authenticate trusted remote sites and provide connectivity using GRE/IPSec tunnels.

- **Dial-in server**—Authenticates individual remote users using TACACS+ and terminate their analog connections.

- **Firewall**—Provides differentiated security for the three different types of remote access.

- **NIDS appliance**—Provides Layer 4 to Layer 7 monitoring of key network segments in the module.

Threats Mitigated

The threats mitigated by the VPN Module are as follows:

- **Network topology discovery**—Only Internet Key Exchange (IKE) and Encapsulating Security Payload (ESP) are allowed into this segment from the Internet.

- **Password attack**—OTP authentication reduces the likelihood of a successful password attack.

- **Unauthorized access**—Firewall services after packet decryption prevent traffic on unauthorized ports.

- **Man-in-the-middle**—Mitigated through encrypted remote traffic.

- **Packet sniffers**—A switched infrastructure limits the effectiveness of sniffing.

E-Commerce Module

The last couple of chapters were largely about the E-Commerce Reference Architecture. This is a very important architecture to have multiple layers of security in because so much of a business now relies on its public World Wide Web presence. Because of need for enhanced security, organizations are implementing the SAFE E-Commerce module to give them an end-to-end security solution with built-in interoperability and reliability. Figure 4-12 depicts the components in the SAFE E-Commerce module architecture.

Figure 4-12 *The SAFE E-Commerce Module*

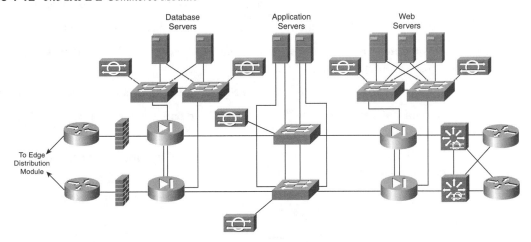

Key Devices

The key devices of the E-Commerce module are as follows:

- **Web server**—Acts as the primary user interface for the navigation of the e-commerce store.

- **Application server**—The platform for the various applications required by the Web server.

- **Database server**—The critical information that is the heart of the e-commerce business implementation.

- **Firewall**—Governs communication between the various levels of security and trust in the system.

- **NIDS appliance**—Provides monitoring of key network segments in the module.

- **Layer 3 switch with IDS module**—The scalable E-Commerce input device with integrated security monitoring.

Threats Mitigated

The threats mitigated by the E-Commerce Module are as follows:

- **Unauthorized access**—Stateful firewalling and ACLs limit exposure to specific protocols.

- **Application layer attacks**—Attacks are mitigated through the use of IDSs.

- **Denial of service**—ISP filtering and rate-limiting reduce DoS potential.

- **IP spoofing**—RFC 2827 and 1918 prevent locally originated spoofed packets and limit remote spoof attempts.

- **Packet sniffers**—A switched infrastructure and HIDS limits the effectiveness of sniffing.

- **Network Reconnaissance**—Ports are limited to only what is necessary, and ICMP is restricted.

- **Trust Exploitation**—Firewalls ensure communication flows only in the proper direction on the proper service.

- **Port Redirection**—HIDS and firewall filtering limit exposure to these attacks.

Summary

You've learned a lot about security throughout this chapter, from why security is needed, to some major attacks and potential solutions for those attacks. You learned about the architecture that has been put together to simplify the application of the security concepts discussed throughout this chapter. If you'd like to continue learning about security concepts, refer to the following links to help take your security knowledge to the next level.

- www.sans.org
- www.cisco.com/go/safe
- www.cert.org

Review Questions

1 What is the SAFE Architecture?

_____

_____

_____

2 What are the Cisco security components of SAFE?

_____

_____

_____

3 What are some common attacks on the Corporate Internet Layer?

_____

_____

_____

4 What are the benefits to implementing intrusion detection?

_____

_____

_____

5 What does AAA stand for?

_____

_____

_____

After reading this chapter, you should be able to perform the following tasks:

- Explain the Internet architecture process.
- Define a Content Delivery Network (CDN).
- Define the components of a CDN.
- Explain some of the CDN Architectures that apply CDN components.

CHAPTER 5

Content Delivery Networks

As the Internet continues to grow and evolve, more and more data must be delivered from place to place. Many feature-rich applications are also being deployed to enhance productivity and accomplish even more with technology. The Internet Business applications that were discussed earlier, such as e-commerce and e-learning, are some of the applications that companies can now deploy to set new standards for their business operations. The challenge is that as more data (applications and files) is added to the network, the greater the potential for a slower user experience.

Content Delivery Networks (CDNs) enhance the end user's experience by overcoming some inherent flaws in the Internet's anatomy and provide a solution to what was once a major challenge. CDNs are architectures in and of themselves that sit on top of, and complement, a Layer 2/Layer 3 architecture. This chapter covers how CDNs increase overall network performance by solving existing challenges, presents the components of a CDN solution, and provides recipe-based solutions that help in deploying a CDN architecture.

Traditional Web Growth

Internet web sites of the world have evolved over time to meet the needs of the end customer. As traffic grew, web sites also had to grow to serve their customer base. In the beginning, to minimize complexity and cost, most web sites began with a Centralized Architecture with one point of presence. A tremendous growth in Internet traffic followed. As the amount of traffic grew, so did the size of content. To accommodate the growth as the web sites' traffic increased, servers and bandwidth were added. Figure 5-1 reflects the central storage growth of a company's World Wide Web presence.

Figure 5-1   *Traditional World Wide Web Growth*

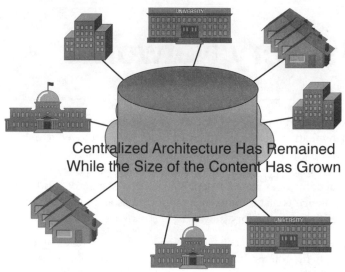

The next section addresses the challenges raised by web site growth.

Anatomy of a Network

Figure 5-2 depicts the Internet's architecture from the ISP network to the home or enterprise network.

Figure 5-2   *Anatomy of a Network*

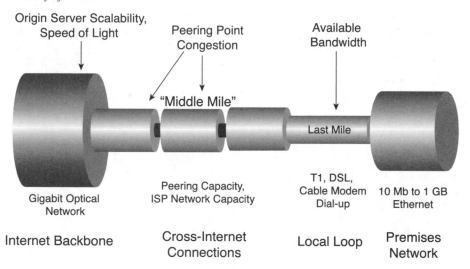

Some have referred to this architecture as the *dumbbell* or the *Q-Tip* because both ends are large while the center is very skinny. This is much like the Internet's architecture. The Internet service provider's (ISP's) network is OC-12/48, Gigabit Ethernet, or 10 Gigabit Ethernet on its backbone while the interconnections with the other ISPs are many times oversubscribed smaller DS-3,OC-3, or OC-12 connections. Because of the oversubscription and smaller bandwidth sizes, these connections, known as *peering points*, represent the middle skinny areas. As you look to the right in figure 5-2 you can see that the next area of interconnection is between the ISP and the enterprise or home. These connections, known as the last mile connections from the incumbent local exchange carrier (ILEC) or competitive local exchange carrier (CLEC), range from 56-kbps dialup to multiple T1 (1.544-Mbps) speed. After the last mile connection is terminated, there is once again more bandwidth on the Ethernet side of the premises enterprise or home network. These Ethernet speeds range from 10 to 100 to 1000 to soon 10,000-Mbps.

Bottleneck Points

What does the connection speed data mean? It means that low bandwidth, oversubscription, and bandwidth congestion points exist where there are skinny points in the picture, at the peering points and in the last mile. Those are the areas where the congestion on the Internet exists. Most of the time, slower infrastructure is cost prohibitive. So, seeing the world as it is and taking a look at what's in place shows an Internet infrastructure with known areas of congestion and a web site/content store architecture that has ballooned in size. Many times this store is in just one location and many users are trying to access it from slower, last mile connections. What if you could alleviate the known congestion points without spending the resources to upgrade the bandwidth in the last mile or the peering points? What if you could also improve the end users' performance significantly at the same time? You can do both with a CDN.

Cisco Content Delivery Networks are the Solution

The number one barrier for e-business applications is bandwidth bottlenecks. The solution is a CDN because it gets the content to the user faster. A CDN can solve both of the bandwidth congestion problems previously discussed by sitting on top of a Layer 2/Layer 3 infrastructure while locating content near the end user and routing user requests to the best source for content delivery to the end user. Large streaming media files, streaming audio, and images are some of the file types that are being pushed close to the end user so they don't have to go over the slower connections to retrieve the data. Instead, that data can be retrieved from a faster local connection. Figure 5-3 shows what happens to the network bottlenecks when a CDN is put in place. As you can see, those bottlenecks have disappeared so that everyone benefits from newly optimized Internet applications with higher performance at a lower cost.

Figure 5-3 *Demonstrating the Pushing of Content to the Edge*

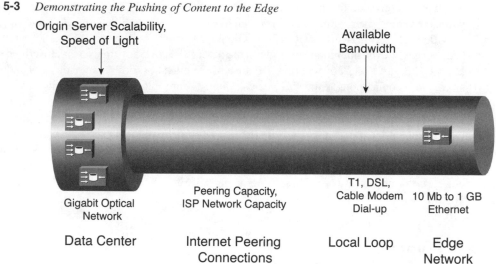

Origin Server Scalability,
Speed of Light

Available
Bandwidth

Gigabit Optical
Network

Peering Capacity,
ISP Network Capacity

T1, DSL,
Cable Modem
Dial-up

10 Mb to 1 GB
Ethernet

Data Center

Internet Peering
Connections

Local Loop

Edge
Network

Cisco's Content Networking Architecture: Components

Through internal developments and acquisitions of breakthrough content networking technologies, Cisco has built a comprehensive architecture for optimizing Web site performance and content delivery. This architecture comprises the five essential technology building blocks along with two complementary technologies that provide the foundation for all of Cisco's existing and future content networking solutions. Table 5-1 describes each one of the components and complementary technologies that make up CDNs. This table provides an overview of each of the components. A more detailed explanation appears later in the chapter.

Table 5-1 *CDN Components*

CDN Component		Purpose
Building Block	Content Distribution and Management	Control the distribution and management of content from the enterprise; the goal is to get the content as close to each user as possible.
	Content Routing	Route the users request for content to the closest available content store or content engine.
	Content Edge-Delivery	Deliver the content quickly from the content engine.
	Content Switching	Receive the user's request and make an intelligent decision as to how to distribute the request across one or multiple servers.
	Intelligent Network Services	Provide more intelligence to the inherent infrastructure components to add more overall value to the infrastructure.

Table 5-1   *CDN Components (Continued)*

CDN Component		Purpose
Complementary Technology	Origin Web Servers	Provide the content that the user is requesting.
	Core Networking	Provide the foundation for all CDNs—the reliable, fast, scalable and manageable Layer 2/Layer 3 infrastructure that CDNs utilize.

Cisco is the only vendor that offers all five CDN solution components. By adding these components to their existing IP networks, organizations can quickly benefit from a variety of new, high-value e-services.

The foundation of a CDN, as listed in Table 5-1, is a highly available Layer 2 and 3 infrastructure. This infrastructure is made reliable by many of the protocols that organizations already run such as HSRP, Spanning Tree, OSPF, EIGRP, and BGP.

After this infrastructure is in place, a content delivery network can be overlaid onto the foundation to begin to allow intelligent networking to take place at the upper layers of the OSI reference model.

Intelligent Network Services

The first component, Intelligent Network Services, is the most readily available and, in many cases, is the enabler for the other components. Intelligent Network Services are tightly integrated with the Layer 2 and Layer 3 infrastructure because the software features for Intelligent Network Services such as QoS, multicast, VPN, and security are available on Cisco routers and switches. For added functionality and performance, external appliances can be purchased to give a company even more intelligence and increased performance.

For example, multicast is a tremendous enabler for an enterprise network because it allows the distribution of one large video file to be made with one stream rather than multiple unicast streams. Companies can easily deploy an e-learning or corporate communications solution without requiring an upgrade of all connections to support the multiple streams because a popular e-learning presentation can be sent once (multicasted) to many people simultaneously.

Content Switching

Content Switching is an essential category to many CDN architectures because of its capability to increase the entire architecture's performance, scalability, and redundancy. You'll hear the term "load balancing" used almost as a synonym with content switching. There is only a small technical difference between load balancing and content switching. However, both accomplish the same outcome—namely distributing requests across multiple servers.

The distinction to be made for load balancing is that the distribution of requests is done with less intelligence than content switching. This intelligence is based on the 7-layer OSI model. Load balancing is handled at Layer 3 and Layer 4, which means that the forwarding decisions are made on the IP address/port number relationship. In most cases, for web switches load balancing occurs on HTTP TCP port 80 and SSL TCP port 443. Figure 5-4 depicts how the load balancer distributes requests across multiple servers, creating more scalability by reducing the load on one server.

Figure 5-4   *Load Balancer Reduces Load Through More Even Request Distribution*

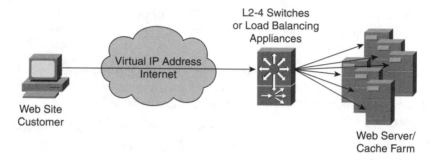

The growing volume and sophistication of e-business-related traffic required a solution that provided increased performance and features. Content switching answered the challenge because of its capability to gather knowledge of the user, device, network, and content. While doing all of this, it is still able to provide deep packet inspection and parsing by using an appliance- or module-based architecture with the increased hardware performance coming from application-specific integrated circuit (ASIC) or network processor-based packet handling.

Content switches are capable of answering these questions:

- Who is requesting the content?

- What content the user is requesting?

- Which server has the content?

- Which server that has the content is best available to serve the content back to the user?

With policies that are implemented at Layer 5 through 7 of the OSI model, the content switch is capable of specifying the policy-based web traffic direction based on full visibility of URLs, host tags, and cookies. This gives a company the flexibility to make forwarding decisions with even more intelligence. Figure 5-5 shows how the Layer 7 content switch is able to distribute the request based on more information, adding more intelligence into the network.

Figure 5-5   *Content Switching Basics*

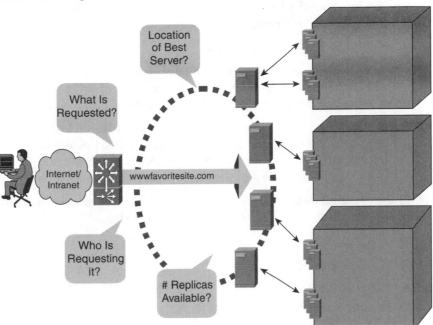

Cisco Content Services Switches

The Cisco CSS 11000 series content services switches are Layer 5/7 aware and provide a robust front-end for web server farms and cache clusters. With unique features for e-commerce, web hosting, and content delivery, the Cisco CSS 11000 series is an important piece in Cisco's end-to-end content networking solution. Cisco's CSS 11000 series switches, powered by Cisco Web Network Services (Web NS) software, offer unique services, including the following:

- Directing web traffic based on full visibility of URLs, host tags, and cookies

- Enabling premium services for e-commerce and web hosting providers

- Strengthening DoS protection, cache/firewall load-balancing, and "flash-crowd" management

Cisco Content Switch Module

The Cisco Content Switching Module (CSM) is a Catalyst 6500 line card that balances client traffic to farms of servers, firewalls, SSL devices, or VPN termination devices. The CSM provides a high-performance, cost-effective load-balancing solution for enterprise and ISP networks. The CSM meets the demands of high-speed Content Delivery Networks, tracking network sessions and server load conditions in real time and directing each session to the most appropriate server. Fault-tolerant CSM configurations maintain full state information and provide true hitless failover required for mission-critical functions.

The CSM provides the following key benefits:

- **Market-leading performance**—Establishes up to 200,000 Layer 4 connections per second (performance might vary based on software versions being run), and provides high-speed content switching while maintaining one million concurrent connections.

- **Outstanding price/performance value for enterprises and ISPs**—Features a low connection cost and occupies a small footprint. The CSM slides into a slot in a new or existing Catalyst 6500 and enables all ports in the Catalyst 6500 for Layer 4 through Layer 7 content switching. Multiple CSMs can be installed in the same Catalyst 6500.

- **Ease of configuration**—Uses the same Cisco IOS Software command-line interface (CLI) that is used to configure the Catalyst 6500 Switch.

Features and Benefits of the CSM

Some of the features and benefits of the Cisco Content Switching Module are as follows:

- **Firewall Load Balancing**—The CSM allows you to scale firewall protection by distributing traffic across multiple firewalls on a per-connection basis while ensuring that all packets belonging to a particular connection go through the same firewall. Both stealth and regular firewalls are supported.

- **URL and Cookie-based Load Balancing**—The CSM allows full regular expression pattern matching for policies based on URLs, cookies, and HTTP header fields. The CSM supports any URL or cookie format allowing it to load balance existing World Wide Web content without requiring URL/cookie format changes.

- **High Performance**—The CSM performs up to 200,000 new Layer 4 TCP connection setups per second (Performance might vary based on software versions being run.). These connections can be spread across 4096 virtual services (16,384 real servers) and all of the ports in a Catalyst 6500 or they can be focused on a single port. This provides a benefit over competitors who use distributed architectures that require all of the ports to be used in order to gain maximum performance.

- **Network configurations**—The CSM supports many different network topologies. A CSM can operate in a mixed bridged and routed configuration allowing traffic to flow from the client side to the server side on the same or on different IP subnets.

- **IP Protocol Support**—The CSM accommodates a wide range of common IP protocols including TCP and User Datagram Protocol (UDP). Additionally, the CSM supports higher-level protocols including Hypertext Transfer Protocol (HTTP), File Transfer Protocol (FTP), Telnet, Dynamic Name Server (DNS), and Simple Mail Transfer Protocol (SMTP).

- **User Session Stickiness**—Whenever encryption or e-commerce is involved, the end user must be consistently directed to the same server (that is, the server where the user's shopping cart is located or the encryption tunnel terminates). The CSM's user session stickiness provides the ability to consistently bring users back to the same server based on Secure Socket Layer (SSL) session ID, IP address, cookie, or HTTP redirection.

- **Load-Balancing Algorithms**—The CSM supports the following load-balancing algorithms:

  — Round robin

  — Weighted round robin

  — Least connections

  — Weighted least connections

  — Source and/or destination IP hash (subnet mask also configurable)

  — URL hashing

- **Quality of Service (QoS)**—Providing differentiated levels of service to end users is important when generating revenue from content. The CSM leverages the Catalyst 6500's robust QoS, enabling traffic differentiation as follows:

  — Correctly prioritizes packets based on Layer 7 rules

  — Directs users who are paying more for services to faster or less loaded servers

- **High availability**—The CSM continually monitors server and application availability using health monitoring probes, inband health monitoring, return code checking, and Dynamic Feedback Protocol (DFP). SNMP server health traps can also be configured. When a real server or gateway failure occurs, the CSM redirects traffic to a different location. Servers can be added and removed without disrupting service and systems can easily be scaled up or down.

- **Connection Redundancy**—Optionally, two CSMs can be configured in a fault-tolerant configuration to share state information about user sessions and provide connection redundancy. In the event the active CSM fails, open connections are handled by the standby CSM without interruption. Users will experience hitless failover which is an important requirement for e-commerce sites and sites where encryption is used.

Content Edge Delivery

Content Edge Delivery consists of edge content engines that seamlessly deliver web, streaming media, or static content faster than traditional servers to clients. This cached content is delivered by Cisco Content Engines with specialized software optimized for content delivery. Content Edge Delivery accomplished from the edge localizes traffic patterns. Content requests are then filled in an optimal manner, improving the end user experience and allowing rich media content over the Internet or corporate network. This is done by having that traffic retrieved from the local corporate network and not over the corporate WAN. This is known as transparent caching. Delivering a client to the most optimal content engine requires the CDN's intelligence to optimize traffic flows. Content Edge Delivery is tightly integrated with the other CDN traffic components discussed throughout this chapter. Today, Cisco Content Engines handle static and streaming media content. In the future, dynamic database content and applications will also be cached.

When a content engine receives a request, it answers the following questions before delivering the content to the end user:

- What's the *best resource* for this request?
- Is my current copy of this content *fresh*?
- If not, go to the origin server and *refresh* it.
- Is there QoS *information* that I should use or alter for these packets?
- Do I have sufficient processing cycles to handle more requests? If not, tell everyone.

Cisco's Content Engine products include the following:

- 507
- 507-AV
- 560
- 560-AV
- 590
- 7320

NOTE   The main difference between each of these Content Engines are disk storage space, throughput, and interface support.

Content Routing or Global Server Load Balancing

Remember Figure 5-1 earlier in the chapter that shows how the size of the server store has grown? The solution, Content Delivery Networking, allows that content to be distributed close to the user so his experience of the content is outstanding rather than good. The category of Content Routing or Global Server Load Balancing, as it's also known, takes care of the intelligent routing of a user request to the best available content engine (this device stores the content). The request is taken in by the content router and the end user is redirected to the best site based on a set of metrics such as delay, topology, server load, and a set of policies such as location of content, enabling the accelerated delivery of web content and streaming media.

As the number of users accessing content on the Internet grows, providing a high level of availability and rapid response from a single location becomes increasingly difficult. The solution to this problem is content routing between multiple data centers or Points of Presence (POPs). Content routing ensures the fastest delivery of content regardless of location, providing the highest availability and site response because the content router is able to sense which content engine, content switch, or point of presence (POP) is the best available to deliver the user's request. This is where a great part of Cisco's CDN intelligence comes from. When a content router takes a look at a request from a user it is essentially asking and answering the following questions:

- What content is requested?

- Where is the user?

- What's the best site *now* based on site and network health-checks?

- Are there other *rules* to factor into this decision?

Cisco's content routing products include the following:

- Content Services Switch 11000

- Content Router 4450

- Content Router 4400

- Cisco 7200 Distributed Director

Content Distribution and Management

How does the content get to all the content engines or content POPs? The answer to that question is through the Content Distribution and Management category. The Content Distribution Manager (CDM) proactively distributes cacheable content from origin servers to content servers at the edges of the network, and keeps the content fresh. This device is a company's central store of content. The CDM enables you to automatically import, maintain copies, and configure content at the edge of the network. From the CDM, an enterprise can globally and centrally provision content to remote locations by using either unicast or multicast, the Intelligent Network Service previously discussed.

Some critical functions include the following:

- Implementing content-specific policies across a global network infrastructure

- Creating virtual CDNs to support multiple discrete clients on a shared services infrastructure

- Transaction logging for automated billing based on actual content service usage

The CDM is continually able to answer the following questions:

- What content can be pre-populated at network edge?

- How should it be distributed (Self-Organizing Distributed Architecture [SODA] or multicast)?

- Which locations should be pre-populated with which content?

- When should content be refreshed?

- How should the service be provisioned and billed?

Cisco's CDM products include the following:

- CDM 4670

- CDM 4650

- CDM 4630

NOTE   The main difference between these models is content storage space. The content must first be loaded into the CDM and then distributed to the content engines, so a CDM with sufficient data storage space is critical.

Figure 5-6 illustrates what happens in Content Delivery architecture from Step 1 to Step 7, and which CDN categories (listed in Table 5-1) take care of each function.

Figure 5-6   *Cisco Content Networking in Action*

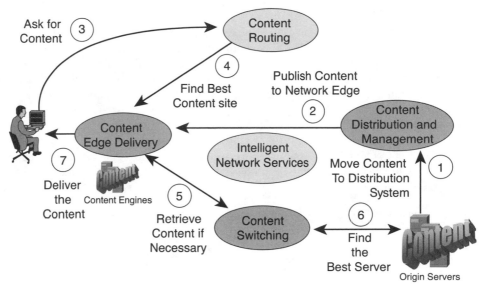

The following detailed list is a description of how the main components can be used.

1   The origin content is pulled to the CDM.

2   The CDM pushes the content to content engines at the edge of the network.

3   The end user makes a request for Content.

4   The request is intercepted by the Content Router, which finds the best site to service that content.

5   The content engine retrieves the content for the end user, if necessary.

6   The Content Switch receives the request and finds the best server to serve that content to the user.

7   The end user receives the content.

Applications of Content Delivery Networking

Transparent Caching

To fully realize the value of caches, enterprises and service providers can implement transparent caching. In transparent caching, the cache intercepts the connection to an origin World Wide Web server, handling all HTTP traffic without requiring explicit browser configuration, easing IT pressures at enterprises and service providers by eliminating the need to preconfigure user browsers. It also removes the problem of users covertly changing their browser settings to bypass the cache because traffic is sent through the cache transparently.

Cisco improved transparent caching by developing Web Cach Communication Protocol (WCCP) and high-performance caches to take full advantage of this Cisco IOS Software-based protocol. WCCP is the open, defacto standard protocol from Cisco that enables a router to redirect content requests to a cache, fully leveraging cache performance and performing basic load balancing across multiple caches in a cluster. Cisco Content Engines are network devices optimized to accelerate content delivery by locally storing frequently accessed content (such as GIFs, JPGs, and MPEGs) and quickly responding to user requests instead of going to the origin server. The combination of Cisco WCCP-Enabled Routers and Content Engines provides a powerful Network Caching Services Solution for accelerating content delivery and reducing WAN bandwidth costs for enterprises and service providers. Figure 5-7 and the associated list that follows illustrate the solution.

Figure 5-7   *Mechanics of Transparent Caching*

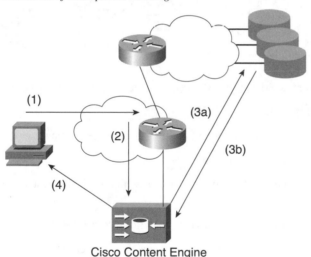

Cisco Content Engine

1   A user requests a World Wide Web page from a browser.

2   The Cisco WCCP-Enabled Router analyzes the request and, based on TCP port number, determines if it should transparently redirect the request to a Cisco Content Engine. Access lists can be applied to control which requests are redirected.

3   If a Cisco Content Engine does not have the requested content, it does one of the following things:

a. It sets up a separate TCP connection to the end server to retrieve the content.

b. The content returns to, and is stored on, the Cisco Content Engine.

4   The Cisco Content Engine sends the content to the end user. From its local storage, the Cisco Content Engine transparently fulfills subsequent requests for the same content.

E-CDN

Cisco System's Enterprise Content Delivery Network (E-CDN) solution enables high-quality, high-bandwidth streaming video, rich audio, large graphics, presentations, and documents to be delivered over corporate wide-area and local-area networks in an efficient manner. It utilizes the Self Organizing Distributed Architecture (SODA) protocol, which takes advantage of existing bandwidth to efficiently route high-bandwidth content over enterprise networks or even over the Internet. This process eliminates network bottlenecks that often accompany the distribution and retrieval of large multimedia and streaming files.

Cisco E-CDN components include a Cisco CDM for centralized media distribution, a Content Router for redirecting client requests to the closest media source, and Cisco content engines (CEs) which poll the Cisco CDM for new content and ultimately fulfill the client browser requests.

Implementing rich media distribution and retrieval in an enterprise environment can enable opportunities across the organization. These opportunities include delivery of rich media (audio/video, large files of any type) across last mile constraints for remote offices. Businesses can use this technology to quickly and cost-effectively distribute e-learning programs, corporate and field communications, software downloads, and so on from one centralized location (corporate HQ) to any number of remote offices or storefronts. This all leads to improved productivity, competitiveness, and a decreased time to market. The E-CDN architecture enhances an enterprise network's scalability, reliability, and built-in redundancy by supporting a rich knowledge exchange environment where employees, partners, and customers can contribute and learn from each other.

Content Filtering Solution

Employees using the Internet for non-business reasons results in lost productivity and wasted network bandwidth and can lead to "hostile work environment" lawsuits. Consequently, many enterprises must monitor, manage, and restrict employee access to non-business and objectionable content on the Internet.

The Children's Internet Protection Act (CIPA) requires that any school or library receiving federal E-Rate funds must have a filtering solution in place. By filtering irrelevant and unwanted Internet content, the Cisco Content Engine can be an effective tool for implementing and enforcing Internet usage policies as well as caching web content to improve delivery and WAN utilization. By deploying a Cisco Content Engine to cache content and using the SmartFilter option to filter non-productive URLs, enterprises can realize a quick return on investment as a result of increased productivity while recapturing network bandwidth and reducing legal liability. The Cisco Content Engine can filter URLs either by a limited internal deny and permit list, which the customer builds and configures, or with the SmartFilter subscription-based URL filtering software.

SmartFilter's Control List is currently composed of two million international URLs in 30 categories. Using automated methods to find and classify these URLs, the list is built and maintained by multi-lingual, multi-cultural Control List Technicians (CLTs), who physically review and categorize World Wide Web pages.

As Figure 5-8 demonstrates, an organization can filter at a local branch office or at headquarters.

Figure 5-8   *Content Filtering*

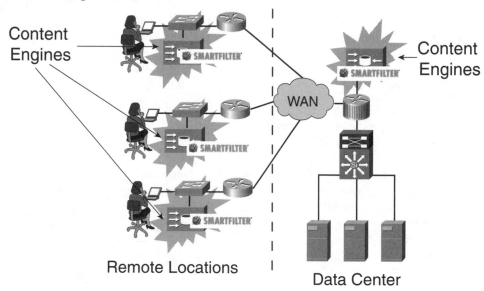

Summary

This chapter shares that Content Delivery Networks are networks in and of themselves. The ingredients of a CDN (the five components that were listed earlier) can be put together in a multitude of ways to form some great recipes, like the three discussed: Transparent Caching, E-CDN, and Content Filtering. As time goes on, new recipes will be created that use different varieties of these ingredients; there might even be another ingredient that comes about. For the near future though, these are the ingredients used to build great content delivery solutions.

Review Questions

1 What is the goal of Content Delivery Networking?

A. Accelerate content delivery

B. Reduce the last mile bottlenecks

C. Improve the user's experience of the content he is retrieving

D. All of the Above

2 What are the five components of a Content Delivery Network?

_____

_____

_____

3 What is content switching/load balancing able to provide a company?

_____

_____

_____

4 How does content routing help a company scale?

_____

_____

_____

After reading this chapter, you should be able to perform the following tasks:

- Define QoS
- Identify characteristics of different traffic types
- Plan for QoS
- Understand how to implement a large-scale QoS policy
- Understand the tools to implement QoS
- Define the different categories of QoS

CHAPTER 6

Quality of Service

Have you ever wondered how all of your Internet traffic gets to where it needs to be in seconds? Have you wondered how voice is delivered over the Internet? One of the answers to those questions is quality of service (QoS). QoS is a set of technologies and configurations that allow a network to provide differentiated services to different network traffic. With QoS, you can increase bandwidth for critical traffic, limit bandwidth for noncritical traffic, and provide consistent network response, among other things. QoS allows an organization to use expensive network connections more efficiently and to prioritize mission-critical applications above non mission-critical applications. QoS's primary goals include managing bandwidth, controlling jitter and latency (required by some real-time and interactive traffic, such as VoIP and video), and improving loss characteristics. Throughout this chapter, you'll learn about QoS, why it's important, how to plan its deployment, some of the ways to implement it, and about the many QoS features that are built into Cisco routers and Switches.

What is QoS?

Have you ever been at a grocery store and been serviced quickly because you had less than 12 items? Imagine having just five items yet standing in line for 30 minutes. Grocery stores have the 12-item-or-less isle because they don't want you to experience a long wait when you are purchasing just a few items. In the networking world, if QoS wasn't available you couldn't guarantee outstanding service to particular traffic types. All traffic would be handled in the same manner. On a router, this queuing method is referred to as First In, First Out (FIFO). Different traffic types must be treated differently to accommodate their varying requirements. Later in this chapter, you'll learn about the different traffic types and how each needs to be accommodated.

You should apply QoS wherever there is congestion on the network. Apply a QoS tool or technique at each congestion point. Later in this chapter, you'll learn what QoS type to apply. Some of the more technical reasons why QoS is needed follow:

- QoS is a critical requirement for WANs with lower link speeds. For that reason, it's important to make sure the traffic is sent in proper order over the narrow WAN pipe. Because of this available bandwidth, low delay and low delay variation requirements are at a premium in a WAN.

- Any time multiple high-speed links terminate in a device and that device uplinks with an oversubscribed or smaller speed link, there is a potential for congestion and a need for QoS. A common scenario on the edge is when multiple 10/100-megabit links terminate at a router that has a single T1 link to the WAN or the Internet. Another common scenario occurs when ten or more 10/100 Mbps high-speed interfaces terminate at a switch with an oversubscribed gigabit uplink. Both of these scenarios can create congestion and often require that packets be reordered at the egress interface.

- Mission-critical applications such as Peoplesoft, Oracle, Citrix, SAP, video, and the growing popularity of Voice over IP in the LAN and WAN, are tremendous drivers for QoS. These applications enable a business to function.

A very large part of what allows Internet system architectures to mature and evolve is the successful implementation of QoS. QoS is an important component to Cisco's widely accepted AVVID Architecture. Because voice, video, and data are now simultaneously riding over the same infrastructure and each traffic type has different requirements, the convergence of voice, video, and data becomes more reliant on QoS.

You can find QoS all around you. It exists in all facets of our lives. The following examples further explain the concept of quality of service.

When you want to send a package across the country very quickly, you often choose a type of service that meets both your needs and the receiver's needs. Maybe you send your package 2nd day air or by top priority, next-day air. In both instances, from the source the package is marked with a level of service and handled accordingly throughout its route to its destination.

The second example has to do with traffic. Is there a lane in driving that gets special service? You most likely answered yes and you thought of the carpool lane. Those that drive with others on a busy highway get a dedicated lane that is usually much less congested. Once again—better service.

Figure 6-1 demonstrates how each lane represents a different traffic type. There's a separate lane for e-mail, video conferencing, mission-critical applications, and file transfers. This traffic segmentation is similar in QoS to each traffic type getting its own queue; however, it is dissimilar to circuit thinking where each type of traffic gets dedicated bandwidth which wastes it for everyone else. Cisco IOS QoS allows a reservation of bandwidth, permitting a reallocation to other classified traffic types, if necessary.

Figure 6-1   *Network Traffic Metaphor*

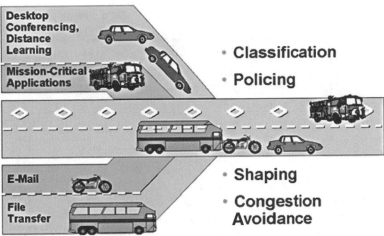

Because there is segmentation, preferential treatment can be applied to traffic that requires it. Mission-critical applications usually have the right-of-way. QoS extends to ensure available bandwidth and minimum delays required by time-sensitive multimedia and voice applications. In addition, it gives network managers control over network applications, improves the cost-efficiency of WAN connections, and enables advanced differentiated services.

The next section explores the different traffic types and their inherent behaviors to better prepare you for planning, implementing, and operating a converged network.

Network Demands Example

On networks today, applications, such as Enterprise Resource Planning (ERP), Voice over IP (VoIP), e-mail, and word processing software operate concurrently. Different users make requests of the network at the same time which can strain the system. QoS policies address these demands by allowing administrators to prioritize and classify each application ensuring that each request gets the attention it requires. Table 6-1 details many of those traffic requirements for the major traffic types.

Table 6-1   *Not All Traffic Is Created Equal*

	Voice	Video	Data (Best-Effort)	Mission-Critical Data
Bandwidth	Low to Moderate	Moderate to High	Moderate to High	Low to Moderate
Random-Drop Sensitivity	Moderate to High	Moderate to High	High (UDP) Low (TCP)	Moderate to High
Delay Sensitivity	High	High	Low	Moderate to High
Jitter Sensitivity	High	High	Low	Low to Moderate

All traffic types are different and use different amounts of bandwidth. For example video takes up more bandwidth than voice. Some applications are more susceptible to delay and latency. TCP-based applications (among others) are more tolerant of random drops than others. Table 6-1 classifies the main traffic types and lists their characteristics. The following two definitions will help you understand the valuable information in this table:

- Delay is the time between the sending and receiving of a packet.

- Jitter is a variation in the delay of received packets.

Packets are sent in a continuous stream with the packets being spaced evenly apart. Because of network congestion, improper queuing, or configuration errors, this steady stream can become "lumpy" or the delay between each packet can vary instead of remaining constant. If the jitter is so great that it causes packets to be received out of a buffering mechanism's range, the out-of-range packets are discarded and dropouts are heard in the audio.

Because of the traffic types' differing characteristics, many different tools exist to reduce delay and jitter and maximize bandwidth utilization. The QoS tool, Weighted Random Early Detection (WRED), takes advantage of certain applications being drop-tolerant. Many of these tools, identified later in the chapter, can be combined to create the QoS policy of choice. Planning and testing are critical to finding the policy that best fits your network. In some cases, modeling successful implementations is all that is needed. This is a feature of the QoS Policy Manager product that gives the administrator pre-defined templates to work from for common scenarios.

Planning for QoS

Implementing QoS is a process that involves reviewing the client's various needs and requirements and designing a solution. Put another way, think about what the client's intended outcome is, its purpose for the outcome, and come up with the steps that must be completed to get the organization to where it wants to be.

The six primary technical planning steps in this process follow:

Step 1   Perform an initial policy needs assessment.

Step 2   Perform a network characterization.

Step 3   Perform an application characterization.

Step 4   Define the service level.

Step 5   Test the policy.

Step 6   Validate the policy.

After you successfully complete the testing and policy validation, it's time to implement that policy. The following section condenses these steps into bite-sized chunks.

Perform an Initial Policy Needs Assessment

The policy needs assessment is the first step in the QoS implementation process's planning phase. It determines where policy should be applied within the system. The policy needs assessment procedure is a two-part method involving a detailed business-critical applications appraisal and a thorough review of existing network architecture. Based on the appraisal of critical applications, you should be able to determine which applications need policy treatment.

Ask the following important questions to gather the information necessary to make your initial QoS decisions:

- What are the business's initiatives?

- What are the business goals?

- What is the time frame for implementation?

- What applications are most important to the business?

The answers to these questions create the foundation from which to launch into what is going on in the network.

Perform a Network Characterization

After you are aware of the client's business policy needs, you can begin to characterize and analyze the network.

Diagram network topology, configurations, and software versions on each device. This gives you an estimate of the number of devices you might need to upgrade to take advantage of some of the latest QoS features; specifically, all network devices (routers, switches, content switches, and the content engines). Next, collect the traffic information such as utilization and traffic flows. You are ready to analyze the information you have gathered for the current traffic and volume flow. Do CPU utilization assessment on each network device during busy periods. This will help you make decisions to distribute QoS features among devices to share load.

Perform an Application Characterization

Application characterization is one of the most important steps yet is done the least. Do not guess based on the information from the business what applications are running and how much bandwidth they are consuming. Guessing requires making lots of assumptions without any valid statistics. These assumptions lead to trouble.

Many other companies are taking control instead of making decisions based on guesswork. Their network teams are now beginning to use the many resources available to them. Tools, such as Network Analysis Modules and RMON Probes, deliver the under-the-hood information required to make the necessary distinctions to begin to implement a sound QoS strategy.

Answer the following questions to get the information needed to build the Application Characterization.

- What are the mission critical applications?

- What background traffic exists?

- How are the applications deployed, and on which servers?

Network analysis tools enable you to answer these questions quickly. For example, the Cisco Catalyst 6500 NAM analysis tool gives network managers visibility into all layers of network traffic by adding remote monitoring functions based on remote monitoring 2 (RMON2) and other advanced Management Information Bases (MIBs). Embedded in the NAM is a World Wide Web-based traffic analyzer application that provides extensive capabilities to analyze traffic in real time for several attributes including hosts, conversations, and applications. Network managers can use this information for fault isolation and troubleshooting, managing network performance, and capacity planning.

Define the Service Level

When designing the client's QoS solution, you must prioritize and classify the information gathered during the Policy Needs Assessment, Network Characterization, and Application Characterization. Using baselining and profile information about each application under study, you can help the client decide how the prioritized application should be ranked in terms of service level (gold, silver, and bronze).

The following list shows one client's service-level decisions for their applications:

- Gold is reserved strictly for voice applications.

- Silver contains the mission-critical traffic.

- Bronze utilizes the best effort for all other traffic.

After the traffic is classified, you must assign service levels to each type of traffic. These business service levels will flow into the QoS configuration on the routers and switches in the network. The service levels consist of the following:

- Bandwidth priority
- Ordering of priority
- What traffic can be dropped
- What traffic cannot be dropped
- Other parameters important to the technical policy that will meet the business goals

Policy Testing and Validation

After designing the QoS solution, policy testing and deployment take place. Testing the policy gives the administrator the ability to change the configuration's approach without bringing much attention to potential mistakes. Follow these procedures to complete a successful test:

Step 1 Create a test environment to run transactions for the applications that need to be tested. Apply the different policies to the routers and the switches in the test environment using the Cisco IOS, QoS Device Manager (QDM), or QoS Policy Manager (QPM), and measure the resulting performance under congestion for the different transactions. This is an important process; however, it can be long because you must interact with the applications to determine if they are performing to your service levels. If they aren't, you need to make changes to the QoS policies.

Step 2 From the results of the tests, determine the "best" policy for each application that gives optimized performance in the face of congested conditions. Document the policy configuration needed at each router and switch.

Step 3 Verify that traffic classified as low priority is still surviving. (This may need to be done in production after implementation.)

After testing and validating the various policies, you should arrive at an optimal QoS configuration for the test environment and for limited deployment. After all of the preceding phases are complete, limited deployment can take place with further testing to follow. An administrator should be ready for applications and traffic interactions that they are not familiar with. Fundamentally, limited deployment is best at first because an administrator can slowly find the unknown applications and begin applying policy to those as well.

After a limited deployment and additional configuration changes to the QoS policies, you can try a larger scale deployment.

Implementing the Larger Scale Policy

Following policy testing and validation, and a limited deployment, preparation is complete for a larger QoS policy implementation. You can deploy QoS in a Cisco environment in many ways:

- QoS Policy Manager (QPM)
- QoS Device Manager (QDM)
- CiscoWorks 2000
- Cisco IOS Software
- Modular QoS Command Line Interface
- Catalyst OS

You can configure the policies on the switches and routers that are in the application traffic's path on an interface or port-by-port basis. These switches and routers will enforce the policies. As a final step, test to validate that classified traffic is behaving according to the set policies. This testing can best be done with a sniffer tool, RMON probes, and **show** commands on the routers and switches. The output presents the information about packet classification and prioritization on every device through the path from source to destination. The next two sections cover the different ways of implementing QoS in more detail.

Deploying QoS

You can configure QoS in an organization in several ways. The main distinction between the different ways is that you can configure QoS on a global basis from one server, QPM, or on a device-by-device basis using tools like Cisco IOS MQC or QDM. Companies can choose to use any combination of the following tools for implementation based on their overall deployment goals or preferences. The main tools are covered in more detail in the following pages.

Deploying QoS Using QPM

Cisco's QPM is designed to provision QoS for voice, video, and data networks and has many useful features to facilitate scaling. A main feature is the set of QPM 2.1 IP Telephony templates which embed the Cisco QoS recommendations for voice into predefined policy device-groups. This simplifies an administrator's task to assigning the devices and interfaces to the corresponding group and clicking on the Deploy button. Furthermore, organizations can tailor these templates to their requirements.

QPM provides users with these main functions:

- A graphical (GUI) configuration interface for Cisco devices

- Easy policy definition and deployment

- IP Telephony templates based on the Cisco IP Telephony QoS Design Guide, which you can find at:

  Cisco AVVID QoS Design Guide-http://www.cisco.com/univercd/cc/td/doc/ product/voice/ip_tele/avvidqos/avvid.pdf

- Centralized policy control and automated policy deployment

- Application of differentiated QoS policy objectives

- Intelligent traffic enforcement

Deploying QoS Using Modular QoS CLI

The Modular QoS CLI or MQC is a way to construct policies that enable end-to-end QoS network wide. It is a template that holds QoS configurations that you can apply to an interface to achieve different service level agreements among different applications or customer sites. MQC contains three different components:

- **class-map** defines which traffic is classified. (Classification is covered in more detail later in this chapter.)

- **policy-map** constructs policies and allocates different network resources for each of the classes defined by class-map.

- **service-policy** attaches policies on an interface.

NOTE   The following support Cisco IOS Software QoS features:

Routers: Cisco 8xx, 16xx, 17xx, 25xx, 36xx, 4xxx, 72xx, 75xx, 85xx, and 12xxx

Switches: Catalyst® 4xxx, 5xxx, and 6xxx

Example 6-1 provides sample syntax of each MQC component available in Cisco IOS Software.

Example 6-1 *MQC Component Configuration*

```
! I: Classify traffic using match option in class-map.
7200-UUT(config)#class-map ?
  WORD       class-map name
  match-all  Logical-AND all matching statements under this classmap
  match-any  Logical-OR all matching statements under this classmap

7200-UUT(config)#class-map TEST ?
  <cr>

7200-UUT(config)#class-map TEST
7200-UUT(config-cmap)#?
QoS class-map configuration commands:
  description  Class-Map description
  exit         Exit from QoS class-map configuration mode
  match        classification criteria
  no           Negate or set default values of a command
  rename       Rename this class-map

7200-UUT(config-cmap)#match ? (What criteria you would like to match on)
  access-group         Access group
  any                  Any packets
  class-map            Class map
  cos                  IEEE 802.1Q/ISL class of service/user priority values
  destination-address  Destination address
  input-interface      Select an input interface to match
  ip                   IP specific values
  mpls                 Multi Protocol Label Switching specific values
 not                   Negate this match result
  protocol             Protocol
  qos-group            Qos-group
  source-address       Source address
! II: Create policies combining various classes.
7200-UUT(config)#policy-map ?
  WORD   policy-map name

7200-UUT(config)#policy-map DEMO
7200-UUT(config-pmap)#?
QoS policy-map configuration commands:
  class        policy criteria
  description  Policy-Map description
  exit         Exit from QoS policy-map configuration mode
  no           Negate or set default values of a command
  rename       Rename this policy-map
  <cr>

7200-UUT(config-pmap)#class TEST
7200-UUT(config-pmap-c)#?
QoS policy-map class configuration commands:
  bandwidth         Bandwidth
```

Example 6-1 *MQC Component Configuration (Continued)*

```
default          Set a command to its defaults
  exit             Exit from QoS class action configuration mode
  no               Negate a command or set its defaults
  police           Police
  priority         Strict Scheduling Priority for this Class
  queue-limit      Queue Max Threshold for Tail Drop
  random-detect    Enable Random Early Detection as drop policy
  service-policy   Configure QoS Service Policy
  shape            Traffic Shaping
  <cr>
  set              Set QoS values
! III: Apply a policy to a desired interface.
7200-UUT(config-if)#service-policy ?
  history  Keep history of QoS metrics
  input    Assign policy-map to the input of an interface
  output   Assign policy-map to the output of an interface

7200-UUT(config-if)#service-policy input ?
  WORD  policy-map name
```

Example 6-2 demonstrates how to attach a service policy to various interface types.

Example 6-2 *Attaching Service Policies to Different Interfaces*

```
! I. an example of attaching to a serial interface:
int serial4/0
   service-policy out VOIP
II. an example of attaching to the sub-interface:
policy-map wred
   class class-default
     random-detect

 int atm6/1/0.1
   service-policy out wred
! III. an example of attaching to the pvc:
policy-map wred
   class class-default
     random-detect

 int atm6/1/0.1
   pvc 1/50
     vbr 512 512
     service-policy out wred
```

NOTE   Make sure none of the classes contain the **bandwidth** command within a policy when attaching a policy to a Frame Relay or ATM subinterface. All the QoS functions other than queuing are supported per ATM or Frame Relay subinterface.

QoS Device Manager

Cisco QoS Device Manager (QDM) 2.0 is a World Wide Web-based network management application that provides an easy-to-use graphical user interface for configuring and monitoring advanced IP-based QoS functionality in Cisco Systems' routers (2600, 3600, 7100, 7200, 7500).

QDM, a World Wide Web-based Java application, is stored in a router's Flash memory. To access QDM, the router must have its embedded HTTP server function enabled. When the client browser makes a connection to the embedded World Wide Web server of this Cisco router, the QDM application is presented as a URL option on the Cisco router menu which, if selected by the user, is uploaded to the Java-enabled client browser. Communication between QDM running on the client World Wide Web browser and the Cisco router occurs over an HTTP session and is based on the Cisco IOS command-line interface (CLI) command syntax. QDM parses this CLI command syntax to present a graphical representation of the QoS configuration to the user and monitor router capabilities.

QoS Application Points

There are many tools for applying QoS. To simplify the understanding of QoS, individual categories of QoS have been created to describe the type of method:

- Classification and Marking
- Congestion Avoidance
- Congestion Management
- Traffic Conditioning
- Link Efficiency Mechanisms

The section that follows describes each category with a brief introduction into the methods of QoS that fall into that category. Figure 6-2 represents the logical flow of categories through a router. To learn more about the topic of QoS, you should consult a focused whitepaper or books on QoS such as *Cisco IOS 12.0* by Mark McGregor or *IP Quality of Service* by Srinivas Vegesna.

Cisco IOS QoS Tools/Categories

Cisco IOS QoS tools are divided into six main categories:

- **Classification and Marking**—This category answers the following questions: How do you identify the packet? Do you put a mark on the packet for other routers or switches to identify? Packet classification features allow you to partition traffic into multiple priority levels, service classes, or service types. This classification is achieved by modifying bits in the packets to allow classification by another device. Classification is recommended to be done as close to the source of the traffic as possible.

Packets can be classified in a variety of ways—Committed Access Rate (CAR), Policy Based Routing (PBR), or Network Based Application Recognition (NBAR) for difficult-to-classify applications. Classification is the first component of the Modular QoS CLI (MQC), the simple, scalable, and powerful QoS framework in Cisco IOS software. The MQC clearly separates classification of the policy applied to the classes from the application of a QoS policy on an interface or sub-interface.

You can also mark packets in a variety of ways (Layer 2—802.1p/Q / ISL, ATM CLP bit, Frame-Relay DE-bit, MPLS EXP bits, and so forth, and Layer 3—IP Precedence, Differentiated Services Code Point (DSCP), and so on) using the MQC's policy-framework component. As an organizing principle, classification should always be done as close to the edge of the network as possible.

- **Congestion Avoidance**—Congestion avoidance adds a tremendous amount of value to a company's QoS strategy because it protects a queue from filling up by dropping packets before the queue gets full. This strategy eliminates packets being tail dropped where the packet coming in is dropped regardless of its type. This can be disastrous for any real-time application.

  The weighted random early detection (WRED) algorithm provides congestion avoidance on network interfaces by providing buffer management and allowing TCP traffic to throttle back before buffers are exhausted. It does this by selectively dropping TCP-based traffic that is of a lower priority based on previous classification. This process helps avoid tail-drops and global synchronization issues, maximizing network utilization and TCP-based application performance. MQC's policy-framework component accommodates WRED.

- **Congestion Management**—A network interface is often congested (even at high speeds, transient congestion is observed) and queuing techniques are necessary to ensure that critical applications get the forwarding treatment necessary. For example, real-time applications such as VoIP, stock trading, and so on, may need to be forwarded with the least latency and jitter (up to a provisioned limit). Cisco's Low-Latency Queuing (LLQ) provides such a solution. For other non-delay sensitive traffic (such as FTP, HTTP, and so forth), other queuing techniques such as CBWFQ, can be used. To round out the congestion management strategies, you can use Weighted Fair Queuing, IP RTP, Custom Queuing, Priority Queuing, or Weighted Round Robin. You can instantiate the queuing techniques using MQC's policy-framework as well.

- **Traffic Conditioning**—Traffic entering a network can be conditioned using a policer or shaper. A policer enforces a rate limit while a shaper smoothes the traffic flow to a specified rate using buffers. A policer enforces by dropping excess packets while a shaper queues excess traffic to send when there is a lull. Once again, mechanisms, such as Committed Access Rate (CAR), Generic Traffic Shaping (GTS), and Frame-Relay Traffic Shaping (FRTS) can be configured within the MQC framework.

- **Link Efficiency Mechanisms**—Streaming video and voice traffic use the Real-Time Protocol (RTP). IP, UDP, and RTP packet headers can be compressed from approximately 40 bytes to two to four bytes. This saves a tremendous amount of bandwidth in low-speed links, and when supporting a large number of media streams. In addition, Frame-Relay Forum specification for frame-fragmentation (FRF.12)) and Cisco Link Fragmentation & Interleaving LFI) can fragment large data packets, interleaving them with RTP packets and maintaining low delay and jitter for media streams.

Table 6-2 lists every QoS technique and the category they fall into.

Table 6-2   *Available Tools and QoS Features*

Classification/ Marking	Congestion Management	Congestion Avoidance	Traffic Conditioners	Link Efficiency	RSVP-Signaled-QoS
DSCP	LLQ	DSCP-compliant-WRED	Policing	cRTP	COPs
IP Precedence	CBWFQ	WRED	Single-Rate Policer	FRF.11	RSVP w LLQ
Set&Match-MQC	WFQ	FWRED	Dual-Rate Policer	FRF.12	RSVP For FR
NBAR	PQ	tail drop	CAR	LFI	Call Admin Control w RSVP
VPN-preclassify	FIFO		Shaping		
TOS	CQ		CBShaper		
CLP	IP RTP Pri		GTS		
DE	PIPQ		FRTS		
DialPeer-Voice via MGCP					
BGP-QPPB					
Policy Based routing					
QoS-group ID					
source/dest IP or MAC add, interfaces, subints.					
IP to ATM CoS					

Figure 6-2 shows where to apply the appropriate technique based on logical flow through the router.

Figure 6-2   *Logical Flow of QoS Categories Through a Router*

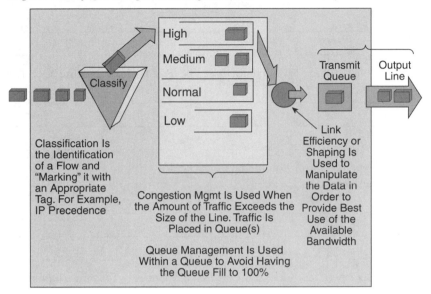

Summary

QoS is becoming more and more necessary as applications are becoming more dynamic and mission critical in nature. As many data networks are being built to handle multiple traffic types like voice, video, and storage, a stronger need will be in place to provide differentiated service with QoS. In this chapter you learned the basics of what it takes to implement QoS on your network. You first learned that it is necessary to identify your current traffic and traffic patterns. After this you can then begin to map out a plan of how and where you are going to apply QoS. You then also learned how you can deploy QoS—either via the command line, an individual GUI, or via a central policy deployment server. You were then exposed to the different categories of QoS and the individual types of tools to be used within each category.

Review Questions

1 What are some ways of deploying QoS?

_____

_____

_____

2 What groups of tools and techniques can be used for implementing QoS features?

_____

_____

_____

3 What technique allows you to mark a packet for identification by all other routers throughout the internetwork?

_____

_____

_____

4 What category of tools does the Low Latency Queuing Technique fall into?

_____

_____

_____

5 What Cisco solution can you use in your QoS deployment planning stage to provide a graph of your top bandwidth users and segments?

_____

_____

_____

6 Why is planning the most important step in QoS deployment?

_____

_____

_____

After reading this chapter, you should be able to perform the following tasks:

- Define network management and its role in a network.

- Describe the FCAPS model and its components. Attribute a given network management goal to a specific component of the FCAPS model.

- Describe fault management's role in a network and identify its five steps.

- Describe performance management's purpose and function. Be able to explain the steps and methods required for performance management.

- Define SNMP and RMON functions in a management system.

- Define the eight basic guidelines for network management and describe their role in a network management system.

- List the metrics for a network system and explain how they are calculated.

- Describe Cisco's Network Management Solutions.

CHAPTER 7

Network Management

Network management is the methodology by which switches, routers, hubs, and other communications equipment that make up a network infrastructure are managed. This methodology includes hardware, software, processes, and, most importantly, people.

Network management is a critical component to the Cisco Internet Architecture. As networks grow in size and complexity, daily maintenance tasks are often overlooked and left behind. Network management tools help network managers by centralizing management, automating routine tasks, and gathering information that facilitates proactively managing the network.

This chapter consists of seven sections. The first three sections discuss the theory and models of network management and how these concepts apply to the Cisco Internet Architecture.

The fourth section provides an in-depth analysis of the four common network management protocols.

The fifth section ties the concepts from the previous sections together into eight network management tasks.

The last two sections discuss network management tools from Cisco and other third-party companies. These tools strive to solve the network management issues arising as networks continue to grow in size and complexity.

Network Management and the FCAPS Model

Any network management solution includes people, processes, and programs which attempt to make the task of managing a network easier. Network management is further explained by looking into the Fault, Configuration, Accounting, Performance, and Security (FCAPS) model.

The FCAPS model was developed by the International Organization for Standardization (ISO). The ISO has been heavily involved in standardizing various network elements including network management, routing protocols, and the OSI Model. The FCAPS model includes five functional areas: fault management, configuration management, accounting management, performance management, and security management. The FCAPS model is designed to make developing and classifying network management tools easier. The model also facilitates understanding the various aspects of a Network Management Systems (NMS).

FCAPS is part of the OSI Telecommunications Management Network (TMN) Architecture. TMN is a network management model defined in ITU-T recommendation M.3100 and related recommendations; it is the standard reference model for management enterprise and service provider networks. TMN specifies a set of standard functions with standard interfaces and includes the full range of the following functions defined in the OSI model:

> Fault Management
> Configuration Management
> Accounting Management
> Performance Management
> Security Management

Fault Management

The "F" in the FCAPS model stands for fault management. Network faults are critical issues common in any network design. Fault management involves identifying the systems, isolating the problem, and completing the steps necessary to solve the problem and test relevant systems to verify that the network is operational. The problem and resolution are recorded in a physical log or in a network management application or tool for future analysis and reference.

Configuration Management

Configuration management is designed to accomplish specific tasks. You will learn about the components that accomplish the following tasks:

- Collect software inventory on software type (Enterprise/IP/etc.), version, and so on.

- Collect hardware inventory on device model, card type, and location, as well as port level information.

- Store configurations on a server for shared access.

- List a device and compare its configuration to others for analysis.

- Install and upgrade device software.

The first and second configuration management tasks are software and hardware inventory, consecutively. Both of these tasks document the existing devices on the network. Just as in a true corporate management position, managing a group is difficult if you don't know the members of that group. The same is true for network management in that knowing the hardware devices and software components in the network is critical. For hardware this includes the model number, cards installed, amount of memory, free slots, ports in use, cable number, and so on. This information is equally important on the software inventory. Important software information might include, software type (Enterprise/IP/etc.), version, free memory, and so on.

The third configuration management task is to monitor and maintain network device configuration to achieve two things: To decrease the amount of time required to manage an individual device and most important, to be able to replicate the existing network should a failure occur to the network as a whole or to an individual device.

The time required to manage each network device increases dramatically as the complexity and the size of the network increase. The fourth configuration management task is to decrease the overall time required to manage a network. To illustrate this point imagine five devices in a hypothetical network called the XYZ network. Each device takes half an hour every week to maintain. Maintenance on a router in the XYZ network includes a configuration archive, a log check, an interface status check, and an occasional reboot. It takes the network manager two and a half hours every week to maintain the five routers. As the number of devices grows to fifty or more, the network manager requires twenty-five hours every week to maintain the network. With relatively simple weekly maintenance, managing a network with more than one hundred devices can be nearly impossible without introducing some form of automation.

Most of the weekly tasks on the XYZ network can be automated with a configuration management tool. Some configuration management tools, such as CiscoWorks 2000, can automatically archive device configuration, check the log or redirect it to a central management system, check the interface status, and e-mail or page the network manager if an anomaly occurs in a device being managed. Configuration management tools also give you a single centralized interface for system management as opposed to connecting to each device individually to maintain its configuration. Configuration management's ability to save time is a critical factor in any Internet system and must be considered as the size and complexity of the system increase.

The fourth task is the capability to replicate the network should a failure occur. If a device fails in a network, replicating the entire configuration without documentation on the device's configuration is difficult, if not impossible. Documentation is even more important if an entire site, such as a data center, fails because of a natural disaster. In such an event, information such as circuit identifiers, network numbers, port information, and so on is required to bring a back-up site online. Though a catastrophic failure is not likely, planning for it ahead of time will minimize the financial loss to your corporation when the disaster occurs. Documentation should include the software configuration, hardware configuration, and any specific application information that is necessary to bring the network back to a functional state.

The fifth configuration management task is to make comparing and analyzing the configuration of multiple devices easier. Configuration management tools can download the configuration from each router or switch on the network and store it in a central location, making it easier for network managers to analyze and compare configurations.

To complete these five tasks, configuration management has the following three core components:

- **Configuration description**—How a network system is interconnected physically and logically. This also includes each device's individual configuration on the network and so forth.

- **Configuration process**—The means by which a network accomplishes changes. This includes changing individual system parameters or physically moving a network device.

- **Configuration result**—The documentation of network changes that will or have been implemented on the network, including old configurations, changes, and the final result.

These components are the means by which configuration management activities are divided.

Configuration Description

Configuration description is comprised of two subcomponents: a logical and physical map of the network.

The logical map shows the association of multiple devices on the network, including their network number and the general speed between the devices. Logical views are necessary to understand how devices are associated and how the network could be better designed.

Physical views show the devices within the network including their physical location, model, cable number, media type, and what patch panel each device uses for connectivity. A complete network map is essential for proper network management. These maps are important in the event of a device failure. During such a failure all the preceding information would be required to install a replacement device with the same software and hardware configuration (cards, cable numbers, media type, and so on) that is required for the device to be operational. Much of the information included in the physical map is also part of the hardware inventory. As such, the hardware inventory list can be helpful when building your network's physical map.

The second subcomponent to configuration description is the individual configuration of each device within the network. While physical and logical maps show a macro view of the network as a whole, device configuration is a micro view of the individual devices that make up the network. Because networks are made of individual components such as routers and switches, you must also look at the configuration of each device, in addition to the hardware and software inventory, to clearly understand the network configuration.

Configuration Process

Configuration process is the component that does the actual hands-on work in configuration management. Configuration processing allows for tools that can automatically change the system parameters or monitor the physical changes of network devices. This component includes two sub categories: configuration and software. Configuration tools modify network device configuration as needed, while software tools update the software to receive additional functionality or to fix possible bugs. Software tools save time and alleviate software maintenance headaches. Software updates can be done by a manual process or handled automatically by the NMS. Manual updates are accomplished by connecting to the device and making the changes piece by piece. Automatic software updates are useful in large networks because they alleviate the need to manually connect to multiple devices, enabling more efficient management of large networks. One of the most common configuration tools in use today is Resource Manager Essentials within the CiscoWorks 2000 suite. It has been specifically designed to automate many of the day-to-day configuration changes that a network manager encounters.

Though configuration changes are simple from a technical perspective, the wrong configuration change can have dramatic effects on a network and on a corporation's business. For this reason, many corporations use a documented change control policy to make sure changes are needed, effective, and in the best interest of the company. A change management process often includes a group or small committee formally reviewing the proposed change. The networking staff implements the change only after it has been approved.

Configuration Results

Configuration results document the changes that will be or have been made on the network. This documentation often includes the device's configuration at the beginning of the process, the individual changes completed on the system or individual devices, and the result on the network and devices within the network. As you will see in the following sections, audit trails are a part of this process.

Configuration Management Tool Functions

As previously mentioned, a number of tools have been developed, such as CiscoWorks 2000 and HP Openview, to make the configuration management task easier. These tools should accomplish the following:

- Create topological maps of the network.
- Back up configuration files.
- Automate and set up configuration changes.
- Enable software distribution.
- Authorize and manage changes.

The "Third Party Network Management Solutions" and "Cisco Network Management Solutions" sections detail specific configuration management tools.

Accounting Management

Accounting management collects network data relating to resource utilization and administration tasks such as directory services. This permits you to track individual and group network resources usage. The collected data allows you to reallocate resources or properly assign network costs as needed.

Accounting management's goal is to measure network resources availability and usage so that the individual or group can be regulated accurately. Regulation allows network managers to allocate network bandwidth and services based on resource capacities. It also maximizes the efficiency of network access across all users. For example, because the Internet is not a key component of their job, the accounting department employees might have limited access to the Internet, while management might be entitled to full system access. Internet resources are conserved for the appropriate users.

The first step in accounting management is to measure the network utilization of all important network resources. This includes the Internet, databases, and file servers. Analyzing the measurements yields what is commonly called a "baseline" for network utilization across all the critical network devices. The baseline includes usage patterns such as the amount of data transferred and duration of individual network access attempts. With usage patterns, quotas can be generated and set for each group or user. After the quotas have been finalized, ongoing measurement can yield billing information. In addition, quotas must be adjusted as network flows change to guarantee optimal resource utilization.

The measurable units in accounting management follow:

- Traffic volume
- Connection duration
- Time of day
- Quality of Service (QoS)
- Fixed costs

Though accounting management is mainly intended to regulate network bandwidth, many of the same tools required for accounting management are also used for performance management and security management.

As previously mentioned, security is a vital component to any Internet systems architecture. In addition to having the appropriate architecture for security, monitoring the user access to network services is also critical. The accounting measures for connection duration and time of day are becoming critical pieces of security information for system administrators and network managers. With these measures, audit trails can maintain security records. Two examples of tools for accounting management include Cisco's Access Control Server (ACS) and Websense by Websense, Inc.

Performance Management

Performance management analyzes and controls network performance including network throughput and error rates. Performance management is closely related to QoS and Service Level Management (SLM). Performance management data is used to trigger events linked to QoS as well as to validate Service Level Agreements (SLAs).

Performance management's goal is to measure and present various aspects of network performance so that it can be monitored and maintained at an acceptable level. Greater detail about performance management appears later in this chapter.

Security Management

Security management is composed of several different specialized systems. These systems have the following functions:

- Identify critical network resources (including systems, files, and other entities).

- Define mappings between sensitive resources and user groups.

- Monitor access to sensitive network resources and log inappropriate activity in audit trails. For example, a security system can monitor access to a file system, deny authentication to users without a correct access code, and log access for future analysis.

Security management is critical to a functional network architecture. Another key component to a security management system is a well-defined security policy. Security policies are essential for a consistent security management implementation throughout the corporate network. Without policies, corporations must rely on users who are prone to forgetting, misapplying, and even abusing security policies. For more information on security policies and the security lifecycle, refer to Chapter 4, "Security Concepts and Design."

Security management's goal is to control access to network resources according to a set security policy. This is important because it prevents unauthorized users from harming the network or accessing sensitive data.

Security systems work by separating network resources into authorized and unauthorized zones. A common example is the separation of the Internet and the local network. For many users, such as those on the Internet, access to internal network resource is inappropriate. For normal internal users, access to privileged systems might also be inappropriate (for example, access to human resources is not allowed for most users outside of human resources). To set up a security system on your network you must identify critical network resources, locate the access points to these resources, secure these access points, and maintain them.

The key elements to network security include the following:

- Analyzing threats and reporting violations and incidents

- Enforcing security policies and access control

- Validating identity

- Encryption

- Creating and updating security policy

As mentioned in Chapter 4, a security policy is critical for a secure Internet architecture. It is also a key component of security management because analyzing and reporting threats is directly tied to the guidelines listed in the security policy.

Security scanner and advisory software can also be used to analyze the network and find non-secure points for those companies who are short on resources or manpower. These tools often include a mapping tool that can contact each device in the network to discover resources and map them in a graphical view. Figure 7-1 shows how scanner software maps the network.

Figure 7-1   *Security Scanner and Advisory Software Can Be Used to Help Companies That Are Short on Time and Staff to Assess Security Risks*

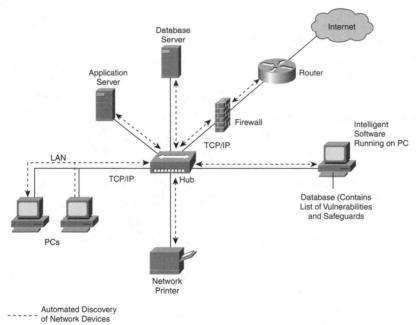

In addition to mapping these tools can scan network devices' communication ports, compare the results against a database, and from that database get suggested safeguards and fixes to security holes.

Fault Management

As previously discussed, fault management ensures that network faults are detected and controlled. This section begins by focusing on the characteristics of fault management, details the steps of fault management, and explains the reasons for fault management.

Most fault management systems have many of the following characteristics:

- Alarm collection and forwarding
- Automated trouble ticket generation
- Assignment of event priority levels
- Status polling
- Event configuration
- Root cause analysis
- Event correlation
- Event notification
- Event filtering
- Network and system status

A fault management system can collect SNMP traps and forward them to another NMS or a trouble ticket system. Sending events to a ticket system assists the network administrator and other network personnel with the ability to automatically assign network faults to specific users based on rules, escalation schemes, and so on. These systems' capabilities are significant because they can assign tickets to the user most able to solve the issue. For example, assigning a new network fault to the user that has the least number of tickets or the individual who has the most experience with the specific subsystem is best. These systems are also popular because they include comments and steps that the user adds to the ticket as he works on the issue.

A fault management system allows easy classification of network faults based on event priority levels. Such classification makes fault management more efficient by directing resources to the most critical network issues.

Status polling is critical in any size network. The days when organizations relied on the user base to first identify network outages are gone. With status polling, all the devices on the network are polled at regular intervals to determine their status. Polling can be accomplished with simple IP pings, SNMP queries, telnet, and so on. When utilizing status polling, network operations can detect possible network outages before the outages disrupt the network users.

Event Handling in a Fault Management System

One of the most useful aspects of fault management is its capability to handle events intelligently. Events are managed with five different capabilities:

- Event configuration
- Root cause analysis
- Event correlation
- Event notification
- Event filtering

Event configuration handles the individual actions for a network event. The configuration for an event might include whether to filter an event, whom to page if the event occurs, or what priority level is assigned to an event.

Root cause analysis is the capability to collect multiple events from a single device and determine the root cause of the messages. For example, if all the interfaces for a specific device appear to be down while the rest of the network is functioning perfectly, you can conclude that the root cause is that the device is down or being rebooted.

Event correlation is important in any fault management system because it associates messages and allows events to be dynamically filtered. For example, if the router for a remote office goes down, the switch also appears to be down to the fault system. Event correlation prevents a second alarm from being sent for the switch failure because it is aware that the switch's parent device, the router, has gone down thus preventing connectivity to the switch.

Event notification, as previously discussed, is the fault system's ability to send pages, e-mail, and so on to an individual, group of individuals, or another event management system.

Event filtering is related to root cause analysis and event correlation. Event filtering prevents erroneous events from reaching the fault management console and overloading the network operations staff to the point where they turn the system off and rely on their intuition and user complaints. Events that might be filtered include unimportant informational events and repetitive messages. Anything that is not considered a true network fault should be filtered so that only relevant events are sent to the console. Although events need to be filtered from the fault console, all event messages must be sent to the event log for accounting and security purposes.

Key Functions in a Fault Management System

For a fault management system to operate as designed, it should accomplish the following functions:

- Monitor network status
- Problem detection and notification
- Problem diagnosis and service restoration

The ability to detect and resolve problems in a network is critical. Many NMS systems have a logical map that shows all the critical systems and their status on the network. This status is indicated with different colors. Green most often indicates a completely operational device or network while red indicates that the device or a device component is down. These systems are also capable of receiving and displaying network events such as a router interface changing status from online to offline. After the NMS has received the event, it can react by sending notifications by e-mail, page, or even a telephone call. In addition to sending a notification, the NMS also changes the affected network device's icon color to indicate that the status has changed.

Although paging can be a useful tool to notify network operations personnel of an outage, it can also be a disaster waiting to happen. Automatic paging must be implemented with extreme care to prevent erroneous pages from overloading the network operations staff. Simple event pages, such as the notification of a device failure, can become a nightmare in a network with 1000 or more network devices, especially if the switch that the fault management system uses for its network connectivity fails. This would trigger 1000 pages, one for each device the fault system cannot reach.

An event can be sent to an NMS several ways; the most common of which are Simple Network Monitoring Protocol (SNMP) and syslog. SN;MP is part of the TCP/IP Suite of protocols; it is used by nearly all network devices including routers and switches. SNMP can alert administrators to fault conditions such as when an interface changes operations status. Syslog messages are system messages on a Cisco router or switch describing different conditions on a device. Syslog messages are sent to a syslog server, which can be isolated or integrated into an NMS. The section on network management protocols goes into more detail on both SNMP and syslog.

After an event has reached the NMS's management console, it must be diagnosed to determine the severity and the steps necessary to correct the problem. The severity of syslog messages is easily discernable by a number indicator on the message. The next step after problem diagnosis is to either bypass the faulty device or resolve the fault on the device itself. Refer to the following list for the fault management steps:

Step 1   Problem determination

Step 2   Problem diagnosis

Step 3   Problem bypass and recovery

Step 4   Problem resolution

Step 5   Problem tracking and control

Where to Implement a Fault Management System

Because faults occur in different systems, many areas exist where fault management can be performed:

- In managing any distributed network system

- In managing any system that can generate SNMP traps

- As the key management/monitoring system in a network operations center

- Within a trouble ticketing system, where the fault handing process can be refined to include advanced reports, such as the most common problem, mean-time-to-repair, and so on

- In conjunction with root cause analysis

Distributed systems by their sheer size require faults to be managed, whether through a simple SNMP-compliant trap program or with a sophisticated NMS that is designed to receive events and alert the network staff to correct the problem. The fault management system is often the main monitoring point for the network operations staff. From a single screen you can see the network's status and manually trigger alerts to specialized network personnel or rely on the automatic alert capabilities within the NMS.

Reasons for Implementing a Fault Management System

Because fault management has many different uses, several reasons exist for network managers to implement fault management:

- Respond to events on the network or system.

- Correlate network and system events.

- Log network and system incidents.

- Link system outages or failures to a trouble ticket system.

- Increase network and system availability by quickly identifying the root cause of a network or system problem.

- Reduce and control network or system costs.

- Provide a visual display of network or system health.

Troubleshooting in a Fault Management System

The most critical topic in fault management is troubleshooting. Network faults can and do occur on a regular basis so the ability to solve the issue after discovery is important.

Failures in a network are characterized by certain symptoms. To users, these symptoms might be the inability to access specific servers, the inability to print, or the inability to access the network at all. To network managers, these symptoms might indicate that specific routes do not appear within the routing table. Each symptom is then traced to one or more problems or causes utilizing various troubleshooting tools and techniques.

When troubleshooting a network environment, a systematic approach works best. This approach consists of three steps: Identify the specific symptoms, list all possible causes of the symptoms, and eliminate the possible causes one by one, going from most to least likely, until the symptoms disappear.

For example, in Cisco routers, you can isolate the cause of a problem with a system's monitoring commands or with a system's test commands and resolve the problem with other commands.

Figure 7-2 illustrates the process flow for the problem-solving model. This flow is not a rigid outline for troubleshooting an Internetwork but instead is a guide that you can change to fit your own specific environment.

Figure 7-2   *Process Flow for Problem-Solving Model*

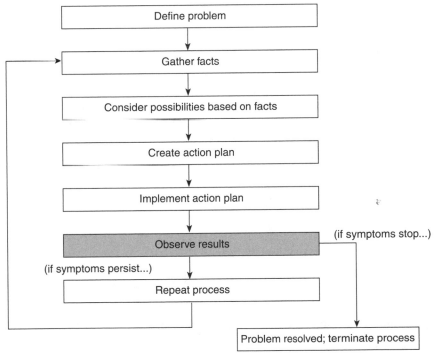

One important aspect of fault management that is not a required part of the troubleshooting model is documentation. Accurate documentation is critical in an Internetwork so that everyone, including the network operations staff, is adequately prepared for network faults before they occur. Only with documentation can the entire network staff work to solve issues quickly and intelligently. The documentation must accurately reflect recent network changes and be detailed to assist with solving complicated issues. Documentation allows everyone to troubleshoot network issues should the need arise.

Performance Management

Performance management deals with many aspects of network performance. Throughput, response time, and line utilization performance is measured. An initial baseline is established as a comparison for subsequent performance measurements. Performance can then be measured for analysis, capacity planning, and to determine if performance is in line with a SLA.

The need for performance management grows as the size and complexity of networks increase. Today's network managers "fight fires," identifying performance problems as they arise. This approach is overwhelming and is also becoming more difficult as complexity increases. When calls to the help desk complain of poor response time, the network manager is often at a loss to find and explain the source of the bottleneck. Unfortunately, network managers often spend little time monitoring network performance until a problem occurs and is reported. This style of performance management is called *reactive performance management*.

Performance management's goal is to measure and present the network's performance to keep the network running smoothly. This methodology is referred to as proactive management. *Proactive management* is the network manager's ability to monitor network performance trends to prevent an increased demand for resources from overloading network capacity. Proactive management is critical for service providers and large enterprise networks that maintain WAN contracts and SLAs. These networks and the customers they support are dependent on the consistent network performance that proactive management provides.

With this in mind, performance management needs to accomplish several functions in order to achieve this goal. The seven main functions of performance management follow:

- Analyze traffic and trending.
- Define managed device performance.
- Profile application traffic flow.
- Grade service performance threshold management.
- Provide a network baseline.
- Analyze infrastructure cost and traffic volume.
- Plan for capacity.

The following three main tasks in performance management accomplish these functions:

Step 1   Establish a network performance baseline.

Step 2   Define the SLA and metrics.

Step 3   Monitor and measure performance.

Establishing a network performance baseline is important because it allows you to more accurately discern any future abnormal measures of performance within the network. A baseline involves collecting network measures over an extended period of time. Routers, switches, and probes attached to the LAN segment or WAN link can collect baseline data. The data is used to determine the normal traffic patterns in the network. Future measures are taken and compared to the baseline to discern whether network performance is at a normal or abnormal level.

An SLA establishes the network's expected performance level. The agreement defines specific metrics that are used to measure the actual service level against those stated as part of the agreement. The most common measures for service level are response time and availability. SLAs are commonly between a service provider and customer. SLAs can also be established between a corporate headquarters and remote offices, or between IS and internal corporate departments. Cisco's Service Management Solution (SMS) is one example of an SLA monitoring tool. SMS can define and validate SLAs on an enterprise or service provider network.

The network's performance is directly linked to the operational state of the network. In addition, the network's status is tied to the condition of its hardware and software components. Faulty software or hardware can severely affect the network's operational state causing an extreme decrease in network performance. Monitoring the network devices' operating environment is important. This includes the temperature, voltage, airflow, and software components, such as buffers, and verifies that they are within operating specifications. Setting thresholds, as well as analyzing and tuning network performance, should always follow measurements.

SNMP and RMON Overview

Four basic protocols manage Cisco equipment:

- Telnet
- SNMP
- RMON
- Syslog

Although not a common network management protocol, Transport Layer Interface (TLI) is also available on some systems. TLI is popular with certain service provider class management platforms. Many more management protocols are available, such as Cisco Discovery Protocol (CDP) and the rising star, HTTP (XML), but the four previously listed are the most common, and the primary topics of this section.

In addition to the protocols listed, several management methods have arisen because of an increased demand on security. The two most common secure management methods are SSH, a standardized management protocol and proposed replacement to Telnet, and out-of-band management, which is more of a methodology than a true protocol. For more information, please refer to the SAFE Architecture on Cisco's web site (www.cisco.com).

This section begins with a brief overview of the four basic management protocols and goes into detail on SNMP, including SNMP versions 1 and 2, SNMP Commands and Events, and MIBs. This section concludes with coverage of RMON.

Telnet

The first basic management protocol is Telnet, also commonly referred to as command-line interface (CLI). Telnet allows direct login into the switch or router's command line to access configuration and monitoring commands. Although Telnet is extremely effective for managing small groups of devices, it is not scalable to a large network.

SNMP

SNMP is an application-layer protocol that facilitates the exchange of management information between network devices. SNMP is based on a request/response model, also known as a manager/agent model. The SNMP manager, as part of a SNMP-compliant tool or Network Management System (NMS), requests information from SNMP agents which are resident processes on the router or switch. To pull the data from the agents, the manager uses the Get and GetNext protocol operations within SNMP. To change a variable's configuration, the SNMP manager uses the Set operation.

Most management information is available through both SNMP and Telnet. Both can gather management information from managed devices. Telnet uses a manual process whereby a telnet session is started and directed at the managed device; SNMP utilizes its ability to pole individual SNMP agents. Two major differences exist between Telnet and SNMP:

- SNMP agents can notify the management system using a Trap, which is an unsolicited piece of management information.

- SNMP gives you the actual data in a numeric format, whereas Telnet presents the information in text, which requires translation for a network management system to be able to understand the data. This unique SNMP characteristic has allowed it to scale to large networks where Telnet is unable to compete.

As previously mentioned, SNMP was developed as part of the TCP/IP Suite of protocols in 1988. SNMP enables network managers to manage network performance, find and solve network problems, and plan for network growth. One of the major advantages of SNMP is its ability to account for and adjust to incompatibilities between network devices. Figure 7-3 shows a sample network; the SNMP components include the manager and the agents (one server, three workstations, and one network router). With these components, SNMP facilitates the exchange of network information between devices.

Figure 7-3   *SNMP Management Protocol*

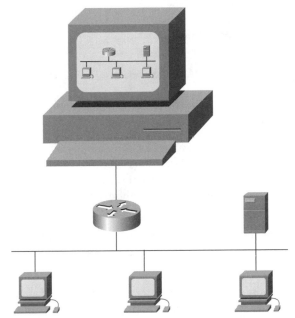

SNMP Facilitates the Exhange of Network Information Between Devices.

Different computers use different data representation techniques which can compromise a network management protocol's ability to exchange information. To solve this issue, SNMP uses a subset of Abstract Syntax Negotiation One (ASN.1). This presentation layer protocol makes information exchange between managed devices more seamless and more tolerant of different communication techniques from diverse systems.

As previously mentioned, SNMP is based on a request/response model, also known as a manager/agent model. The network management system issues a request and the agent on the managed device responds. This behavior is accomplished with the following four protocol operations:

- Get

- GetNext

- Set

- Trap

Figure 7-4 shows the communication between an SNMP manager and an SNMP agent using the various protocol operations.

Figure 7-4 *Communication Between an SNMP Manager and an SNMP Agent Using the Various Protocol Operations*

Flow of Management Operations Requests, Responses,
and Traps Between the Manager and the Agent

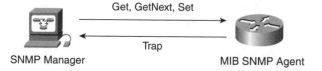

Get, GetNext, Set

Trap

SNMP Manager

MIB SNMP Agent

Get is targeted at one or more management variables on a device. After the management system issues the get, the agent responds with the requested data.

GetNext is similar to **Get**, but only follows the **Get** command or other **GetNext** commands when used. For example, when requesting the first variable from a table or a list on the agent, a single **Get** is sent. Each successive variable on the table or list is requested with a **GetNext** until all variables have been retrieved. (Example: **Get-Response-GetNext-Response-GetNext-Response**…)

Set is targeted at a specific management variable on a device. Instead of requesting information, it changes the parameter. Unlike **Get**, each successive variable is also modified with the **Set** operation.

Trap, unlike the other three operations, is sent from the agent to the management station unsolicited (asynchronously). On the initial agent setup, the management system's IP address is specified so that when a trap condition occurs, an SNMP trap message is sent to the management system. Two of the numerous possible trap conditions are "Link Up" and "Link Down."

Any SNMP managed network consists of three components:

- Managed devices

- Agents

- Network management systems (NMSs)

A managed device is a network node that contains the SNMP agent on a managed network. Managed devices collect and store management information and make this information available to an NMS using SNMP. Managed devices are sometimes called network elements; they can be routers, switches, bridges, access servers, computer hosts, or printers.

An agent is a network management software module, such as Cisco IOS Software, that resides in a managed device. An agent has local knowledge of management information and translates this information into a form compatible with SNMP.

An NMS executes and runs applications that monitor and control managed devices. NMSs provide the bulk of the processing and memory resources required for network management. One or more NMSs must exist on any managed network.

SNMP-managed network components fit together, as illustrated in Figure 7-5.

Figure 7-5   *Relationship of SNMP-managed Network Components*

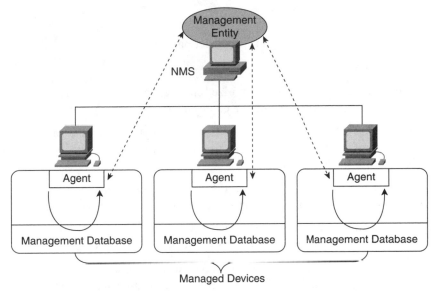

An SNMP Managed Network Consists
of Managed Devices, Agents, and NMSs.

SNMP Versions 1 and 2

SNMP version 1 was the initial release of the SNMP protocol. To correct several weaknesses in that first release, SNMP version 2 was published as a set of proposed Internet standards in 1993, five years after the initial SNMP release. As with SNMPv1, SNMPv2 functions within the Structure of Management Information (SMI) specifications. SMI defines the rules for describing management information. SNMPv2 was designed to address the following two SNMPv1weaknesses:

- Weak security

- Inability to perform bulk data transfers

To solve the bulk data transfers issue, the **GetBulk** protocol operation was added to SNMPv2. A **GetBulk** operation selects multiple elements for retrieval by the agent. The agent in turn sends multiple responses. This alleviates the need for multiple **GetNext** requests and makes the SNMP management process slightly more efficient. Despite the slightly improved performance realized with the addition of the **GetBulk** command, larger data transfers are still time consuming and resource intensive.

SNMPv2 attempted to address SNMPv1's weak security but, unfortunately, neither have a true authentication mechanism. This opens up several vulnerabilities:

- Masquerading
- Modification of information
- Message sequence and timing modifications
- Disclosure

Masquerading occurs when an unauthorized entity attempts to perform management operations by assuming the identity of an authorized management entity.

Modification of information is the unauthorized attempt to alter a message generated by an authorized entity so that the message causes unauthorized accounting management and configuration management operations.

Message sequence and timing modifications occur when an unauthorized entity reorders, delays, or copies and replays a messages generated by an authorized entity.

Disclosure results when an unauthorized entity extracts values stored in managed objects or learns of events by monitoring exchanges between managers and agents.

These security vulnerabilities have been solved with the recent development of the SNMP version 3 (SNMPv3) standard. SNMPv3 uses authentication and encryption to secure the session between NMS and agent.

SNMP Commands and Events

Instead of defining a large set of commands, all SNMP operations are controlled through a simple four-command format:

- NMS uses the **read** command to monitor managed devices. The NMS examines different variables that are maintained by managed devices.

- NMS uses the **write** command to control managed devices. The NMS changes the values of variables stored within managed devices.

- Managed devices use the **trap** command to report events to the NMS asynchronously. When certain types of events occur, a managed device sends a trap to the NMS.

- NMS uses **traversal** operations to determine which variables a managed device supports and to gather information sequentially in variable tables, such as a routing table.

All Cisco devices generate traps that send error and status events to the NMS. In addition to the default SNMP trap events, Cisco devices can also send syslog messages through SNMP.

There are three main event types:

- SNMP traps

  — Public and private SNMP Traps

  — Syslog SNMP traps

- Syslog messages

- Platform events

All Cisco devices send SNMP traps. Because most Cisco devices support the standard RMON alarm and default event groups, additional localized polling of any management variable can be configured within a device to monitor thresholds and generate SNMP traps as needed.

Cisco routers can send syslog messages through SNMP. This feature enhances SNMP traps' ability to send unsolicited messages by increasing the number of supported events.

Any Cisco device can generate syslog messages. Fortunately, Unix uses a UDP-based logging mechanism that is identical to the Cisco IOS implementation. This allows any Unix host to act as a syslog server (preferably a Unix Management Station). When a syslog management server receives a message, it is given a timestamp, a facility, a severity, and a textual description. Microsoft's family of Windows products can also act as a syslog server with third-party programs, such as Kiwi Syslog Deamon. Kiwi Syslog Deamon has many of the same features as those included with the UNIX operating system.

The SNMP management system generates platform events as a result of remotely polling specific variables and applying thresholds to these variables. Event correlation engines and performance management applications can also trigger SNMP traps to be sent to their corresponding management system.

After an event reaches the management system, the NMS performs the following four activities to filter, classify, and display events before they are added to the logging facility:

- **Event collection**—The basis for a comprehensive event collection engine is to feed it as many events as possible to obtain the maximum amount of filtering and correlation. A high-performance event collection engine is required to accept all events received from both SNMP traps and syslog messages.

- **Event knowledge**—A comprehensive explanation of the event and how it relates to the device's operation must accompany processed and reported events. Event knowledge is a critical component to any event system because it permits the translation of the event into usable information or data for the network administrator. As with event filtering, if the event is not relevant or the event is not understood, it will be ignored.

- **Event filtering**—When there are excessive and/or repetitive events, the NMS can become cluttered and useless to the network operators. This may result in the system being deactivated and the operators relying on their intuition and user complaints, rather than the NMS. Provide an effective means to reduce the number of events reported to network operators by removing repetitive messages (for example, identical messages repeated within a given time period), and eliminate low-priority events (for example, events not deemed as requiring operator notification). The event filters must be set up properly and reviewed periodically to insure their continued effectiveness.

- **Event correlation**—After events are filtered, assess the critical nature of an event as it relates to a device or to other events. For example, an event that alerts you that a router has gone down might be ignored temporarily if you know the router is restarting as a result of a software error. However, if the router does not come back online after five minutes, the NMS should notify the operator immediately.

Figure 7-6 shows the relationship among the four activities performed by the NMS to filter, classify, and display events before they are added to the logging facility.

From left to right, the following steps occur:

1 SNMP passes events to the filter, through which they are passed to the normalization engine.

2 The normalization engine combines the different event types with information from the event knowledge database.

3 The event correlation engine attempts to make intelligent filtering decisions regarding the incoming events.

Figure 7-6   *Relationship Among SNMP-managed Network Components*

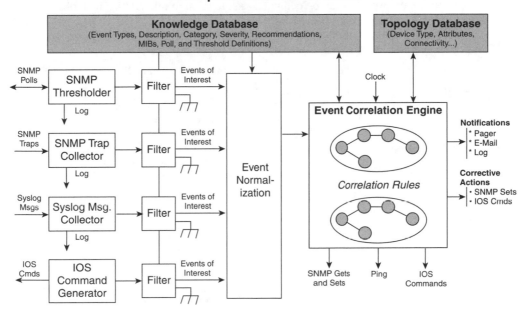

The event correlation engine is composed of several correlation rules that can drop events, pass them straight through, or pass them straight through only if one or more other events occur within a specific time period. Different defined scopes for correlation can limit the number of devices that are tied to a specific rule. These scopes include a single device, a type of device, or all devices, depending on your requirements. Correlation rules can make use of a physical or logical topology map to gain a greater understanding of the network. These maps help accelerate the process of isolating a faulty device. A correlation engine can also actively make additional requests to other systems to gain information for the correlation rule. For example, a rule might require a specific interface to go down before sending an event to the NMS. The correlation engine can poll that interface and, based on the results, trigger or filter an event.

Every event correlation system (ECS) has its own method of mapping Cisco events to its own internal event model. Third-party correlation engines might require custom programming or scripts, depending on their capabilities.

Because most fault management is focused on detecting network faults and performing root cause analysis, this book places less emphasis on automating corrective action.

MIB

SNMP uses a Management Information Base (MIB) concept to identify specific variables on managed agents. An MIB can be defined as a collection of related managed objects residing in a virtual information store. An MIB achieves the following:

- Presents a hierarchically organized collection of information

- Accesses through the use of management protocols such as SNMP and RMON

- References managed objects and object identifiers

Figure 7-7 shows the MIB hierarchy which is depicted as a tree with a nameless root.

Figure 7-7   *MIB Hierarchy*

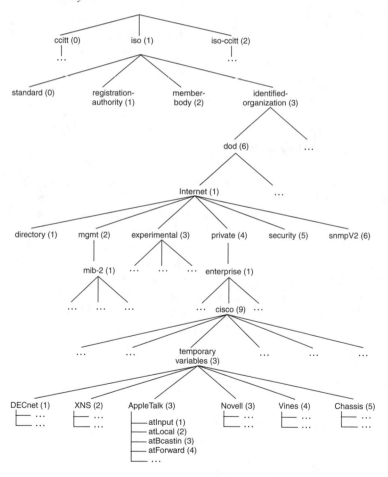

Top-level MIB object IDs belong to different standards organizations while low-level object IDs are allocated by associated organizations. Vendors define private branches that include managed objects for products. Non-standard MIBs are typically found in the experimental branch. This hierarchy allows network management protocols like SNMP or RMON to easily identify and manipulate objects (variables) managed by SNMP agents.

Managed objects or variables are referenced with unique names called Object Identifiers (Object IDs). Object IDs are composed of the numbers or names that make up the MIB tree beginning at the top and proceeding downward to the object's location within the tree. For example, the variable Atinput's Object ID (the total number of AppleTalk packets received by a router) in number format is 1.3.6.1.4.1.9.3.3.1.

With the use of a hierarchy and Object IDs, MIBs allow SNMP to easily request and manipulate variables on network devices.

RMON

The third basic network management protocol is Remote Monitoring (RMON). RMON is designed to remotely monitor traffic patterns on network links. RMON is based on SNMP, has its own SNMP MIB, and uses the same basic manager/agent model. The RMON agent is similar to the SNMP agent in that they both reside on the end device, and they both utilize SNMP to communicate with the manager. Unlike the SNMP agent, the RMON agent has a dedicated data collection and monitoring engine; the RMON agent is also known as a RMON engine. The RMON manager acts as a central point of control for setting collection rules and receiving collected data and notifications from the remote agents. Only two different RMON groups exist:

- RMON, commonly referred to as RMON 1, collects data within OSI Layer 1 and 2 for data-link information, such as frame rates.

- RMON 2 collects data from Layer 3 and above for network and application layer information.

RMON has over 200 managed objects. These objects are divided into more than 20 functional groups. Figure 7-8 shows 20 of the common RMON groups.

Figure 7-8   *20 Common RMON Groups*

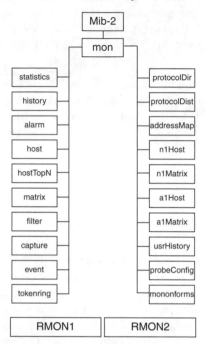

Like SNMP, RMON has both a console and a remote agent. The remote agents can also be called monitors or probes. RMON probes can monitor a network LAN segment or a WAN link and transmit the statistics back to a RMON-compliant console. Remote RMON probes are often standalone devices that devote significant resources to monitoring a network. Figure 7-9 shows the relationship between the RMON probe and the RMON console.

Syslog

The last basic management protocol is syslog. Syslog is used by network devices to send unsolicited messages to a management station. Syslog is similar to SNMP's traps, but unlike SNMP, syslog is only used for event notification. Because of its specialized function, syslog offers a richer set of notification features than SNMP traps provide. For example, syslog permits a network manager to control the notification level based on the type of event. This level can be tuned to provide more or less detail based on requirements. Syslog can also use a gateway on Cisco devices called the syslog MIB which makes receiving all events through SNMP possible. In some situations, this removes the need for a dedicated syslog server but it can also overload the SNMP server with informational events.

Figure 7-9   *RMON Probe/RMON Console Relationship*

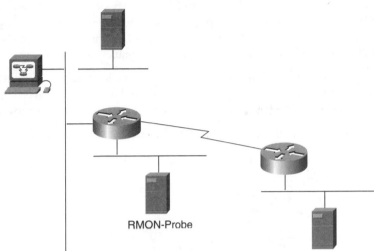

RMON-Probe

Eight Guidelines for Managing a Network

Using the following eight guidelines for good network management practices helps to ensure a successful network management implementation:

- Start with a good design and secure physical location.

- Identify critical ports and leave the rest alone.

- Set up fault monitoring.

- Collect baseline data.

- Define and set thresholds.

- Adjust thresholds.

- Reduce baseline data collection.

- Revisit and gather baseline data regularly.

These guidelines have been developed in conjunction with the FCAPS model. When the two are used together you ensure a strong structure for effective network management.

Starting with a Good Design and Secure Physical Location

The following components make up a good network design and a secure physical location:

- Secure access to wiring closets and data closets. Simply closing the door is no longer enough to protect a corporation's valuable data resources.

- Document the physical network, including the network equipment and the wiring. Network personnel should be able to correlate each device with a corresponding port located on a switch or router. Proper physical documentation of the network permits easy identification of the cable used to connect each device. Accurate documentation is not just a good idea; it greatly eases the maintenance and troubleshooting processes.

- Define and adhere to move/add/change policies in which all network modifications are documented, and planned in advance when possible. Physical maps and inventories should always reflect the latest changes and important notes about the network inventory.

Network documentation should always include a physical network design, as shown in Figure 7-10.

Figure 7-10 *A Basic LAN's Physical Design*

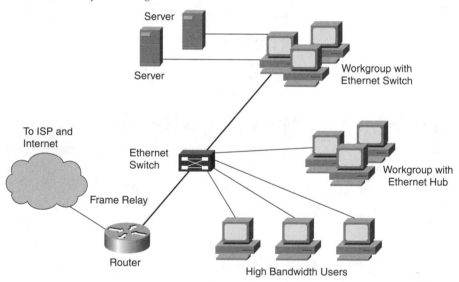

Identifying Critical Ports and Leaving the Rest Alone

Monitoring all the switched ports in the network is not practical. Critical ports, or ports that are critical to the business's operation, need to be identified and monitored. The remaining ports, including most user ports, don't require identification and monitoring. To monitor the status and performance of switch ports, use SNMP- and RMON-based tools. Examples of these tools include CiscoWorks, nGenius Real Time Monitor, Internetwork Performance Monitor, HP Openview, Netscout, Concord, and InfoVista.

After you have identified the critical ports, they should be documented, physically marked, and maintained through all moves/changes. The critical ports list also needs to be updated as new ports are added to the network. If this is not done, network operators might react to port conditions that were once critical but have now lost their importance because of an undocumented change.

Setting Up Fault Monitoring

Fault monitoring consists of availability monitoring, SNMP trap logging and processing, and syslog message logging and processing. Configure network devices for SNMP access, SNMP trap generation, and syslog message generation with timestamps. The following three steps set up fault management on network devices:

Step 1   Availability Monitoring

Step 2   Setting up SNMP traps

Step 3   Setting up syslog

Collecting Baseline Data

Establishing a baseline is key to capacity planning within the network. Capacity planning, as its name implies, is the ability to plan for network growth before the network is affected by too many requests for services. Capacity planning is a proactive approach to network improvement instead of a reactive approach where additional bandwidth is added only after the traffic outpaces the network's ability to meet the demand. Capacity planning is accomplished with a thorough understanding of the network baseline, which contains a picture of the traffic flows through the network, and by comparing this baseline to the network performance that has been monitored over a specific time period. The network demand can then be predicted and capacity can be adjusted prior to the demand surpassing the supply. A couple common capacity planning tools are NetScout's nGenius Capacity Planner, and Concord Communications' eHealth Suite.

In addition to capacity planning, a baseline is also essential to establish performance management thresholds. In a performance management system, thresholds are established and events notifications arc sent to the NMS when the threshold is violated. Baselining is a reoccurring process that needs to be performed at least once a quarter. This will maintain an accurate picture of network performance and traffic flows through the network.

Prior to establishing a baseline, you must first determine what systems and information you need to monitor. Some examples include the following:

- CPU utilization

- Buffer utilization

- Memory consumption

- Interface utilization

- Error rate, particularly cyclic redundancy check (CRC) errors

- Multicast traffic

- Broadcast traffic

After you establish a baseline, it becomes part of the process as you proceed with the fifth guideline, defining and setting thresholds.

Defining and Setting Thresholds

Thresholds are primarily utilized with the RMON management protocol. The RMON alarm and event groups allow thresholds to be established and utilized by the RMON agent (residing on a probe, router, or switch) to send an SNMP trap to an NMS when one of the thresholds is violated.

To generate useful alarms, reasonable thresholds need to be defined. While this might sound easy, the process is not always straightforward. If the system permits, define two thresholds. The first should alert operations personnel when conditions are problematic and the second threshold should alert them when conditions return to normal. Figure 7-11 shows how the SNMP traps generated by Cisco switches and routers provide useful information on potentially harmful environmental conditions, processor status, and port status.

Figure 7-11 *SNMP Trap Information Generated by Cisco Switches and Routers—*
Rising and Falling Threshold Over Time

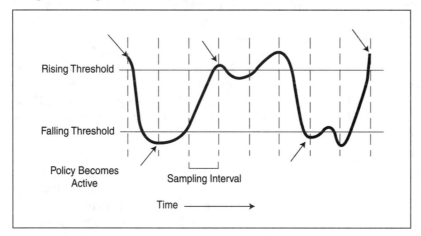

Adjusting Thresholds

Monitor and collect performance data for several weeks after the thresholds are created. By analyzing this data and the alarm rate, the thresholds' effectiveness can be determined and adjusted accordingly. Threshold adjustment is a constant process as the network grows and changes. Thresholds should be examined to determine their effectiveness at least once every three months

Reducing Baseline Data Collection

After baselines are established, data collection from the network device is no longer needed. Instead of actively polling the device for network statistics, the device now generates alarms if a defined threshold is violated. Simple ICMP echo (pings) and SNMP polling are still needed because if a device fails it is not able to advertise its own failure. In general, you can disable RMON history collection when the baselining phase is completed. This setup reduces CPU and memory consumption on the switch or router. Although history collection can be disabled, you should continue monitoring the critical switch ports.

Revisiting and Gathering Baseline Data Regularly

Because networks change in size and complexity, you must poll network device on a regular basis to maintain the baseline measures. In addition to fault detection, baseline data can also be used to study network growth over time and gauge the switched network's performance. Capacity planning comes into play when the network device is actively polled for network statistics. Because performance management and, specifically, capacity planning require continual polling of RMON statistics, RMON history collection might need to be continued after the baselining is complete. In certain environments it is best to establish a rotating period of RMON history collection while other at other times it is best that RMON be disabled.

Third-Party Network Management Tools

This section discusses Cisco and third-party network management solutions. The primary distinction of third-party network management from Cisco's solutions is their vast flexibility in terms of device support. Third-party tools can manage many different device types and diverse systems by default; for more detailed management these tools often support plug-ins. This capability often makes third-party tools very flexible. As you will see in the next section, while third-party tools are flexible, Cisco's network management tools have robust support in terms of fault management, configuration management, and so on for Cisco devices. Because of these specialized features, Cisco's tools are compatible only with Cisco devices; third-party networking gear is not supported.

Many third-party network management tools on the market today are capable of acting as solid platforms for network management. Of these tools, three comprise the majority of Network Management Systems in use today:

- Hewlett Packard's Openview

- IBM's Tivoli/Netview

- Computer Associate's Unicenter TNG

Although these Network Management Systems come from different vendors, they basically provide the same primary services:

- Heterogeneous SNMP polling and trap management

- Topology mapping

- Inventory and asset tracking

- Fault and event correlation

Hewlett Packard's Openview

Hewlett Packard's Openview provides in-depth management of wide-ranging network resources and applications. The various modules that make up Openview provide administrators with the tools necessary to maintain an efficient network that contributes to their long-term business success. Openview provides the following:

- An application service view that shows the logical relationship between the application and the underlying infrastructure that supports it

- Industry-leading application response time measurement that monitors true end-user experience

- Complete management of Service Level Agreements (SLAs), including reports that accurately portray service performance

- Application-specific, out-of-the-box management extensions for leading Enterprise Resource Planning (ERP), messaging, and database applications

- Integrated SNMP management of various network devices, including Cisco switches and routers

- Device discovery and automated topology mapping capabilities

IBM's Tivoli/Netview

NetView meets the needs of large-scale network managers by providing scalability and flexibility to manage mission-critical environments. NetView discovers TCP/IP networks, displays network topologies, correlates and manages events and SNMP traps, monitors network health, and gathers performance data.

NetView accomplishes this by doing the following:

- Providing a scalable distributed management solution

- Quickly identifying the root cause of network failures

- Building collections to manage critical business systems

- Integrating with leading vendors, such as Cisco

- Maintaining device inventory for asset management

- Measuring availability and providing fault isolation for problem control and management

- Reporting on network trends and analysis

Computer Associate's Unicenter TNG

Unicenter TNG provides a single point of control for administering virtually every hardware, software, and non-IT critical resource regardless of vendor. TNG's end-to-end management capabilities optimize system availability, improve overall performance, and even predict when system outages might occur. Unicenter TNG includes the following features:

- Breadth and depth of covered platforms, software, and applications
- Totally integrated open architecture
- Virtually unlimited scalability
- Intelligent capability through Neugents
- Graphic user interface

Cisco Network Management Solutions

Cisco is actively involved in developing network management solutions for Internet architectures. This involvement began with a few network management tools and has grown into a full suite of products that are designed to efficiently manage network devices and Internet architecture. The following section discusses Cisco's network management solutions and their place in the five functional areas of network management as outlined by the FCAPS model.

The following list outlines Cisco's current network management solutions:

- CiscoWorks 2000 Bundles
  - LAN Management Solution (LMS)
  - Routed WAN Management Solution (RWAN)

    IPM

    ACL Manager
  - Service Level Management Solution (SMS)

    Service Level Manager

    Service Collection Managers
  - VPN/Security Management Solution (VMS)

    CSPM
- QoS Policy Manager (QPM)
- Cisco Network Registrar (CNR)
- Cisco Secure User Registration Tool (URT)
- Cisco Secure Access Control Server (ACS)

Figure 7-12 shows the product bundles and the individual applications that are part of the Cisco network management solutions.

Figure 7-12 *Cisco Network Management Solution Product Bundles/Applications*

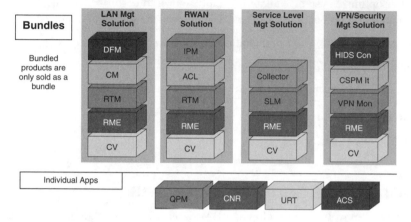

CiscoWorks 2000 Bundles

Cisco's current CiscoWorks version, CiscoWorks 2000, is not an individual product but a set of solutions referred to as bundles. There are currently four of these bundles including LMS, RWAN, SMS, and the VMS. Each bundle is composed of multiple network management tools. For example, LMS is a collection of tools such as Resource Manager Essentials (RME), CiscoView, Campus Manager (CM), nGenius Real Time Monitor (RTM), and Device Fault Monitor (DFM). The LMS bundle has many of the same components found in other bundles, such as those in the RWAN bundle, for example. The components that are shared between the bundles are in addition to unique components that are only available as part of the individual bundles. For example, the Internetwork Performance Monitor (IPM) and ACL Manager tools can only be purchased from Cisco as part of the RWAN bundle.

All of the tools within CiscoWorks 2000 are accessible through a web interface except Cisco Secure Policy Manager (CSPM). Because these applications are browser-accessible, administrators have the freedom to access network tools from anywhere within the network. CiscoWorks 2000's use of web-enabled tools has vastly simplified the network management task.

LAN Management Solution (LMS)

CiscoWorks 2000 LMS is designed for networks that are primarily based on a LAN environment. LMS, like the other three bundles, is composed of several components. The components within LMS are designed to provide all the tools necessary for a network administrator to easily monitor and manage a Cisco LAN infrastructure. LMS includes the following components:

- Resource Manager Essentials (RME)
- CiscoView
- Campus Manager (CM)
- nGenius Real Time Monitor (RTM)
- Device Fault Monitor (DFM)

LAN Management Solution's first component, RME is the core to CiscoWorks LMS because of its inventory management capability. In addition to LMS having many components, there are several subcomponent tools within RME including:

- Inventory Manager
- Device Configuration Manager
- Software Image Manager
- Change Audit Service
- Availability Manager
- Syslog Analyzer

With these tools, RME is capable of performing two of network management's functions: fault management and performance management. Fault management is performed with the Availability Monitor and Syslog Analyzer subcomponents. Availability Manager's "reachability dashboard" quickly determines the operational status of critical routers and switches. From the Availability Monitor, you can drill down on a particular device to view historical details about its response time, availability, reloads, protocols, and interface status.

Syslog Analyzer gathers and analyzes syslog messages from Cisco devices. It can generate reports that are based on user-defined filters that highlight specific errors or severity conditions and help identify when specific events, such as a link-down or device reboot, occurred.

Four of the preceding tools make RME one of the most capable configuration management tools available for Cisco devices. The first tool is Inventory Manager. This tool builds an up-to-date inventory database that houses device information such as hardware model, software version, amount of DRAM, and so on. The second tool, Device Configuration Manager, archives and analyzes device configurations. One Device Configuration Management tool feature is its ability to archive the device's configuration on a regular basis. This capability is especially valuable if a network device fails. Normally, without access to a failed device, the configuration is lost. Device Configuration Manager can pull the failed device's configuration from the central database and apply it to the replacement hardware.

Another tool closely related to Device Configuration Manager is Change Audit. Change Audit maintains a central database of network changes in terms of the time applied, the actual modification to the configuration, what user modified the configuration, and how the user accessed the device (CLI or CiscoWorks). This tool is useful to a network manager when multiple administrators are changing device configurations on a regular basis.

The last tool within RME is Software Inventory Manager. Like the configuration tools just mentioned, Software Inventory Manager is a configuration management tool. It greatly simplifies the version management and routine deployment of software updates to Cisco routers and switches through wizard-assisted planning, scheduling, downloading, and monitoring software updates. To secure this process to prevent unauthorized upgrades, scheduled jobs can be controlled through a signoff process which allows a manager to authorize a technician's activities before initiating the upgrade.

The next component in the LMS bundle, CiscoView is one of the oldest and most popular tools in the CiscoWorks family. CiscoView displays a physical view of a device chassis, color-coding modules and ports for at-a-glance status. Monitoring capabilities display performance and other statistics. Configuration capabilities allow comprehensive changes to Cisco switches which include general device configuration and interface configuration. For Cisco routers, CiscoView has the ability to monitor but configuration capabilities are limited to the individual interfaces.

The third component is Campus Manager (CM). For those of you familiar with the old CiscoWorks for Switched Internetworks (CWSI), Campus Manager is its replacement. Campus Manager is a graphical tool that is composed of three network management tools. The Topology Services tool creates a variety of topological maps and tabular summaries of network devices. Within the topological maps, right-clicking on individual network devices can launch other network management tools such as CiscoView and RME. Topology Services can also define and maintain VLANs and VTP domains in a campus network.

User Tracking is an accounting management tool that scans for end-user hosts on the network and records their IP address, MAC address, switch port, user name, and so on. After this data has been gathered it is presented in a tabular format that can be sorted and queried which allows network administrators to easily find users on the network.

The third tool in Campus Manager is Path Analysis. Path Analysis is a fault management tool similar to the Cisco CLI utility "traceroute." Path Analysis diagrams the data's path through the network in terms of Layer 2 and Layer 3 hops. This tool allows network administrators to easily troubleshoot connectivity issues on a network.

CiscoWorks 2000 LMS's fourth component is nGenius Real Time Monitor (RTM). This application is the performance management tool within the LMS bundle. RTM utilizes RMON agents including probes, switches, and routers, to gather network throughput statistics. These statistics are graphed so network administrators have a visual reference for their network's performance. With probes, higher-level data, such as application flows, can be analyzed to determine the demand on individual services on the network. RTM can store statistics for 30 days which, in most cases, is sufficient. When long-term statistics are needed to accurately gauge performance, a third-party capacity planning solution is required such as those available from Netscout, Concord, and InfoVista.

The final component in the LMS bundle is Device Fault Monitor (DFM). DFM is a real-time fault analysis and reporting tool for Cisco devices. Cisco devices are polled with ICMP pings, and monitored by SNMP trap reception and MIB interrogation. MIB interrogation refers to querying the SNMP variables on a network device. DFM has all the important fault management usability features including the following:

- Alarm collection and forwarding
- Automated trouble ticket generation
- Assignment of event priority levels
- Status polling
- Event configuration
- Root cause analysis
- Event correlation
- Event notification
- Event filtering
- Network and system status

Routed WAN Management (RWAN) Solution

RWAN is designed specifically for WAN Networks. Although RWAN was developed for a WAN environment, RWAN and LMS share three common components: RME, CiscoView, and nGenius. In addition to these, RWAN has two unique components: Internetwork Performance Monitor (IPM), and ACL Manager.

IPM is a performance management tool that allows network administrators to monitor network response time and resource availability. IPM does this with the Service Assurance Agent (SA Agent or SAA). The SA Agent (formerly called the RTR Agent) is a network management tool that resides within Cisco IOS software in a Cisco router. The SA Agent generates "synthetic traffic" which is measured in terms of response time and success rate (availability), and reported to the IPM system. Synthetic traffic is "synthetic" because the router itself generates the traffic rather than a network user. To get the most accurate response time measure, synthetic traffic is designed to closely resemble user traffic.

The SA Agent can generate traffic from common protocols such as HTTP, FTP, SNMP, DHCP, ICMP (Echo), DLSw, and so on. In addition to monitoring network response time and success rate, these protocols can also monitor network services such as web pages, FTP sites, and others. This ability to monitor network services is becoming more critical as additional services are added to the network. To monitor advanced network services such as SAP, SMTP, IP/TV, LDAP, and so on, Cisco has developed specific scripts. These scripts emulate client transactions, gathering more application-level performance information.

The artificial traffic that the SA Agent generates can be directed at any node on the network including workstations. In addition to response time and success rate, the SA Agent can calculate the following measures:

- Latency
- Jitter (for UDP jitter operation type only)
- Availability
- Errors
- Packet loss

Figure 7-13 depicts how the Cisco router, acting as an IPM source device, measures network performance to a target device across the network.

Figure 7-13 *Cisco Router as IPM Source Device*

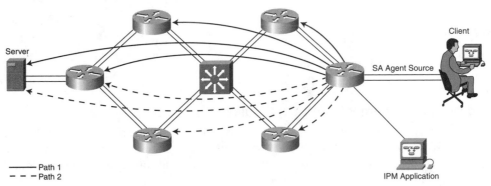

After the agent calculates these metrics, they are reported to the IPM system where they are graphed.

IPM is an excellent tool to monitor how your network is performing as a whole. It is also useful as a fault management tool when you receive reports of slow response time. In addition to plotting statistics on graphs, IPM can configure the SA Agent to proactively send SNMP trap alerts when a defined threshold is violated.

The second unique component to RWAN is ACL Manager. This tool manages network access lists on Cisco devices. ACL Manager allows network administrators to develop and distribute access lists from a central location. It also allows access lists to be defined in templates. Using these templates, common network access lists can be implemented on network devices with the click of a button. ACL Manager also has the ACL optimization utility, ACL Optimizer. ACL

Optimizer allows you to input your current rule set and it will go through the rules and calculate the most efficient access lists. The optimization utility can be very beneficial as you implement access lists in your network.

Service Management Solution (SMS)

SMS is a performance management solution designed to monitor and manage enterprise and service provider SLAs. SMS defines and monitors SLAs specifying traffic type, endpoints, and thresholds against key parameters such as latency, packet loss, and jitter. SMS sets real-time traps allowing administrators to quickly detect and correct possible service degradation. SMS has two core components: Service Level Manager (SLM) and SLM Collection Manager(s). Like LMS and RWAN, SMS also contains CiscoView.

Service Level Manager is the management and monitoring brains of SMS. SLM includes applications for creating, managing, and reporting on SLAs and system management functions. SLM Collection Managers are distributed software agents that provide job management and collect and aggregate service level data. To collect service level data, SMS utilizes SA Agents also used by Internetwork Performance Monitor (IPM).

VPN/Security Management Solution (VMS)

VMS is the security management bundle within the CiscoWorks 2000 family. VMS manages Cisco security devices including VPN routers and concentrators, PIX Firewalls, and Cisco's Network and Host IDS systems. All of these devices are managed through VMS's three unique components: VPN Monitor, Cisco Secure Policy Manager (CSPM), and Cisco IDS Host Console. VMS also utilizes CiscoView and RME to deliver configuration management services to security-centric devices.

VMS's VPN Monitor collects, stores, and reports on IPsec-based, site-to-site, and remote access VPNs. Devices can be graphically monitored from a web browser which displays the status of their IPsec VPN implementations. In addition, VPN Monitor provides drill down and graphing capabilities for problem analysis.

VMS's Cisco Secure Policy Manager (CSPM) is capable of monitoring and managing Cisco firewalls, IP security (IPSec) virtual private network (VPN) routers, and network-based Intrusion Detection System (IDS) sensors. CSPM's simple GUI allows administrators to visually define high-level security policies for multiple Cisco firewalls and VPN routers. These policies can be distributed throughout the network from a central location, completely eliminating the costly and time-consuming practice of manual implementation. CSPM also provides basic system auditing functions, including real-time alarm notification and a web-based reporting system. CSPM can also configure and monitor intrusion detection sensors, including IDS appliances and Cisco Catalyst 6000 line cards.

The Cisco IDS Host Console allows network managers to monitor and manage remote host IDS sensors from a central location. In addition to managing individual host policies, the IDS

Console can change policies by group thus simplifying policy implementation and allowing uniform policy configuration across host sensors. The host console can also monitor real-time security alerts and provide additional event analysis information for network administrators.

QoS Policy Manager (QPM)

QPM is a standalone configuration management product. QPM, the centralized management entity for intelligent network-wide QoS, simplifies the deployment of intelligent network services in an Internet architecture. Even with advanced, intelligent network devices, manually deploying QoS policies on a network-wide basis can be an error-prone, time-consuming process. QPM automates the steps associated with policy definition, validation, configuration, and deployment. Using the QPM GUI, you can quickly and reliably deploy QoS policies without requiring a detailed understanding of QoS mechanisms.

Cisco Network Registrar (CNR)

Cisco Network Registrar (CNR) is a full-featured DNS/DHCP system that provides scalable naming and addressing services for enterprise and service provider networks.

Access Control Server (ACS)

ACS is Cisco's primary accounting management solution. ACS offers centralized command and control for all user authentication, authorization, and accounting from a web-based, graphical interface. After controls have been created, ACS distributes those controls to hundreds or thousands of access gateways in your network. In addition, ACS acts as a centralized Remote Access Dial-In User Service (RADIUS) or TACACS+ server system. This allows you to control the authentication, authorization, and accounting (AAA) of users accessing corporate resources through the network. Using the AAA, ACS acts as both an accounting management solution and a security management solution.

Summary

Network management, as described in this chapter, is the methodology by which switches, routers, hubs, and other communications equipment that make up a network infrastructure are managed. This methodology includes the hardware, software, processes, and people that manage the network. Network management is divided into five functional areas known as the FCAPS Model. This model incorporates the following:

Fault management
Configuration management
Accounting management
Performance management
Security management

Cisco, as well as other third-party companies, offers several network management solutions that assist in the management of your network. The solutions include HP Openview, CiscoWorks 2000 LMS, CiscoWorks 2000 RWAN, and others. These systems use four common network management protocols that facilitate communication from the managed devices to the managing system. These protocols include Telnet, syslog, RMON, and, most importantly, SNMP. By using proper network management techniques, you can maximize the efficiency of your network and contribute to the overall success of your company.

Review Questions

1 What are the five functional areas of network management?

A. Application Management

B. Configuration Management

C. Security Management

D. Performance Management

E. Fault Management

F. Accounting Management

G. Protocol Management

2 What are the five steps in fault management?

A. Problem Bypass and Recovery

B. Problem Determination

C. Problem Analysis

D. Problem Diagnosis

E. Problem Resolution

F. Problem Isolation

G. Problem Tracking and Control

3 What are configuration management's three core components?

A. Configuration Records

B. Configuration Management

C. Configuration Process

D. Configuration Result

E. Configuration Analysis

F. Configuration Description

4 List at least three common characteristics of fault management.

_____

_____

_____

5 Which of the following are NOT management protocols?

A. Telnet

B. RMON

C. NTP

D. Syslog

E. SNMP

F. FTP

G. CLI

6 What are the four basic protocol operations in SNMP Version 1?

A. Set

B. Test

C. GetNext

D. Trap

E. Confirm

F. Commit

G. Get

7 Which of the following is a correct SNMP MIB Object Identifier?

A. 1.3.6.1.4.1.9.3.12.1

B. 1.3.6.1.4.1.9.X.3.1

C. 13.6.1.4.1.9.3.3.1

D. A.3.6.1.4.1.9.3.3.1

E. 1.3.6.1.4.1.9.3.3.1-2

F. 1.3.6.1.4.1.9.3.3.1

G. 100.1.3.6

8 List the eight guidelines for managing a network.

_____

_____

_____

9 List three common third-party network management systems.

_____

_____

_____

10 Which of the following is NOT a Cisco network management solution?

A. Ciscoworks 2000 LMS

B. URT

C. VMS

D. Ciscoworks 2000 RWAN

E. Cisco TFTP

F. QoS Policy Manager

G. CNR

After reading this chapter, you should be able to perform the following tasks:

- Understand the Service Level Management Chain.

- Define Business Synchronization.

- Define Service Level Definitions.

- Define SLA and SLM.

- Define SLAs and explain what they define for the customer and for the service provider.

- Define the two types of SLAs.

- Describe the need for an SLA to specify characteristics.

- List and define the common core requirements and metrics for generic network infrastructure.

- Explain how SLA metrics interface with business metrics.

- Discuss the overall meaning and elements of SLM, its relationship to different vendors and third-party initiatives, and how critical Cisco's SLM solution has become to e-business.

- Describe Service Assurance Agent.

- Understand what QOS Policy Manager and Internetwork Performance Monitor give an organization.

CHAPTER 8

Service Level Agreements

Chapter 1, "Internet System Architecture Overview," discussed the Internet business solutions that organizations implement to help lower overall costs and increase productivity. Because many of these solutions are business-critical, customers request that there be levels of assurance to guarantee uptime which, in turn, assures the continuance of revenue, savings, or a continued convenience to their user population.

Documents that guarantee solution availability are called Service Level Agreements (SLAs). As Internet-enabled applications become more common in implementing business processes, delivery of guaranteed service, either by a service provider or IT department, becomes crucial to a company's operation and survival. In many cases, a company requires an SLA before it will implement an application or an infrastructure where it is ultimately not responsible for the service uptime.

This chapter covers what SLAs are and what they include—service level definitions. The chapter explains the different SLAs and details a sample SLA. The chapter also discusses ways to manage the SLAs that have been put in place to measure the service being delivered to the end customer.

Service Level Management Chain

SLAs specify services that are required for a business process to be effective and to meet goals and contracts set with the business's external constituents (customers, suppliers, business partners, and employees).

For example, business applications must meet functional and integration requirements and applications must be available and must meet expectations. To meet these information technology (IT) service goals, IT organizations look to internal and external suppliers. To have confidence in meeting SLAs, the IT organization breaks down service requirements into its components and measures those components.

For internal suppliers, these components are called *service level objectives*. These objectives are often used to measure the effectiveness of an IT process and its people. For external suppliers, contracts are put in place with set expectations on supplier performance. Service level objectives and contracts are set within the organization in hopes of meeting the business's needs.

Figure 8-1 shows the Service Level Management Chain.

Figure 8-1   *Service Level Management Chain Figure*

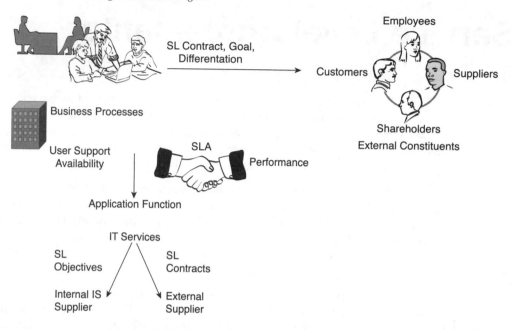

Business Synchronization

To achieve synchronization, the business provides competitive products and services to its customers. To keep promises made to customers and build customer satisfaction, each department within the enterprise must work in sync with each other.

For example, a company that promises a product shipment within 24 hours of a customer order must have its forecasting, order processing, purchasing, materials planning, manufacturing, shipping, and invoicing departments synchronized to meet that promise. These business processes are enabled by the IS organization, which must provide the quality of service (QoS) required to meet the overall business objective. The business unit and IT organization use SLAs to define QoS goals. SLAs help to direct each department, vendor, or employee contribution to the business goals.

Figure 8-2 introduces the concept of business synchronization.

Figure 8-2   *Business Synchronization Figure*

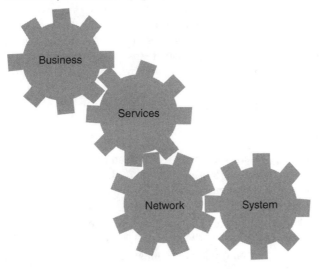

Figure 8-3 shows a graph of SLA expectations.

Figure 8-3   *Setting Expectations Figure*

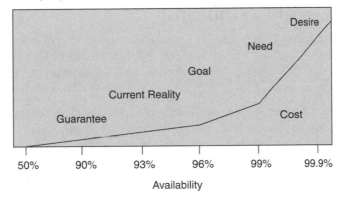

Setting Expectations

End users' service levels reflect the interworking of components, services, and management domains. The end result reflects the infrastructure's ability to deliver service and depends on the business's application requirements, the application's design, and the other services being delivered by shared resources. Wishful thinking by either those delivering or those consuming the service will not guarantee availability levels.

IT organizations should consider certain points of availability when discussing service levels with business managers. Business managers' desires are frequently padded with uncertainty and a delivery margin. You can improve service level goals through targeted process improvements and investments; however, guarantees to business managers should be set slightly below what can be delivered. This approach helps synchronization by forcing businesses to understand their needs more carefully and by using business justification to fund improvements in what IT can deliver.

Measuring the User's View

Fewer than five percent of large enterprises today measure end-to-end application availability. This will change as businesses pressure IS organizations for higher availability levels to meet business objectives. Reporting will continue to be largely a manual process supported with automated tools to collect outage data, users affected, and location affected. Reporting remains a manual effort primarily because of impact analysis. Just because an application is down does not mean that the business process is totally down nor does it mean that users cannot perform other tasks. This measure of impact on productivity must come from the user base and should be a measure of downtime's real impact. In web-based applications, this would identify users logged on at the time of outage and potential revenues lost.

What is a Service Level Definition?

Service level definitions provide goals for all IT personnel and can be used as a metric in the overall service quality. You can also use service level definitions as a tool for prioritizing IT projects and budgets, aligning IT initiatives with business goals. They also provide a way to evaluate vendor and carrier performance.

Without a service level definition and measurement, the organization does not have clear goals. Users can govern Service satisfaction with little differentiation between applications, server/client operations, and network support. Budgeting can be more difficult because the end result is not clear to the organization. The network organization tends to be more reactive in nature in improving the network and support model. The service level definition solution, a must for today and beyond, has a clear vision of the service level outcomes in mind, who is affected by those outcomes, and why the service level definition is there. This way all those in the organization know the potential results of all scenarios and the service's importance.

Cisco recommends the following steps to building and support a service level model:

1 Analyze technical goals and constraints.

2 Determine the availability budget.

3 Create application profiles detailing critical applications' network characteristics.

4 Define availability and performance standards and common terms.

5 Create a service level definition that includes availability, performance, service response time, mean time to resolve problems, fault detection, upgrade thresholds, and escalation path.

6 Collect metrics and monitor the service level definition.

Creating and Maintaining SLAs

Service level definitions are an excellent building block because they help create a consistent level of service throughout the organization and improve availability. The next step is SLAs which align business objectives and cost requirements directly to service quality. Recall that SLAs are the contractual agreement to guarantee service quality. The well-constructed SLA serves as a model for efficiency, quality, and synergy between the user community and support group by maintaining clear processes and procedures for network issues or problems. SLAs are made up of service level objectives, some of which follow:

- Define the service to be provided.

- Negotiate achievable performance objectives that satisfy the user.

- Develop appropriate means to measure performance.

- Implement a reporting system that shows if objectives are being achieved.

- Plan improvements to the service.

When a customer implements an SLA, they receive the following benefits:

- SLAs establish two-way accountability for service meaning that users and application groups are both accountable for the network service. If users don't help create an SLA for a specific service and communicate business impact to the network group then they could actually be accountable for the problem.

- SLAs help determine standard tools and resources needed to meet business requirements. Deciding how many people and which tools to use without SLAs is often a budgetary guess. The service can be overengineered which leads to overspending or under-engineered which leads to unmet business objectives. Tuning SLAs helps achieve a balanced optimal level.

- The documented SLA creates a clearer vehicle for setting service level expectations.

After creating your service level definitions and your SLA, take the following recommended steps:

Step 1 Evaluate the prerequisites for SLAs.

Step 2 Determine the parties involved in the SLA.

Step 3 Determine the service elements.

Step 4 Understand customer business needs and goals.

Step 5   Define the SLA required for each group.

Step 6   Choose the SLA's format.

Step 7   Develop SLA workgroups.

Step 8   Hold workgroup meetings and draft SLAs.

Step 9   Negotiate the SLA.

Step 10   Measure and monitor SLA conformance.

Internal and External SLAs

SLAs impact many different parts of an enterprise. Just as measuring the performance of the quality and effectiveness of WAN links and applications provided by outside companies is important, it is equally as important to have a mechanism by which to measure how effectively your internal systems and departments are performing. You must differentiate between internal and external SLAs. Internal and external SLAs both have predefined parameters and thresholds that the service provider has agreed to adhere to. The general format is often the same.

- **Internal SLA**—An agreement between individual workgroups within the same organization. These workgroups rely on each other to succeed in their individual tasks. These SLAs focus mostly on individual processes.

- **External SLA**—An agreement between two different organizations that work in a service provider-to-customer relationship.

The difference between internal and external SLAs is very important because they measure fundamentally different things. External SLAs provide verification of Service Level Contracts (SLCs) that have been agreed upon with outside service providers. For example, a commitment by a service provider to provide a certain amount of bandwidth to an enterprise for a certain price is an external SLA. If the link is congested and the service provider is unable to fulfill the contract, a provision usually exists for a financial rebate to the enterprise. This creates an incentive to the service provider to prove that it is in compliance, and is also an incentive for the enterprise to verify when there is a violation.

Internal SLAs demonstrate the following differences in comparison to their external counterparts:

- Internal SLAs are defined as "service level objectives," while external SLAs are written contracts.

- Internal SLAs are not legally binding contracts.

- Internal SLAs foster greater alignment toward business goals.

- Internal SLAs are more difficult to enforce.

Sample External Service Level Agreement

Most major service providers offer a wide range of SLAs to their customers. These tend to be network-oriented guarantees such as network availability, round-trip packet latency, and maximum packet loss. The following list shows parameters from a large service provider's actual external SLA.

- Guarantees connections to the user's premises, where dedicated connections are used, at 99.999 percent.

- Other customers are guaranteed 99.9 percent uptime.

- Network outages of up to an hour result in three days' credit and over an hour credits one extra day for each additional hour.

- Customers must request a billing adjustment if their network is down but need not open a trouble ticket when the network is down because the network is continually monitored. If an outage occurs, the service provider proactively notifies them.

- Maximum average latency on the backbone is given as 70 ms round-trip, with 10 percent of the monthly bill credited if this is exceeded.

- The backbone is used at 65 percent capacity.

- SLAs are automatically offered to new customers, but existing customers must request them.

- A 99.9–100 percent uptime end-to-end guarantee is available to VPN customers, with an average round-trip delay of 75 ms.

- This large ISP offers a 100 percent firewall availability guarantee for its VPN services.

- Two levels of service are offered. The first gives a 25 percent rebate if a security problem occurs and notifies the customer within two hours. The second gives a 50 percent rebate and notifies the customer within 30 minutes.

- This large ISP offers access to reports as a service to its Frame Relay customers. Frame Relay Performance Manager allows customers to choose from a number of products to monitor their network performance. This allows customers to access performance reports and other management statistics from a platform maintained by the ISP using a web-based browser.

SLAs allow service providers to identify and define premium services to their customers. Providing added value to the customer can increase the service provider's revenue stream. Service providers add value by delivering extra services such as Enterprise VPN, Managed CDN, and transparent wireless access to enterprise applications, to name a few. Another real-world example of a premium service is a WAN carrier monitoring network utilization for their customers as part of the SLA's network performance characteristics. Using the collected data, the provider can offer capacity planning to the customer by using chart technical analysis of the information to look for trends. This can be classified as a premium service.

Figure 8-4 shows where in a network SLAs can apply.

Figure 8-4   *LA Application in a Network*

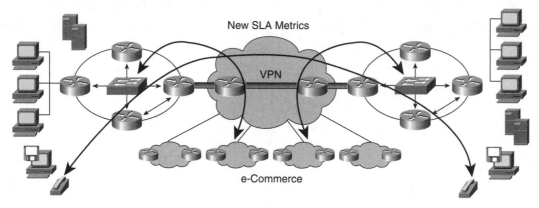

Common Core Requirements and Metrics of an SLA

Providers often have varying SLA definitions for the same service depending on each customer's requirements. Because SLA contract details vary, a better way to organize, or chunk, the categories those details fall into is needed. Core parameters for generic network infrastructure SLAs are listed in the sections that follow.

Administrative Requirements

The following are administrative requirements for network infrastructure SLAs:

- Describe the service.
- Identify the customer target group.
- List conditions for use (operational times and maintenance windows).

Technical Dependencies

Technical dependencies are details of customer-provided infrastructure such as system hardware, applications, and operating systems. They also include anything that might impact the service levels that are outside the service provider's control.

Functional Dependencies

The service function must be described in a manner that is easily understood by the customer. A definition of the target group and conditions for using the service should also be included.

Network Availability Metrics

Conditions of network availability metrics follow:

- Identify the maximum time that the system is unavailable to the customer because of faults.

- Faults are determined by the maximum downtime during the month as a percentage of total possible availability and the maximum downtime in a single outage.

- Identify under what conditions the system is deemed unavailable.

Network Performance Metrics

Conditions of network performance metrics follow:

- Identify maximum network response time.

- Identify QoS parameters.

- Identify network performance exception criteria; for example, the number of times a user can exceed a Frame Relay committed information rate (CIR) in any given time period.

Operation Level Metrics

Conditions of operation service level metrics follow:

- Response time to customer calls

- Time limits to commence escalation procedures

- Mean time to fault identification

- Mean time to repair

Cost

Cost conditions include the following:

- Cost summary for each identified level of service offered by the provider

- Details of penalties incurred by provider for SLA default

Design Integration

Many enterprises realize the importance of choosing a single vendor for an infrastructure, as shown in Figure 8-4, for integration, scalability, support, and overall cost reasons. However, networks sometimes end up with components from different vendors.

The next couple of sections discuss Service Level Management when there are multiple third-party vendors and how SLM solutions can work to support an enterprise.

SLM Integration

Delivering SLAs requires SLM when a given service has several components. Although different vendors have different definitions and capabilities for managing service levels, only one definition and capability is meaningful to customers: end-to-end management of all aspects that relate to the service or application's connectivity, performance, and availability.

Third-Party Integration Initiatives

In the era of e-business, no single vendor can measure all components from all layers of the communication and application stack that are relevant to SLM. SLM solutions must lend themselves to easy integration with third-party vendor and enterprise service management applications and capabilities. Table 8-1 lists some typical vendor SLM products.

Table 8-1 *Typical Vendor SLM Products*

Service Type	Vendor/Product
Network and system service level and performance reporting tools	InfoVista, Concord, Cisco Internet Performance Monitor, Net IQ- Webtrends
End-to-end SLM	Cisco Service Level Manager
QoS management services	Cisco QOS Policy Manager
Correlation and event SLM	Micromuse/Netcool/Cisco InfoCenter, HP OpenView

Cisco Service Management Tools

Tools are available to complete, along with technology, the SLA requirements and parameters that were set forth earlier in this chapter. These tools empower an organization by putting some control in its hands to achieve the availability numbers it has predefined. The next few sections discuss the features of quality SLA management tools as well as specific products that assist in the deployment and operation of continuous service.

Many SLM tools accomplish the same task. To simplify the process of selecting the product that is best for you, the following list distills a set of organizing principles of quality tools that will allow you to choose the appropriate tool. This list can be a reference for you for the future.

Qualities of Outstanding Service Management Tools:

- Ease of use

- Ability to measure key network and system components

- Configurable elements that meet the unique business requirements of the environment in which they operate

- Ability to correlate and present information in an understandable and meaningful way

- Provide root cause analysis to help operations staff find and resolve a problem that is causing a decline in service performance

- Ability to define constraints and thresholds that allow operations staff to see areas of the system that are failing service level criteria

- Reporting capabilities

- Periodic reports and analyses for both technical and executive review

- A relational database to review historical information in the event of contract disputes

Cisco Service Management Solution

Cisco continues working toward its vision of total service management: an end-to-end solution for evaluating and rating end-user services using multiple diverse data sources and open, standards-based interfaces. Cisco realizes this vision with the CiscoWorks2000 Service Management Solution (SMS) and other complementary technologies and applications. The following sections discuss SMS and other applications that help an enterprise or service provider report on the availability of their network.

CiscoWorks2000 SMS manages service levels between enterprises and internal or external service providers to ensure high-quality, economic delivery of converged network services. CiscoWorks2000 SMS defines and monitors SLAs, specifying traffic type, endpoints, and thresholds against key parameters such as latency, packet loss, and jitter.

By leveraging XML import and export functions and open XML application programming interfaces (APIs), CiscoWorks2000 SMS ensures consistent definition and representation of SLAs between systems and organizations. Its leverage of Cisco IOS Software-based probe technologies suits it perfectly to showing that a network can support new technologies such as VoIP, mission-critical e-business applications, and VPNs. The same tests can be applied after service deployment to verify successful service delivery against SLAs.

CiscoWorks2000 SMS brings together the core elements required for end-to-end service level management, including the following:

- **CiscoWorks2000 server components**—Provide base-level services and capabilities, such as a server desktop, database, inventory management, device credentials, device capabilities, and web server software.

- **Service Level Manager 2.0**—Includes applications for creating, managing, and reporting on SLAs and system management functions.

- **SLM Collection Managers**—Distributable software agents that provide job management and the collection and aggregation of service level data generated by the Cisco IOS Service Assurance Agent (SAA).

- **Cisco IOS Service Assurance Agent**—Measures a wide range of service level metrics, and is now an integral part of the Cisco IOS Software.

Use of Cisco IOS Software Technology to Measure Network Service Level Performance

Delivering on SLAs requires that service providers have the ability to isolate performance metrics on a hop-by-hop basis so they can quickly troubleshoot network bottlenecks and boost network performance.

Having performance information about each network service better positions service providers to offer hosted application services. Customers of these services often demand specific QoS levels on par with what they are accustomed to experiencing when services are delivered locally.

To fulfill these requirements, service providers can use a performance monitoring capability embedded in Cisco IOS Software called the Cisco Service Assurance Agent (SA Agent). Compared with running a separate monitoring appliance at each customer location and at the access link termination point in a point of presence (POP), this feature scales much better in a service provider environment from a cost, management, and training perspective. Cisco edge routers with Cisco SA Agent monitor thousands of operations simultaneously across routed IP networks, Multiprotocol Label Switching (MPLS) virtual private networks (VPNs), and Layer 2 Frame Relay and ATM networks.

Figure 8-5 shows the information that SAA can provide a service provider.

Figure 8-5   *Service Information Provided by the SAA to a Service Provider*

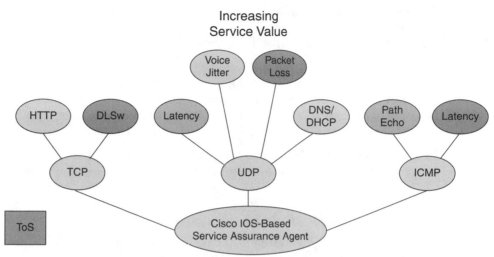

Each network function monitored by the Cisco SA Agent is called an *operation* or a *probe*. A sampling of the operations that the agent monitors for response time includes the following:

- UDP jitter, which is the degree of delay and delay variability in one direction of a user transmission; this is particularly useful in delivering voice-over-IP (VoIP) services, because service providers can isolate network congestion spots that can interfere with voice service quality

- File Transfer Protocol (FTP)

- Internet Control Message Protocol (ICMP) path jitter and echo, for hop-by-hop performance isolation and troubleshooting

- Hypertext Transfer Protocol (HTTP)

- Domain Name Service (DNS)

- Dynamic Host Control Protocol (DHCP)

- Frame Relay and ATM

Configuration Considerations

Service providers can use Cisco SA Agent to set network thresholds. For example, the network can be set to trigger an SNMP trap or another Cisco SA Agent operation if a delay reaches a certain number of milliseconds. A Cisco SA Agent component called Application Performance Monitor (APM) enables a service provider to monitor specific applications such as various e-mail applications, directory services, and enterprise-resource-planning (ERP) applications. This capability is beneficial when the provider wants to offer application-specific service guarantees or hosted application services.

Benefits Summary

Cisco SA Agent was first available in Cisco IOS Software Release 12.0(5)T. The probes for UDP jitter, FTP, and SNMP support became available in Cisco IOS Software Release 12.1(1)T. MPLS VPN, Frame Relay, ATM, ICMP path jitter and echo, and APM support was first available in Cisco IOS Software Release 12.2(2)T.

To enhance scalability when monitoring a large number of customer premises equipment (CPE) devices, Cisco recommends running Cisco SA Agent on a dedicated "shadow" router located in network aggregation POPs. The shadow router is generally a smaller router than the primary edge router that offloads the monitoring processing overhead from the primary router.

Cisco recommends running a probe from the POP to each CPE. For measuring performance between POPs, Cisco recommends a fully meshed Cisco SA Agent probe configuration.

Cisco Internetwork Performance Monitor

Cisco Internetwork Performance Monitor (IPM) Version 2.1 is a network response time and availability troubleshooting application. It is available as one of the network management applications within the CiscoWorks2000 Routed WAN Management Solution. This tool enables network engineers to validate performance metrics that are defined within SLAs. This is done by measuring network utilization through real-time and historical reports.

After an IPM collector is configured and deployed in the source router, IPM continuously collects performance information based on the parameters of the defined collector for the following service level performance metrics:

- **Latency**—The amount of time it takes a packet to travel from source to destination. Together, latency and bandwidth define a network's speed and capacity.

- **Jitter**—Any distortion of a signal or image caused by poor synchronization. Jitter is relevant to applications such as VoIP.

- **Availability**—The amount of time the network is available to the end user.

- **Errors**—Corruption of data during transmission resulting from collisions, frame checks, or cyclical redundancy check (CRC) errors.

- **Packet loss**—Data packets that are not received by the end station.

Troubleshooting Network Response Time and Availability Problems

IPM 2.1 enables the network engineer to manage network response time problems proactively. IPM notifies the network engineer when network response time degrades or a monitored link becomes unavailable, and helps pinpoint the link causing the problem.

Troubleshooting Features

IPM provides the following performance troubleshooting features:

- Identification and analysis of all paths between two devices in a network

- Analysis of each hop in the path between two networked devices

- Real-time and historical graphical reports of response time between two network devices

- Proactive notification with a Simple Network Management Protocol (SNMP) trap when response time exceeds predefined thresholds; an SNMP trap is a pro-active event generated by a network device to notify a management system of a problem on the network

- Proactive notification with an SNMP trap when a link becomes unavailable

Troubleshooting Network Response Time Threshold Violations

IPM enables the continuous monitoring of response time between network device pairs using Cisco IOS Service Assurance (SA) Agent technology. This tool is often used to provide advanced notification when SLA metrics are violated or exceeded. The thresholds that IPM configures on the router can be tuned to the appropriate level of sensitivity based on the following configuration parameters:

- **Rising thresholds**—Notification occurs when the response time value rises above a specified level.

- **Falling thresholds**—Notification occurs when the response time value falls below a specified level.

- **Immediate thresholds**— Notification occurs when one sample violates the threshold.

- **Intermittent threshold**—Notification occurs based on the threshold being satisfied a specified percentage of the time.

- **Average threshold**—Notification is based on the threshold being exceeded an average amount of times. In this case, notifications are not issued until a specified number of samples have been taken.

- **Consecutive threshold**—Notification is based on the sampled response time violating the threshold a specified number of consecutive times.

Cisco QoS Policy Manager Version 2.0

The need for high availability and predictable performance for business-critical applications combined with the demand for advanced voice and media services mandates differentiated handling of network traffic. By leveraging existing and newly integrated Cisco IOS QoS mechanisms in LAN and WAN switching equipment, Cisco QoS Policy Manager (QPM) enables network administrators to protect critical applications through centralized policy control and automated policy deployment.

An integral part of Cisco content networking, and an intelligent network architecture that dynamically recognizes Internet business applications, QPM provides differentiated services to web-based applications, voice traffic, web hosting, and business-critical processes.

Features at a Glance

A few Cisco QPM 2.0 features follow:

- **Centralized policy control**—An easy-to-use graphical user interface (GUI) eliminates device-by-device configuration for configuring, modifying, and deploying QoS for LAN and WAN routing and switching equipment.

- **Differentiated service for application traffic**—QPM simplifies configuration of traffic classification, bandwidth reservation, and QoS enforcement policies used by Cisco devices to achieve service level differentiation.

- **Enhanced application-level classification**—Support for a newly released, integrated packet inspection engine within Cisco IOS Software extends IP packet classification to content-based application signaling, World Wide Web URLs, and dynamic protocols.

- **Voice QoS configuration**—Rapid configuration of advanced voice QoS features provides absolute priority to voice traffic.

- **Guaranteed network service**—Resource Reservation Protocol (RSVP) signaling is configured across the enterprise network for real-time applications such as voice, video, and audio, that need guaranteed throughput and latency.

- **Policy domain configuration**—Intelligent interface grouping allows you to selectively enable QoS mechanisms for LAN or WAN policy domains.

- Add the following to immediately precede the Review Questions section:

Summary

In this chapter you learned what an SLA is and why it's important to achieve two-way accountability of service. As Internet applications continue to increase productivity and become the essential functioning components of the business, an agreement between providers of the service is necessary to push toward continuous availability. Service Level Agreements, as you've learned, become the business process glue that holds together the process of continuous service.

Review Questions

1 What is a Service Level Agreement?

_____

_____

_____

2 What are the two types of SLAs?

_____

_____

_____

3 What are the benefits of an SLA?

_____

_____

_____

4 What is Service Assurance Agent (SAA)?

_____

_____

_____

5 Who are some third-party companies that provide Service Management applications?

_____

_____

_____

Answers to the Chapter Review Questions

Chapter 1 Review Questions

1 What is an Internet system architecture?

Answer: An Internet System Architecture is an architecture that has been designed and optimized to support Internet-based applications.

2 What are the six types of Internet business solutions?

Answer: Customer Care, e-commerce, Supply Chain Management, e-learning, Workforce Optimization, and e-publishing.

3 How does Lands' End apply the principles of the New World Customer Care Architecture?

Answer: Lands' End changed its Call Center to a Contact Center, enabling its customers to communicate in a multitude of ways (through e-mail, chat, voice, or browser).

4 What are some ways that companies can leverage the e-learning solution?

Answer: Companies can leverage the e-learning solution by employing distance learning, HR training, new hire training, meeting distribution, media (recorded video and voice) distribution, and corporate communications.

5 What Cisco architecture solution makes up the e-learning architecture?

Answer: Cisco Enterprise Content Delivery Network and IP/TV Broadcast Servers make up the e-learning architecture.

6 Companies use the IP Contact Center Architecture Solution to improve what part of their business?

Answer: Companies use the Cisco IP Contact Center to increase the quality of their customer interactions, increase the effectiveness of their contact center agents, and decrease their overall costs.

7 What solution seamlessly integrates suppliers, manufacturers, and purchasers?

Answer: Supply Chain Management

Chapter 2 Review Questions

1 Name the four major types of network connectivity in an Internet infrastructure.

Answer: Campus network, WAN, switched connectivity, and Internet connectivity.

2 What does "hitless" mean in terms of the Internet Systems Architecture?

Answer: The term hitless means that no system user would notice any outage and no network packets would get lost as a result of a change.

3 Define availability.

Answer: Availability refers to the amount of time a system is available to users.

4 Define capacity.

Answer: Capacity is defined as the data-carrying capability of a circuit or network, and is usually measured in bits per second (bps).

5 Define utilization.

Answer: Utilization can be defined as the percentage of total available capacity in use.

6 What three pieces of a switch should you consider when choosing a switch?

Answer: Queueing model, switching implementation, and Switch fabric.

7 What does the term "stickiness" mean?

Answer: Stickiness is the ability of a system to be able to keep all of a client's requests coming back to the same server in a server farm.

8 What are the three goals of security?

Answer: Maintain integrity, protect confidentiality, and assure availability.

9 What does a "stateful" firewall do?

Answer: A stateful firewall maintains a list of active connections and keeps track of this information.

10 What is out-of-band management?

Answer: Out-of-band management is management that puts management traffic onto a separate network than the production traffic, such as having a separate management VLAN.

11 Define QoS.

Answer: QoS is a set of technologies and configurations that allow a network to provide differentiated services to different network traffic.

Chapter 3 Review Questions

1 Define high availability.

Answer: High availability is defined as the continuous operation of computing systems.

2 What are the three facets of high availability that need to be considered when designing a highly available system?

Answer: Uptime, performance and accessibility.

3 How many minutes per year is a "five nines" system down for at the very most?

Answer: Five

4 What are the five steps for designing or customizing high-availability solutions?

Answer:

Define an up-front availability objective based on business requirements.

Follow a top-down approach beginning with overall high-availability goals.

Develop an availability model.

Compose a development road map.

Perform design verification.

5 What are the two design approaches to high availability?

Answer: Designs based on fault-tolerant devices and designs based on redundant topologies.

6 What objectives should be met when composing a development roadmap?

Answer:

Step-by-step availability improvement.

Plans to minimize service outages.

Provisions for maintenance and upgrades without downtime.

Plans to minimize recovery time.

Plans to minimize high-availability environment restoration time.

Contingent recovery plan.

7 What are MTBF and MTTR?

Answer: Mean time before failure and mean time to repair.

8 What Layer 2 technologies can be used to provide automatic recovery of lost connections?

Answer: Spanning Tree, ISL trunking, and 802.1Q trunking.

9 What is the standards based version of Cisco's HSRP?

Answer: VRRP

Chapter 4 Review Questions

1 What is the SAFE Architecture?

Answer: The Cisco SAFE architecture is a proven, detailed security blueprint that is built on the Cisco AVVID (Architecture for Voice Video and Integrated Data) Infrastructure. The SAFE architecture combines leading Cisco security solutions with a rich ecosystem of complementary programs, products, partners, and services. The architecture is a layered modular design built to allow companies to stay within their budget as they migrate to a secure infrastructure framework.

2 What are the Cisco security components of SAFE?

Answer:

Cisco PIX Firewall

Cisco Intrusion Detection Sensor and Module

Cisco Host-Based Intrusion Detection

Cisco VPN 3000 Concentrator

Cisco IOS VPN Routers

Cisco Access Control Server

Cisco VMS (VPN Management Solution)

3 What are some common attacks on the Corporate Internet Layer?

Answer:

Application layer attacks

Virus

Trojan Horse

Password attacks

Denial-of-Service attacks

IP Spoofing

Network Reconnaissance

Trust Exploitation

Port Redirection

4 What are the benefits to implementing intrusion detection?

Answer:

IDS Highlights:

- **Advanced attack identification and classification capabilities**
- **Anti-IDS evasion techniques, including IP fragmentation reassembly, TCP streams reassembly, and Unicode web deobfuscation**
- **Cisco's Countermeasure Research Team (C-CRT) is a team of renowned security experts that has over 65 percent secret or top-secret government clearances with backgrounds in the USAF, National Security Agency, Central Intelligence Agency, DoD, DOE, NSA, and CIA**
- **Patent-Pending SME (Signature Micro-Engine) technology delivering the ability to customize and tune signatures**
- **Active Update Technology for automating application and signature updates**
- **Active Response Capabilities to shun on Cisco routers, switches, and firewalls**
- **Integrated Solution: "plug-and-play" solutions include both the hardware and software package**

Key Benefits:

- **Ubiquitous business protection**
- **Market-leading, patented innovation**
- **Powerful enterprise management and monitoring**
- **Unmatched accuracy and reliability**
- **Scalable sensing performance**
- **Investment protection**
- **Highest performance**

5 What does AAA stand for?

Answer: Authentication, Authorization, and Accounting.

Chapter 5 Review Questions

1 What is the goal of Content Delivery Networking?

A. Accelerate content delivery

B. Reduce the last mile bottlenecks

C. Improve the user's experience of the content he is retrieving

D. All of the Above

Answer: D

2 What are the five components of a Content Delivery Network?

Answer:

Content Switching

Content Routing

Content Distribution and Management

Content Edge Delivery

Intelligent Network Services

3 What is content switching/load balancing able to provide a company?

Answer: Content switching intelligently load balances traffic across servers in a data center or point of presence (POP) based on the content's availability and the load on the server. The result is a consistently positive experience for web site users.

4 How does content routing help a company scale?

Answer: Content routing redirects an end user to the best site based on a set of metrics, such as delay, topology, and server load, and a set of policies, such as content location, enabling the accelerated delivery of web content and streaming media. Content routing ensures the fastest delivery of content regardless of location, providing the highest availability and site response time.

Chapter 6 Review Questions

1 What are some ways of deploying QoS?

Answer:

Use QoS Policy Manager (QPM)

Use the Cisco IOS Software Command-Line Interface (Modular QoS CLI)

Use QoS Device Manager

Use Catalyst OS

Use CiscoWorks 2000

2 What groups of tools and techniques can be used for implementing QoS features?

Answer:

Classification

Congestion Management

Congestion Avoidance

Traffic Shaping and Policing

Signaling

Link Efficiency Mechanisms

3 What technique allows you to mark a packet for identification by all other routers throughout the internetwork?

Answer: At Layer 2, you can mark packets with 802.1p/Q / ISL, ATM CLP bit, Frame-Relay DE-bit, and MPLS EXP bits. At Layer 3, you can mark packets with IP Precedence or Differentiated Services Code Point (DSCP). All of this is done using Modular QoS CLI's policy-framework component.

4 What category of tools does the Low Latency Queuing Technique fall into?

Answer: Congestion Management

5 What Cisco solution can you use in your QoS deployment planning stage to provide a graph of your top bandwidth users and segments?

Answer: Network Analysis Module

6 Why is planning the most important step in QoS deployment?

Answer: You must review the client's various needs and requirements *before* designing a solution.

Chapter 7 Review Questions

7 What are the five functional areas of network management?

A. Application Management

B. Configuration Management

C. Security Management

D. Performance Management

E. Fault Management

F. Accounting Management

G. Protocol Management

Answer:

E. Fault Management

B. Configuration Management

F. Accounting Management

D. Performance Management

C. Security Management

8 What are the five steps in fault management?

A. Problem Bypass and Recovery

B. Problem Determination

C. Problem Analysis

D. Problem Diagnosis

E. Problem Resolution

F. Problem Isolation

G. Problem Tracking and Control

Answer:

B. Problem Determination

C. Problem Diagnosis

A. Problem Bypass and Recovery

E. Problem Resolution

G. Problem Tracking and Control

9 What are configuration management's three core components?

A. Configuration Records

B. Configuration Management

C. Configuration Process

D. Configuration Result

E. Configuration Analysis

F. Configuration Description

Answer:

C. Configuration Process

D. Configuration Result

F. Configuration Description

10 List at least three common characteristics of fault management.

Answer:

Alarm collection and forwarding

Automated trouble ticket generation

Assignment of event priority levels

Status polling

Event configuration

Root cause analysis

Event correlation

Event notification

Event filtering

Network and system status

11 Which of the following are NOT management protocols?

A. Telnet

B. RMON

C. NTP

D. Syslog

E. SNMP

F. FTP

G. CLI

Answer:

C. NTP

F. FTP

12 What are the four basic protocol operations in SNMP Version 1?

A. Set

B. Test

C. GetNext

D. Trap

E. Confirm

F. Commit

G. Get

Answer:

A. Set

C. GetNext

D. Trap

G. Get

13 Which of the following is a correct SNMP MIB Object Identifier?

A. 1.3.6.1.4.1.9.3.12.1

B. 1.3.6.1.4.1.9.X.3.1

C. 13.6.1.4.1.9.3.3.1

D. A.3.6.1.4.1.9.3.3.1

E. 1.3.6.1.4.1.9.3.3.1-2

F. 1.3.6.1.4.1.9.3.3.1

G. 100.1.3.6

Answer:

F. 1.3.6.1.4.1.9.3.3.1

14 List the eight guidelines for managing a network.

Answer:

Start with a good design and secure physical location.

Identify critical ports and leave the rest alone.

Set up fault monitoring.

Collect baseline data.

Define and set thresholds.

Adjust thresholds.

Reduce baseline data collection.

Revisit and gather baseline data regularly.

15 List three common third-party network management systems.

Answer:

HP Openview

Unicenter TNG

IBM's Tivoli

16 Which of the following is NOT a Cisco network management solution?

A. Ciscoworks 2000 LMS

B. URT

C. VMS

D. Ciscoworks 2000 RWAN

E. Cisco TFTP

F. QoS Policy Manager

G. CNR

Answer:

E. Cisco TFTP

Chapter 8 Review Questions

1 What is a Service Level Agreement?

Answer: A Service Level Agreement (SLA) is a predefined agreement as to the terms of service expected. The term SLA can mean different things to different people. A network administrator might interpret SLA to mean that his wide-area network (WAN) connection to the Internet must be available 99.9 percent of the time. A business unit manager might interpret SLA to mean that his connection to Cisco.com should respond in a reasonable amount of time.

2 What are the two types of SLAs?

Answer: Internal and External

3 What are the benefits of an SLA?

Answer: SLAs establish two-way accountability for service, meaning that users and application groups are both accountable for the network service. If users don't help create an SLA for a specific service and communicate business impact to the network group, they could actually be accountable for the problem.

SLAs help determine standard tools and resources needed to meet business requirements. Deciding how many people and which tools to use without SLAs is often a budgetary guess. The service might be overengineered, which leads to overspending, or underengineered, which leads to unmet business objectives. Tuning SLAs helps achieve that balanced optimal level.

The documented SLA creates a clearer vehicle for setting service level expectations.

4 What is Service Assurance Agent (SAA)?

Answer: An SAA is an active performance-monitoring agent embedded in Cisco IOS Software. It measures performance by sending out one or more synthetic packets to a target router, similar to ping's functionality. SAA uses the timestamp information on both the source and target (depending on the type of operation) to calculate performance metrics (that is, jitter, latency, and response time).

5 Who are some third-party companies that provide Service Management applications?

Answer: InfoVista, Concord, Net IQ- Webtrends, Micromuse/Netcool/Cisco InfoCenter, HP OpenView

Index

Numerics

3DES, 118
802.1Q standard, 33

A

access control, 127
    authentication, 127–128
    authorization, 129
    defending against IP spoofing, 104
    mitigating IP spoofing threats, 104
access VPNs, 115–117
accounting management, 182
administrative requirements for SLAs, 228
agents, 195
ANS.1 (Abstract Syntax Negotiation One), 193
APM (Application Performance Monitor), 233
application characterization, performing, 164
application layer attacks, 108
application servers, 13
ARPANET, 3
ASA (Adaptive Security Algorithm), 113
ASICs (Application Specific Integrated Circuits), 31
    reducing latency from load balancing, 36
assessing QoS policy needs, 162–163
    defining service levels, 164–165
    performing application characterization, 164
    performing network characterization, 163
asymmetric encryption, 119
attacks
    application layer, 108
    detecting with IDS, 44–45
    DoS, 104, 106
    IP spoofing, 103
        defense mechanisms, 104
    man-in-the-middle, 107
    network reconnaissance, 109
    packet sniffers, 102
        defense mechanisms, 103
    password, 106–107
    port redirection, 110
    Trojan horse, 110
    trust exploitation, 109
    unauthorized access, 110
    viruses, 110
authentication, 127
    biometrics, 128
    defending against packet sniffers, 103
    OTP, 128
    username/password, 128
authorization, 129
automatic paging, 187
availability, 27. *See also* high availability systems
    downtime, 75
    five nines, 75
    with Cisco Internet Systems Architecture, 63
AVVID (Architecture for Voice, Video, and
   Integrated Data)
    customer care service integration, 10
    QoS, 160

B

backend World Wide Web applications, 13
bandwidth, capacity, 28
best practices for maintaining high availability, 88
biometrics, 128
bottleneck points in Q-Tip architecture, 143
brute-force attacks, 106
buffering techniques, 30
building
    Cisco SAFE architecture, 129
        Corporate Internet module, 134–135
        E-Commerce module, 137–138
        Enterprise module, 130–131
        Management module, 131, 133
        Remote Access VPN module, 136–137
        Server module, 133–134
    service level model, 224
bundles, 210
bus architecture fabric, 32
business application servers, 13
business solutions
    customer care, 7
        IPCC, 9–10
        Land's End, 8–9
        service integration, 8

e-commerce, 11
World Wide Web service components, 12–13
e-learning, 15–17
case study, Genuity, 17–18
e-publishing, 20–21
supply chain management, 14
workforce optimization, 19–20
business synchronization, 222
reporting, 224
SLA expectations, setting, 223

C

CAs (certification authorities), 119
caching, transparent, 154
CANI (Constant and Neverending Improvement), 98
capacity, 28, 62
CCS (Cisco Content Smart Switches), 36
CDM (Content Distribution Manager), 53, 151–152
CDNs (Content Delivery Networks), 51, 53–54, 143
components, 144–145
CDM, 151–152
Content Edge Delivery, 150
Content Routing, 151
Content Switching, 145–149
Intelligent Network Services, 145
E-CDN, 155
e-learning solutions, 17
transparent caching, 154
central storage growth (Internet), 141
CERT (Computer Emergency Response Team), 105
CIS (Customer Interaction Suite), Lands' End customer care solution, 8
Cisco AVVID (Architecture for Voice, Video and Integrated Data)
customer care service integration, 10
QoS, 160
Cisco CSS 11000 series content service switches, 147
Cisco e-CDNs (enterprise CDNs), e-learning solutions, 17
Cisco host-based IDSs, features of, 126
Cisco Internet Reference Architecture
content engines, 46, 49–54
Content Routers, 55, 60

content switches, 34–37, 40
firewalls, 41–43
IDS, 44–45
Layer 3 switches, 28–29
redundancy, 32–34
sizing, 30–32
perimeter routers, 26–27
Cisco Internet System Architecture
connectivity, types of, 29
Cisco Internet Systems Architecture
benefits of using, 61
availability, 63
capacity, 62
connectivity, 62
manageability, 64
QoS, 63–64
security, 63
server placement, 60
Cisco IOS
QoS tools, 170–172
SAA (Service Assurance Agent), 232
Cisco IPM (Internetwork Performance Monitor), 234–235
Cisco network management solutions, 209
CiscoWorks2000 bundles, 210–216
CNR (Cisco Network Registrar), 216
QPM, 216
Cisco network-based IDS, features, 125
Cisco PIX firewall, exclusive features, 112–117
application awareness, 113
DoS Guards, 113
FragGuard, 114
intrustion detection, 114
NAT options, 115
redundancy, 116
site-to-site VPNs, 115–116
standards-based IPSec, 115
stateful inspection, 113
TCP intercept, 114
Virtual Reassembly, 114
VPN acceleration, 116
Cisco QPM (QoS Policy Manager), 235–236
Cisco SAFE architecture, 95, 129
Corporate Internet module, 134–135
E-Commerce module, 137–138
Enterprise module, 130–131
Management module, 131–133

Remote Access VPN module, 136–137
Server module, 133–134
Cisco Secure Policy Manager, 123
CiscoWorks 2000 SMS, 231–232
classification tools (QoS), 170–171
CLTs (Control List Technicians), 156
Comer, Gary C., 8
commands (SNMP), 196
comparing redundant and non-redundant topologies, 81–83
components
of Cisco Internet Reference Architecture
content engines, 46–54
Content Routers, 55, 60
content switches, 34–40
firewalls, 41–43
IDS, 44–45
Layer 3 switches, 28–34
perimeter routers, 26–27
of Internet system architecture, 25
Computer Associates, Inc., Unicenter TNG, 209
confidentiality, 96
congestion avoidance
buffering traffic, 30
Cisco IOS QoS tools, 171
connectivity
types of, 29
with Cisco Internet Systems Architecture, 62
Content Edge Delivery, 150
content engines, 46, 49, 51, 53–54
CDM, 53
CDNs, 51
content routers, 55, 60, 151
content switches, 34–40, 145–146
CSM, 147–149
maintaining session state, 40
control plane, 36
Corporate Internet module, Cisco SAFE architecture, 134–135
corporate training, e-learning solutions, 15–17
Genuity case study, 17–18
correlation rules, 199
cost-benefit analysis, total cost of ownership model, 72–74
creating SLAs, 225
crossbar switch fabric, 32
cryptography, defending against packet sniffers, 103

CSM (Cisco Content Switch Module), 147–149
customer care solutions, 7
Land's End, 8–9
service integration, 8–10

D

data encryption, 118–121
data traffic, QoS requirements, 161
DDoS (distributed denial-of-service) attacks, 105
decision-making process, Layer 3 switching, 31
decryption, 118–119, 121
defending against IP spoofing attacks, 104
defining
objectives for high availability systems, 76–77
security polices, 98–99
service levels (QoS), 164–165
delay, 162
Deming, Edward, 7
deploying large-scale QoS implementation, 166
with Modular QoS CLI, 167–168
with QoS Device Manager, 170
with QPM, 166–167
DES (Data Encryption Standard), 118
designing
highly available systems
defining objectives, 76–77
development road map, 78
EtherChannel, 86
failover mechanisms, 87–88
HSRP, 86–87
load balancers, 84
recovery procedures, 89–91
Spanning Tree, 85–86
top-down approach, 77
verifying design, 79
VRRP, 86–87
Internet system architecture. guidelines, 28
SLM solutions, integrating components from various vendors, 230
detecting
attacks with IDS, 44–45
failed components, 91
development road map, achieving high availability objectives, 78

devices, 44
  availability, 27
  CDN components, 144–145
    CDM (Content Distribution Manager), 151–152
    Content Edge Delivery, 150
    Content Routing, 151
    Content Switching, 145–149
    Intelligent Network Services, 145
  Cisco Internet Reference Architecture components
    content engines, 46–54
    Content Routers, 55, 60
    content switches, 34–37, 40
    firewalls, 41–43
    IDS, 44–45
    Layer 3 switches, 28–34
    perimeter routers, 26–27
  fault tolerant, building highly available systems, 80
  hitless upgrades, 26
  shadow routers, 234
  VPN access support, 122
Digital IDs, 119
digital signatures, 121
director console (IDS), 45
disclosure (SNMP), 196
distributed switching, 31
DMZ (demilitarized zone), 43
DNS Guard feature (Cisco PIX firewall), 113
DNS mode (Content Routers), 56
  request processing, 57, 60
documentation
  network policies, 76
  security policies, 98
    defining, 98–99
    implementing, 100
    improving, 101
    monitoring, 100
    testing, 100
DoS attacks, 104–106
downtime, 75
  MTBF, 80
  outages, tracking causes of, 78

dumbbell architecture, 143
  bottleneck points, 143
  ISPs, 143
Dynamic NAT translation, 115

E

e-business solutions
  customer care, 7
    IPCC, 9–10
    Land's End, 8–9
    service integration, 8
  e-commerce, 11
    World Wide Web service components, 12–13
  e-learning, 15–17
    Genuity case study, , 17–18
  e-publishing, 20–21
  supply chain management, 14
  workforce optimization, 19–20
E-CDN (Enterprise CDN), 155
E-Commerce architecture
  non-redundant design, 83
  redundant design, 83
E-Commerce module, Cisco SAFE architecture, 137–138
e-commerce solutions, 11
  World Wide Web service components, 12–13
ECS (event correlation system), 199
e-learning solutions, 15, 17
  Genuity case study, 17–18
employee training, e-learning solutions, 15–17
encryption, 118–119, 121
  public keys, 120
  VPN access, Cisco device support, 122
Enterprise module (Cisco SAFE architecture), 130–131
entitlement engines, 13
e-publishing solutions, 20–21
EtherChannel, 86
  impact on bandwidth, 33
event correlation engine, 199
events
  handling, 186–187
  SNMP, 197–199

examples of external SLAs, 227–228
exclusive Cisco PIX features
        application awareness, 113
        DoS Guards, 113
        FragGuard, 114
        intrusion detection, 114
        NAT options, 115
        redundancy, 116
        site-to-site VPNs, 115–116
        standards-based IPSec, 115
        TCP intercept, 114
        Virtual Reassembly, 114
        VPN acceleration, 116
external connections of World Wide Web, 13
external SLAs, 226
        example, 227–228
extranet VPNs, 118

F

failover mechanisms, 87–88
failover mode (Cisco PIX firewall), 116–117
failure analysis, 89
failure detection, 91
fault management
        event handling, 186–187
        necessity of, 188
        placing systems, 188
        status polling, 185
        troubleshooting, 189
fault tolerance
        designing highly available systems, 80
        in highly available systems, 89
FCAPS (Fault, Configuration, Accounting,
    Performance, and Security) model, 177
        accounting management, 182
        configuration management, 178–181
                description, 180
                process, 181
                results, 181
                tools, 181
        fault management, 178
        performance management, 183
        security management, 183
feasibility of five nines availability, 75

features of Cisco IDSs
        host-based, 126
        network-based, 125
FIB (forwarding information base), 31
FIFO queuing, 159
filtering URLs, content filtering, 155–156
financial considerations of redundant systems,
    72–74
firewalls, 41–43, 111
        Cisco PIX, 112
                exclusive features, 112–117
        DMZ, 43
        packet filtering, 111
        stateful, 42, 112
five nines availability, 75
fixed-size buffers, 30
Flood Defender feature (Cisco PIX firewall), 113
flow-based switching, 31
FragGuard (Cisco PIX), 114
fragmentation of customer care services, 7
front end World Wide Web applications, 12
functional dependencies of SLAs, 229
functionality of perimeter routers, 27

G

general-purpose application servers, 13
Genuity, e-learning case study, 17–18
Get requests (SNMP), 194
GetBulk operation (SNMP), 196
GetNext requests (SNMP), 194
goals
        of Internet system architecture, 5
        service level definitions, 224
growth of Internet technologies, 3
Guard features of Cisco PIX, 113
guidelines of network management, 203–207

H

hash algorithms, 118
head of line blocking, 30
Hewlett Packard Openview, 208
HIDS (Host-based IDS), 108

high availability systems, 72
    E-Commerce architecture
        non-redundant design, 83
        redundant design, 83
    EtherChannel, 86
    designing
        defining objectives, 76–77
        design verification, 79
        development road map, 78
        top-down approach, 77
    failover mechanisms, 87–88
    five nines, 76
    HSRP, 86–87
    implementing
        with fault tolerant devices, 80
        with redundant topologies, 80, 83
    load balancers, 84
    MTBF, 80
    non-network considerations
        operational best practices, 88
        power consumption, 89
        server fault tolerance, 89
    Spanning Tree, 85–86
    VRRP, 86–87
hitless upgrades, 26
Host Sensor 2.0, 126
host-based IDS features, 126
HSRP (Hot-Standby Routing Protocol), 86–87
HTTP requests, load balancing, 37

I

IBM Tivoli, 208
IDEA (International Data Encryption Algorithm),
    119
IDSs (Intrusion Detection Systems), 44–45,
    122–123
    director console, 45
    features
        host-based, 126
        network-based, 125
    sensors, 123–124
        placement, 125

implementing
    high availability systems
        with fault tolerant devices, 80
        with redundant topologies, 80–83
    large-scale QoS deployment, 166
        business synchronization, 222–224
        service level definitions, 224
        with Modular QoS CLI, 167–168
        with QoS Device Manager, 170
        with QPM, 166–167
    security policies, 100–101
improving security policies, 101
infrastructure of ISP networks, 143
input queuing, 30
integrating
    customer care services
        benefits of, 8
        IPCC, 9–10
    SLM components from various vendors, 230
integrity, 96
Intelligent Network Services, 145
interaction enablers, 13
internal SLAs, 226
Internet, central storage growth, 141
Internet Systems Architecture, 3–5, 25
    benefits of using, 61
        availability, 63
        capacity, 62
        connectivity, 62
        manageability, 64
        QoS, 63–64
        security, 63
    goal of, 5
    server placement, 60
intranet VPNs, 118
intrusion detection (Cisco PIX), 114
IP spoofing, 103
    defense mechanisms, 104
IPCC (Cisco IP Contact Center), 9–10
IPM (Internetwork Performance Monitor), 234–235
ISO (International Standards Organization), FCAPS
    model, 177
ISP's, network infrastructure, 143

J

jitter, 162
job training, e-learning solutions, 15–17

K

KAIZEN, 19
Kiwi Syslog Deamon, 197
Knowledge Bases, 80

L

Land's End, customer care services, 8–9
large-scale QoS deployment, 166
    with Modular QoS CLI, 167–168
    with QoS Device Manager, 170
    with QPM, 166–167
latency, load balancing induced, 36
Layer 3 switches, 28–29
    redundancy, 32, 34
    sizing, 30, 32
        queuing model, 30
        switch fabric, 32
        switching implementation, 31
life cycle model of security, 99
link efficiency mechanisms, 172
LMS (LAN Management Solution), 210–213
load balancers
load balancing, 84
    content switches, 34, 36–37, 40
    HTTP requests, 37
    latency, 36
logical network maps, 180

M

maintaining
    high availability, operational best practices, 88
    session state, 40
    SLAs, 225
manageability, Cisco Internet Systems
   Architecture, 64

managed devices, 194
Management module (Cisco SAFE architecture),
   131–133
management protocols
    RMON, 201–202
    SNMP, 192–193
        Get requests, 194
        GetNext requests, 194
        Set operations, 194
        traps, 194
        versions, 195
    syslog, 202
    Telnet, 192
manager/agent model, 192
man-in-the-middle attacks, 107
marking tools (QoS), 170–171
masquerading, 196
measuring
    high availability, MTBF, 80
    service level performance, 232–233
media streams, link efficiency mechanisms, 172
message digest algorithms, 119
MIBs (Management Information Bases), 201
mission-critical data, QoS requirements, 161
mitigating security threats
    application layer attacks, 108
    DoS attacks, 106
    IP spoofing, 104
    network reconnaissance, 109
    packet sniffers, 103
    password attacks, 107
    unauthorized access, 110
modification of information, 196
Modular QoS CLI, large-scale QoS deployment,
   167–168
monitoring
    security policies, 100
    SLAs, 191
monitoring tools, failure detection, 91
MTBF (meantime between failure), 80
MTTR (meantime to repair), 80
multi-switch deployment with EtherChannel, 34

N

NAT options (Cisco PIX), 115
network analysis tools, 164
network availability metrics (SLAs), 229
network characterization, performing, 163
network management
    FCAPS model, 177
        accounting management, 182
        configuration management, 178–181
        fault management, 178
        performance management, 183
        security management, 183
    guidelines, 203–204, 206–207
    policy documentation, 76
    RMON, 201–202
network performance metrics (SLAs), 229
network reconnaissance, 109
network response time thresholds,
    troubleshooting, 235
network-based IDS
    features, 125
    sensors, 123–124
NIDS (Network-based IDS), 108
NMSs (Network Management Systems)
    Cisco solutions, 209
        CiscoWorks 2000 bundles, 210–216
        CNR, 216
        QPM, 216
    fault management
        event handling, 186–187
        necessity of, 188
        placing systems, 188
        status polling, 185
        troubleshooting, 189
    performance management, 190–191
    RMON, 201–202
    SNMP, 192–193
        commands, 196
        disclosure, 196
        events, 197, 199
        Get requests, 194
        GetNext requests, 194
        MIBs, 201
        modification of information, 196
        Set operations, 194
        syslog messages, 197
        traps, 194
        versions, 195
    Telnet, 192
non-redundant design (E-Commerce
    architecture), 83
n-tier model, 25

O

Object Identifiers, 201
objectives for high availability systems, defining,
    76–77
Old World system architecture, 3
online services
    customer care, 7–8
        IPCC, 9–10
        Land's End, 8–9
    e-commerce, 11
        World Wide Web service components,
            12–13
    e-learning solutions, 15, 17
        Genuity case study, 17–18
    e-publishing solutions, 20–21
    supply chain management solutions, 14
    workforce optimization solutions, 19–20
Openview (Hewlett Packard), 208
operation level metrics (SLAs), 229
operational best practices, maintaining high
    availability, 88
OTPs (one-time passwords), 103
    authentication, 128
outages, tracking causes of, 78
output queuing, 30

P

packet filtering, 111
packet sniffers, 102
    defense mechanisms, 103
password attacks, 106–107
PAT (Port Address Translation), 115
peering points, 143

performance
 capacity, 28, 62
 of service levels, measuring, 232–233
 SLA metrics, 229
 troubleshooting with IPM, 234
performance management, 183, 190–191
performing
 application characterization, 164
 network characterization, 163
 QoS policy needs assessment, 162–163
perimeter routers, 26–27
physical network maps, 180
placement
 of fault management systems, 188
 of IDS sensors, 125
 of servers, Cisco Internet Systems
  Architecture, 60
policies
 documenting, 76
 QoS
  defining service level, 164–165
  performing application
   characterization, 164
  performing needs assessment, 162–163
  performing network characterization, 163
  testing, 165
 SLAs, 77
port redirection, 110
power consumption in highly available systems, 89
proactive management, 190
probes (RMON), 202
productivity, KAIZEN, 19
programs, 123
promiscuous mode (packet sniffers), 102
public key encryption, 118
 CAs, 119
 certificates, 120
publishing, e-publishing solutions, 20–21

Q

QoS (quality of service), 160
 application characterization, performing, 164
 business synchronization, 222
  reporting, 224
  setting SLA expectations, 223

Cisco IOS tools, 170–172
large-scale deployment procedures,
 166–168, 170
link efficiency mechanisms, 172
necessity of, 159–160
network characterization, performing, 163
policies
 needs assessment, 163
 testing, 165
requirements for traffic types, 161
service levels, defining, 164–165
SLAs
 administrative requirements, 228
 cost, 229
 creating, 225
 external, 226–228
 functional dependencies, 229
 internal, 226
 network availability metrics, 229
 network performance metrics, 229
 operation level metrics, 229
 technical dependencies, 228
traffic conditioning, 172
with Cisco Internet Systems Architecture,
 63–64
QoS Device Manager, large-scale QoS deployment,
 170
QPM (QoS Policy Manager), 166, 216, 235–236
 large-scale QoS deployment, 166–167
Q-Tip architecture, 143
 bottleneck points, 143
 ISPs, 143
quality assurance, Edward Deming, 7
queuing, 30, 159

R

reactive performance management, 190
read command (SNMP), 196
recovery procedures, implementing, 89–91
redundancy. *See also* high availability systems
 E-Commerce architecture, designing, 83
 highly available systems, designing, 80, 83
 impact on total cost of ownership, 72–74

Layer 3 switches, 29–34
single point of failure, 83
VRRP, 86–87
Remote Access VPN module (Cisco SAFE
architecture), 136–137
request/response model, 192
requirements of service level objectives, 221
retail services
Land's End customer care solution, 8
supply chain management solutions, 14
retrieving static Web server content, content engines,
49–54
revenue loss from security downtime, 97
RFC 2196, security policies, 97
RMON (Remote Monitor), 201–202
RSA Data Security, Inc, 119
RWAN (Routed WAN Management) solution,
213–214

S

SAA (Cisco IOS Service Assurance Agent),
232–233
SAFE architecture. *See* Cisco SAFE architecture
scalability, 28
security
access control, 127
attacks
application layer, 108
DoS, 104–106
IP spoofing, 103–104
man-in-the-middle, 107
network reconnaissance, 109
packet sniffers, 102–103
password, 106–107
port redirection, 110
Trojan horse, 110
trust exploitation, 109
unauthorized access, 110
viruses, 110
Cisco SAFE architecture, building, 129–138
Cisco Internet Systems Architecture, 63
confidentiality, 96
effect on revenue, 97

firewalls, 41–43, 111
Cisco PIX, 112–117
DMZ, 43
packet filtering, 111
stateful, 42
stateful inspection, 112
IDSs, 44–45, 122–123
director console, 45
host-based, 126
network-based, 125
sensors, 123–124
integrity, 96
life cycle model, 99
perimeter router functionality, 27
policies, 97–98
defining, 98–99
implementing, 100
improving, 101
monitoring, 100
testing, 100
update notification system, 45
VPNs, 117
Cisco device support, 122
data encryption, 118–119, 121
security management, 183
selecting QoS policies
defining service level, 164–165
performing application characterization, 164
performing needs assessment, 162–163
performing network characterization, 163
validation, 165
sensors
host-based, attack recognition database,
126–127
IDS, 45, 123–125
Server module (Cisco SAFE architecture), 133–134
servers
fault tolerance, 89
placement using Cisco Internet Systems
Architecture, 60
service level definitions, 164–165, 224
service level objectives, 221
session state, maintaining, 40
Set operation (SNMP), 192–194
shadow routers, 234
shared-memory fabric, 32

shared-memory queues, 31
shunning, 45
single point of failure, 83
    eliminating, 91
site-to-site VPNs, 115–116
sizing Layer 3 switches
    queuing model, 30
    switch fabric, 32
    switching implementation, 31
SLAs (service-level agreements), 77
    administrative requirements, 228
    business synchronization, 222
        reporting, 224
        setting expectations, 223
    cost, 229
    creating, 225
    external, 226
        example, 227–228
    functional dependencies, 229
    internal, 226
    network availability metrics, 229
    network performance metrics, 229
    operation level metrics, 229
    service level objectives, 221
    service levels
        defining, 164–165
    technical dependencies, 228
SLM (service-levelmanagement)
    design integration, 230
    tools, 231
        CiscoWorks 2000 SMS, 231–232
        IPM, 234–235
        QPM, 235–236
SmartFilter, 156
SMS (Service Management Solution), 215
SNMP (Simple Network Management Protocol),
    187, 192–193
    commands, 196
    disclosure, 196
    events, 197, 199
    Get requests, 194
    GetNext requests, 194
    masquerading, 196
    MIBs, 201
    modification of information, 196
    Set operations, 194
    syslog messages, 197

traps, 194
versions, 195
SODA (Self Organizing Distributed
    Architecture), 155
Spanning Tree, 85–86
splintered customer care services, 7
standards-based IPSec (Cisco PIX), 115
stateful failover, 116
stateful firewalls, 42
stateful inspection, 112–113
stateless failover, 116
static NAT translation, 115
status polling, 185
stickiness, maintaining session state, 38–40
supply chain management solutions, 14
switch fabric, 32
switching implementation, 31
symmetric-key encryption, 118
SYN attacks, 39
syslog, 202
syslog messages, 187, 197

T

TCP intercept (Cisco PIX), 114
technical dependencies of SLAs, 228
Telnet, 192
testing
    QoS policies, 165
    security policies, 100
third-party network management tools, 207
    Openview (Hewlett Packard), 208
    Tivoli (IBM), 208
    Unicenter TNG (Computer Associates), 209
thresholds, troubleshooting network response time,
    235
throughput, 42
Tivoli (IBM), 208
TLI (Transport Layer Interface), 191
TMN (Telecommunications Management Network)
    Architecture, FCAPS model, 177–178
        accounting management, 182
        configuration management, 178–181

fault management, 178
performance management, 183
security management, 183
tools
Cisco IOS QoS, 170–172
configuration management, 181
network analysis, 164
SLM, 231
CiscoWorks 2000 SMS, 231–232
IPM, 234–235
QPM, 235–236
third-party network management, 207
Openview (Hewlett Packard), 208
Tivoli (IBM), 208
Unicenter TNG (Computer
Associates), 209
top-down approach, high availability system
design, 77
topologies, redundant versus non-redundant, 81–83
total cost of ownership, 72, 74
traffic
load balancing, 84
content switches, 34–40
QoS, 160–161
traffic conditioning, Cisco IOS QoS tools, 172
training employees, e-learning solutions, 15–18
transparent caching, 150, 154
trap command (SNMP), 194–196
traversal command (SNMP), 196
Trojan horse attacks, 110
troubleshooting
fault management systems, 189
with IPM, 234
trust exploitation, 109
tunneling, 117
Cisco device support, 122
data encryption, 118–119, 121
two-factor authentication, 103

U

unauthorized access, 110
unavailbility. *See* downtime
Unicenter TNG (Computer Associates), 209
Unified Internet system architecture, 5
update notification systems, 45

upgrades, hitless, 26
URLs, filtering, 155–156
user management, 13
username/password authentication, 128
utilization, 28

V

validating QoS policies, 165
variable-size buffers, 30
verifying high availability design, 79
Vesperman, Ann, 8
video traffic
link efficiency mechanisms, 172
QoS requirements, 161
Virtual Reassembly (Cisco PIX), 114
viruses, 110
VMS (VPN/Security Management Solution), 215
voice traffic
link efficiency mechanisms, 172
QoS requirements, 161
VPNs, 117
acceleration, 116
Cisco device support, 122
data encryption, 118–121
VRRP (Virtual Router Redundancy Protocol),
86–87
vulnerable network locations, IDS sensor
placement, 125

W-Z

WCCP (Web Cache Communication Protocol), 154
Web servers
content engines, 46–54
Content Routers, 55, 60
placement, 60
workforce optimization solutions, 19–20
World Wide Web
cental storage growth, 141
services, 12
WRED (Weighted Random Early Detection),
162, 171
write command (SNMP), 196

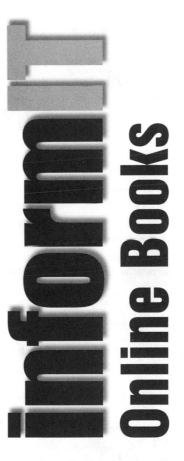

Cisco Press Solutions

Cisco Internet Applications and Solutions Self-Study Guide: Cisco Internet Solutions Specialist

Michael Wilkes
1-58705-066-8 • AVAILABLE NOW

Based on the content of the Cisco Internet Solutions Specialist (CISS) Application Essentials and the Applications Solutions courses, *Cisco Internet Applications an Solutions Self-Study Guide: Cisco Internet Solutions Specialist* takes the reader step-by step through the process of application design, identifying the necessary building bloc to facilitate the creation of company-appropriate Internet solutions. Focused on providing broad overview of applications deployment and management, this self-study guide addresses a number of Cisco Internet business solutions and the benefits organization can realize through the implementation of customer care, e-commerce, e-learning, and supply-chain management systems.

E-Support

Andrew Connan and Vincent Russell
1-58720-052-X • AVAILABLE NOW

Learn what eSupport is and how it can help your business. This book consists of non-technical, conversational, and easy-to-read interviews with the experts. Setting up an eSupport system isn't cheap or simple, but you can use this book's informatic as a guide to setting up a successful eSupport system, or improving the one you've got.

High Availability Network Fundamentals

Chris Oggerino
1-58713-017-3 • AVAILABLE NOW

High Availability Network Fundamentals discusses the need for and the mathematic of availability, then moves on to cover the issues affecting availability, including hardware, software, design strategies, human error, and environmental consideration After setting up the range of common problems, it then delves into the details of how design networks for fault tolerance and provides sample calculations for specific system Also included is a complete, end-to-end example showing availability calculations fc a sample network.

Performance and Fault Management

Paul Della Maggiora, Kent Phelps, Christopher Elliott, James Thompson, Robert Pavone
1-57870-180-5 • AVAILABLE NOW

Performance and Fault Management is a comprehensive guide to designing and implementing effective strategies for monitoring performance levels and correctng problems in Cisco networks. It provides an overview of router and LAN switch operations to help you understand how to manage such devices, as well as guidance on the essential MIBs, traps, syslog messages, and show commands for managing Cisco routers and switches.

CCNA Certifications

Interconnecting Cisco Network Devices

Edited by Steve McQuerry
1-57870-111-2 • AVAILABLE NOW

Based on the Cisco course taught worldwide, Interconnecting Cisco Network Devices teaches you how to configure Cisco switches and routers in multiprotocol internetworks. ICND is the primary course recommended by Cisco Systems for CCNA #640-607 preparation. If you are pursuing CCNA certification, this book is an excellent starting point for your study.

Cisco CCNA Exam #640-607 Certification Guide

Wendell Odom
1-58720-055-4 • AVAILABLE NOW

Although it's the first step in the Cisco Career Certifications, the Cisco Certified Network Associate (CCNA) exam is a difficult test. The recent additions of performance-based questions have made it even more challenging. Your first attempt at becoming Cisco certified requires a lot of study and confidence in your networking knowledge. When you're ready to test your skills, complete your knowledge of exam topics, and prepare for exam day, you need the preparation tools found in *Cisco CCNA Exam #640-607 Certification Guide* from Cisco Press.

Cisco CCNA Exam #640-607 Flash Card Practice Kit

Eric Rivard
1-58720-048-1 • AVAILABLE NOW

CCNA test time is rapidly approaching. You've learned the concepts, you have the experience to put them into real-world use, and now you want to practice, practice, practice until exam time. *Cisco CCNA Exam #640-607 Flash Card Practice Kit* gives you three methods of proven late-stage CCNA exam preparation in one package: more than 350 flash cards, 550+ practice exam questions, 54 study sheets

The CD-ROM contains 350+ flash cards and more than 550 practice test questions. Flash cards are downloadable to Palm OS and Pocket PC handheld devices.

CCNA Practical Studies

Gary Heap, Lynn Maynes
1-58720-046-5 • AVAILABLE NOW

CCNA Practical Studies is a guide for students and instructors alike to gaining essential hands-on experience in networking lab environments. An equally effective supplement to concept-based study guides or as a stand-alone reference for applying CCNA knowledge, this text provides lab-executable scenarios that cover the entire range of CCNA topics. Starting at the physical layer of the OSI model, your students are presented with a layered approach to learning how to build a small network. Each chapter tackles a major subject area such as router configuration, routing protocols, bridging and switching, ISDN, access lists, and IPX. Each subject presents a mini-lab, walking them through the lab scenario and explaining in detail the commands used, why the authors chose the specific commands, and the resulting configurations.

Cisco Security Specialist

Managing Cisco Network Security

Mike Wenstrom
1-57870-103-1 • AVAILABLE NOW

Managing Cisco Network Security focuses on implementing IP network security and contains a wealth of case study material, configuration examples, command summaries, helpful tables and diagrams, and chapter-ending review questions, making this book an effective preparation tool for the MCNS portion of the Cisco Security Specialist certification, part of the new Cisco Qualified Specialist certification track.

Cisco Secure PIX Firewalls

David Chapman and Andy Fox
1-58705-035-8 • AVAILABLE NOW

Whether you are preparing for the Cisco Security Specialist 1 certification or simply want to understand and make the most efficient use of PIX Firewalls, *Cisco Secure PIX Firewalls* provides you with a complete solution for planning, deploying, and managing PIX Firewall protected networks.

Cisco Secure Virtual Private Networks

Andrew Mason
1-58705-033-1 • AVAILABLE NOW

Cisco Secure Virtual Private Networks provides you with the knowledge to plan, administer, and maintain a virtual private network (VPN). Learn how to reduce network cost, enable network scalability, and increase remote access efficiency by deploying Cisco-based VPNs. You will also learn how to configure and test IPSec in Cisco IOS Software and PIX Firewalls; secure remote access connections to corporate networks with IPSec; create a secure tunnel to a Cisco VPN Concentrator and PIX Firewall; and configure the Cisco VPN Concentrator, Cisco router, and PIX Firewall for interoperability.

Cisco Secure Intrusion Detection System

Earl Carter
1-58705-034-X • AVAILABLE NOW

Cisco Secure Intrusion Detection Systems provides a clear explanation of why network security is crucial in today's converged networking environment, how the Cisco Secure Intrusion Detection System (CSIDS) improves the security on a network, and how to install and configure CSIDS. The CSIDS is a real-time, network-based IDS designed to detect, report, and terminate unauthorized activity throughout a network. The industry's first and now the market-leading IDS, CSIDS is the dynamic security component of Cisco's end-to-end security product line.

CISCO SYSTEMS

CISCO SYSTEMS/PACKET MAGAZINE
ATTN: C. Glover
170 West Tasman, Mailstop SJ8-2
San Jose, CA 95134-1706

Place
Stamp
Here

☐ **YES!** I'm requesting a **free** subscription to *Packet*™ magazine.

☐ No. I'm not interested at this time.

☐ Mr.
☐ Ms.

First Name (Please Print)   Last Name

Title/Position (Required)

Company (Required)

Address

City   State/Province

Zip/Postal Code   Country

Telephone (Include country and area codes)   Fax

E-mail

Signature (Required)   Date

☐ I would like to receive additional information on Cisco's services and products by e-mail.

1. Do you or your company:
A ☐ Use Cisco products   C ☐ Both
B ☐ Resell Cisco products   D ☐ Neither

2. Your organization's relationship to Cisco Systems:
A ☐ Customer/End User   E ☐ Integrator   J ☐ Consultant
B ☐ Prospective Customer   F ☐ Non-Authorized Reseller   K ☐ Other (specify):
C ☐ Cisco Reseller   G ☐ Cisco Training Partner
D ☐ Cisco Distributor   I ☐ Cisco OEM   _____

3. How many people does your entire company employ?
A ☐ More than 10,000   D ☐ 500 to 999   G ☐ Fewer than 100
B ☐ 5,000 to 9,999   E ☐ 250 to 499
C ☐ 1,000 to 4,999   F ☐ 100 to 249

4. Is your company a Service Provider?
A ☐ Yes   B ☐ No

5. Your involvement in network equipment purchases:
A ☐ Recommend   B ☐ Approve   C ☐ Neither

6. Your personal involvement in networking:
A ☐ Entire enterprise at all sites   F ☐ Public network
B ☐ Departments or network segments at more than one site   D ☐ No involvement
C ☐ Single department or network segment   E ☐ Other (specify):
                                                              _____

7. Your Industry:
A ☐ Aerospace   G ☐ Education (K–12)   K ☐ Health Care
B ☐ Agriculture/Mining/Construction   U ☐ Education (College/Univ.) L ☐ Telecommunications
C ☐ Banking/Finance   H ☐ Government—Federal   M ☐ Utilities/Transportation
D ☐ Chemical/Pharmaceutical   I ☐ Government—State   N ☐ Other (specify):
E ☐ Consultant   J ☐ Government—Local   _____
F ☐ Computer/Systems/Electronics

CPRESS

PACKET

Packet magazine serves as the premier publication linking customers to Cisco Systems, Inc. Delivering complete coverage of cutting-edge networking trends and innovations, *Packet* is a magazine for technical, hands-on users. It delivers industry-specific information for enterprise, service provider, and small and midsized business market segments. A toolchest for planners and decision makers, *Packet* contains a vast array of practical information, boasting sample configurations, real-life customer examples, and tips on getting the most from your Cisco Systems' investments. Simply put, *Packet* magazine is straight talk straight from the worldwide leader in networking for the Internet, Cisco Systems, Inc.

We hope you'll take advantage of this useful resource. I look forward to hearing from you!

Cecelia Glover
Packet Circulation Manager
packet@external.cisco.com
www.cisco.com/go/packet

PACKET